CBSE X 2021

Chapter and Topic-Wise
Solved Papers
2011-2020
Social Science

CL MEDIA (P) LTD.

Edition : 2021

© **PUBLISHER**

No part of this book may be reproduced in a retrieval system or transmitted, in any form or by any means, electronics, mechanical, photocopying, recording, scanning and or without the written permission of the publisher.

Administrative and Production Offices

Published by : **CL Media (P) Ltd.**

A-45, Mohan Cooperative Industrial Area,
Near Mohan Estate Metro Station,
New Delhi - 110044

Marketed by : **G.K. Publications (P) Ltd.**

A-45, Mohan Cooperative Industrial Area,
Near Mohan Estate Metro Station,
New Delhi - 110044

ISBN 978-93-89718-92-8

Typeset by : CL Media DTP Unit

For product information :

Visit :- **www.gkpublications.com**

or

Email :- **gkp@gkpublications.com**

Social Science

Unit I : History

India and the Contemporary World-II

Unit II : Geography

Contemporary India-II

Unit III : Political Science

Democratic Politics II

Unit IV : Economics

Understanding Economic Development

PREFACE

Class X Board Exams are a race against time. You must know how to manage time efficiently if you want to ace your exams. At Career Launcher, we understand the struggle of attempting such a crucial examination for the first time and the pressure that comes along with it. Which is why, our Chapter and Topic-Wise Solved Papers for Social Science have been designed to help you become acquainted with the exam pattern and hone your time management skills, both at the same time.

Exclusively designed for the students of CBSE Class X by highly experienced teachers, the book provides answers to all actual questions of Social Science Board Exams conducted from 2011 to 2020. The solutions have been prepared exactly in coherence with the latest marking pattern; after a careful evaluation of previous year trends of the questions asked in Class X Boards and actual solutions provided by CBSE.

The book follows a three-pronged approach to make your study more focused. The questions are arranged Chapter-wise so that you can begin your preparation with the areas that demand more attention. These are further segmented topic-wise and eventually the break-down is as per the marking scheme. This division will equip you with the ability to gauge which questions require more emphasis and answer accordingly. Apart from this, several value-based questions have also been included.

At the end of the book, solved paper of 2020 Board exam has been provided for you to practice and become familiar with exam pattern.

We hope the book provides the right exposure to Class X students so that you not only ace your Boards but mold a better future for yourself. And as always, Career Launcher's school team is behind you with its experienced gurus to help your career take wings.

Let's face the Boards with more confidence!

Wishing you all the best,

Team CL

Blueprint & Marks Distribution

COURSE STRUCTURE
CLASS X (2020–21)

Theory Paper

Time: 3 Hrs.			Max. Marks : 80
No.	**Units**	**No. of Periods**	**Marks**
I	India and the Contemporary World – II	60	20
II	Contemporary India – II	55	20
III	Democratic Politics – II	50	20
IV	Understanding Economic Development	50	20
	Total	215	80

<table>
<tr><td colspan="2">Unit 1: India and the Contemporary World – II</td><td>60 Periods</td></tr>
<tr><td colspan="2" align="center">Themes</td><td align="center">Learning Objectives</td></tr>
<tr>
<td colspan="2">

Section 1: Events and Processes:

1. The Rise of Nationalism in Europe:
- The French Revolution and the Idea of the Nation
- The Making of Nationalism in Europe
- The Age of Revolutions: 1830-1848
- The Making of Germany and Italy
- Visualizing the Nation
- Nationalism and Imperialism

2. Nationalism in India:
- The First World War, Khilafat and Non - Cooperation
- Differing Strands within the Movement
- Towards Civil Disobedience
- The Sense of Collective Belonging

</td>
<td>

- Enable the learners to identify and comprehend the forms in which nationalism developed along with the formation of nation states in Europe in the post-1830 period.
- Establish the relationship and bring out the difference between European nationalism and anti-colonial nationalisms.
- Understand the way the idea of nationalism emerged and led to the formation of nation states in Europe and elsewhere.

- Recognize the characteristics of Indian nationalism through a case study of Non-Cooperation and Civil Disobedience Movement.
- Analyze the nature of the diverse social movements of the time.
- Familiarize with the writings and ideals of different political groups and individuals.
- Appreciate the ideas promoting Pan Indian belongingness.

</td>
</tr>
</table>

Section 2: Livelihoods, Economies and Societies: Any **one theme** of the following:

3. The Making of a Global World:

- The Pre-modern world
- The Nineteenth Century (1815-1914)
- The Inter war Economy
- Rebuilding a World Economy: The Post-War Era

- Show that globalization has a long history and point to the shifts within the process.
- Analyze the implication of globalization for local economies.
- Discuss how globalization is experienced differently by different social groups.

4. The Age of Industrialization:

- Before the Industrial Revolution
- Hand Labour and Steam Power
- Industrialization in the colonies
- Factories Come Up
- The Peculiarities of Industrial Growth
- Market for Goods

- Familiarize with the Pro- to-Industrial phase and Early – factory system.
- Familiarize with the process of industrialization and its impact on labour class.
- Enable them to understand industrialization in the colonies with reference to Textile industries.

Section 3: Everyday Life, Culture and Politics:

5. Print Culture and the Modern World:

- The First Printed Books
- Print Comes to Europe
- The Print Revolution and its Impact
- The Reading Mania
- The Nineteenth Century
- India and the World of Print
- Religious Reform and Public Debates
- New Forms of Publication
- Print and Censorship

- Identify the link between print culture and the circulation of ideas.
- Familiarize with pictures, cartoons, extracts from propaganda literature and newspaper debates on important events and issues in the past.
- Understand that forms of writing have a specific history, and that they reflect historical changes within society and shape the forces of change.

Unit 2: Contemporary India – II	55 Periods
Themes	**Learning Objectives**

1. Resources and Development:
  • Types of Resources
  • Development of Resources
  • Resource Planning in India
  • Land Resources
  • Land Utilization
  • Land Use Pattern in India
  • Land Degradation and Conservation Measures
  • Soil as a Resource
  • Classification of Soils
  • Soil Erosion and Soil Conservation
	• Understand the value of resources and the need for their judicious utilization and conservation.

2. Forest and Wildlife
  • Biodiversity or Biological Diversity
  • Flora and Fauna in India
  • Vanishing Forests
  • Asiatic Cheetah: Where did they go?
  • The Himalayan Yew in trouble
  • Conservation of forest and wildlife in India
  • Project Tiger
  • Types and distribution of forests and wildlife resources
  • Community and Conservation
Note: The chapter 'Forest and Wildlife' to be assessed in the Periodic Tests only and will not be evaluated in Board Examination.
	• Understand the importance of forests and wild life in one environment as well as develop concept towards depletion of resources.

3. Water Resources:
  • Water Scarcity and The Need for Water Conservation and Management
  • Multi-Purpose River Projects and Integrated Water Resources Management
  • Rainwater Harvesting
	• Comprehend the importance of water as a resource as well as develop awareness towards its judicious use and conservation.

4. Agriculture:

- Types of farming
- Cropping Pattern
- Major Crops
- Technological and Institutional Reforms
- Impact of Globalization on Agriculture

- Explain the importance of agriculture in national economy.
- Identify various types of farming and discuss the various farming methods; describe the spatial distribution of major crops as well as understand the relationship between rainfall regimes and cropping pattern.
- Explain various government policies for institutional as well as technological reforms since independence.

5. Minerals and Energy Resources

- What is a mineral?
- Mode of occurrence of Minerals
- Ferrons and Non-Ferrons Minerals
- Non-Metallic Minerals
- Rock Minerals
- Conservation of Minerals
- Energy Resources
  - Conventional and Non-Conventional
  - Conservation of Energy Resources

- Identify different types of minerals and energy resources and places of their availability
- Feel the need for their judicious utilization

6. Manufacturing Industries:

- Importance of manufacturing
- Contribution of Industry to National Economy
- Industrial Location
- Classification of Industries
- Spatial distribution
  Industrial pollution and environmental degradation
- Control of Environmental Degradation

- Bring out the importance of industries in the national economy as well as understand the regional disparities which resulted due to concentration of industries in some areas.
- Discuss the need for a planned industrial development and debate over the role of government towards sustainable development.

7. Life Lines of National Economy:	
• Transport – Roadways, Railways, Pipelines, Waterways, Airways • Communication • International Trade • Tourism as a Trade	• Explain the importance of transport and communication in the ever-shrinking world. • Understand the role of trade and tourism in the economic development of a country.

Unit 3: Democratic Politics – II	50 Periods
Themes	**Learning Objectives**
1. Power Sharing: • Case Studies of Belgium and Sri Lanka • Why power sharing is desirable? • Forms of Power Sharing	• Familiarize with the centrality of power sharing in a democracy. • Understand the working of spatial and social power sharing mechanisms.
2. Federalism: • What is Federalism? • What make India a Federal Country? • How is Federalism practiced? • Decentralization in India	• Analyse federal provisions and institutions. • Explain decentralization in rural and urban areas.
3. Democracy and Diversity: • Case Studies of Mexico • Differences, similarities and divisions • Politics of social divisions *Note: The chapter 'Democracy and Diversity' to be assessed in the Periodic Tests only and will not be evaluated in Board Examination.*	• Analyse the relationship between social cleavages and political competition with reference to Indian situation.
4. Gender, Religion and Caste: • Gender and Politics • Religion, Communalism and Politics • Caste and Politics	• Identify and analyse the challenges posed by communalism to Indian democracy. • Recognise the enabling and disabling effects of caste and ethnicity in politics. • Develop a gender perspective on politics.

5. **Popular Struggles and Movements:**
   - Popular Struggles in Nepal and Bolivia
   - Mobilization and Organization
   - Pressure Groups and Movements

   Note: The chapter 'Popular Struggles and Movements' to be assessed in the Periodic Tests only and will not be evaluated in Board Examination.

   - Understand the vital role of people's struggle in the expansion of democracy.

6. **Political Parties:**
   - Why do we need Political Parties?
   - How many Parties should we have?
   - National Political Parties
   - State Parties
   - Challenges to Political Parties
   - How can Parties be reformed?

   - Analyse party systems in democracies.
   - Introduction to major political parties, challenges faced by them and reforms in the country.

7. **Outcomes of Democracy:**
   - How do we assess democracy's outcomes?
   - Accountable, responsive and legitimate government
   - Economic growth and development
   - Reduction of inequality and poverty
   - Accommodation of social diversity
   - Dignity and freedom of the citizens

   - Evaluate the functioning of democracies in comparison to alternative forms of governments.
   - Understand the causes for continuation of democracy in India.
   - Distinguish between sources of strengths and weaknesses of Indian democracy.

8. **Challenges to Democracy:**
   - Thinking about challenges
   - Thinking about Political Reforms
   - Redefining democracy

   Note: The chapter 'Challenges to Democracy' to be assessed in the Periodic

   - Reflect on the different kinds of measures possible to deepen democracy.
   - Promote an active and participatory citizenship.

<table>
<tr><td colspan="2">Tests only and will not be evaluated in Board Examination.</td></tr>
<tr><td>Unit 4: Understanding Economic Development</td><td>50 Periods</td></tr>
<tr><td>Themes</td><td>Objectives</td></tr>
<tr><td>

1. **Development:**
   - What Development Promises - Different people different goals
   - Income and other goals
   - National Development
   - How to compare different countries or states?
   - Income and other criteria
   - Public Facilities
   - Sustainability of development

2. **Sectors of the Indian Economy**:
   - Sectors of Economic Activities
   - Comparing the three sectors
   - Primary, Secondary and Tertiary Sectors in India
   - Division of sectors as organized and unorganized
   - Sectors in terms of ownership: Public and Private Sectors

3. **Money and Credit:**
   - Money as a medium of exchange
   - Modern forms of money
   - Loan activities of Banks
   - Two different credit situations
   - Terms of credit
   - Formal sector credit in India
   - Self Help Groups for the Poor

4. **Globalization and the Indian Economy:**
   - Production across countries
   - Interlinking production across countries

</td><td>

- Familiarize with concepts of macroeconomics.
- Understand the rationale for overall human development in our country, which includes the rise of income, improvements in health and education rather than income.
- Understand the importance of quality of life and sustainable development.

- Identify major employment generating sectors.
- Reason out the government investment in different sectors of economy.

- Understand money as an economic concept.
- Understand the role of financial institutions from the point of view of day-to- day life.

- Explain the working of the Global Economic phenomenon.

</td></tr>
</table>

• Foreign Trade and integration of markets • What is globalization? • Factors that have enabled Globalisation • World Trade Organisation • Impact of Globalization on India • The Struggle for a fair Globalisation	
5. Consumer Rights: *Note: Chapter 5 'Consumer Rights' to be done as Project Work.*	• Gets familiarized with the rights and duties as a consumer; and legal measures available to protect from being exploited in markets.

PROJECT WORK
CLASS X (2020–21)

(05 Periods)   **05 Marks**

1. Every student has to compulsorily undertake any one project on the following topics:

Consumer Awareness

OR

Social Issues

OR

Sustainable Development

2. Objective: The overall objective of the project work is to help students gain an insight and pragmatic understanding of the theme and see all the Social Science disciplines from interdisciplinary perspective. It should also help in enhancing the Life Skills of the students.

    Students are expected to apply the Social Science concepts that they have learnt over the years in order to prepare the project report.

    If required, students may go out for collecting data and use different primary and secondary resources to prepare the project. If possible, various forms of art may be integrated in the project work.

3. The distribution of marks over different aspects relating to Project Work is as follows:

S. No.	Aspects	Marks
a.	Content accuracy, originality and analysis	2
b.	Presentation and creativity	2
c.	Viva Voce	1

4. The projects carried out by the students in different topics should subsequently be shared among themselves through interactive sessions such as exhibitions, panel discussions, etc.

5. All documents pertaining to assessment under this activity should be meticulously maintained by concerned schools.

6. A Summary Report should be prepared highlighting:

- objectives realized through individual work and group interactions;
- calendar of activities;
- innovative ideas generated in the process ;
- list of questions asked in viva voce.

7. It is to be noted here by all the teachers and students that the projects and models prepared should be made from eco-friendly products without incurring too much expenditure.

8. The Project Report should be handwritten by the students themselves.

9. Records pertaining to projects (internal assessment) of the students will be maintained for a period of three months from the date of declaration of result for verification at the discretion of Board. Subjudiced cases, if any or those involving RTI / Grievances may however be retained beyond three months.

SOCIAL SCIENCE (CODE NO. 087)
QUESTION PAPER DESIGN CLASS X
(2020-21)

Time: 3 Hours			Maximum Marks : 80
Sr. No.	Competencies	Total Marks	% Weightage
1	**Remembering and Understanding:** Exhibiting memory of previously learned material by recalling facts, terms, basic concepts, and answers; Demonstrating understanding of facts and ideas by organizing, comparing, translating, interpreting, giving descriptions and stating main ideas	28	35%
2	**Applying:** Solving problems to new situations by applying acquired knowledge, facts, techniques and rules in a different way.	14	17.5%
3	**Formulating, Analysing, Evaluating and Creating:** Examining and breaking information into parts by identifying motives or causes; Making inferences and finding evidence to support generalizations; Presenting and defending opinions by making judgments about information, validity of ideas, or quality of work based on a set of criteria; Compiling information together in a different way by combining elements in a new pattern or proposing alternative solutions.	32	40%
4	**Map Skill**	6	7.5%
		80	100%

Note: Teachers may refer 'Learning Outcomes' published by NCERT for developing lesson plans, assessm ent framework and questions.

- 02 Items from History Map List and 04 from Geography Map List
- Internal Assessment: 20 Marks

INTERNAL ASSESSMENT

	Marks	Description	
Periodic Assessment	10 Marks	Pen Paper Test	**5 marks**
		Assessment using multiple strategies For example, Quiz, Debate, Role Play, Viva, Group Discussion, Visual Expression, Interactive Bulletin Boards, Gallery Walks, Exit Cards, Concept Maps, Peer Assessment, Self-Assessment, etc.	**5 marks**
Portfolio	5 Marks	☐ Classwork and Assignments ☐ Any exemplary work done by the student ☐ Reflections, Narrations, Journals, etc. ☐ Achievements of the student in the subject throughout the year ☐ Participation of the student in different activities like Heritage India Quiz	
Subject Enrichment Activity	5 Marks	☐ Project Work	

LIST OF MAP ITEMS
CLASS X (2020-21)

A. HISTORY (Outline Political Map of India)

Chapter - 3 Nationalism in India - (1918 - 1930) for Locating and Labelling / Identification

1. **Indian National Congress Sessions:**
   a. Calcutta (Sep. 1920)
   b. Nagpur (Dec. 1920)
   c. Madras (1927)

2. **Important Centres of Indian National Movement**
   a. Champaran (Bihar) - Movement of Indigo Planters
   b. Kheda (Gujarat) - Peasant Satyagrah
   c. Ahmedabad (Gujarat) - Cotton Mill Workers Satyagraha
   d. Amritsar (Punjab) - Jallianwala Bagh Incident
   e. Chauri Chaura (U.P.) - Calling off the Non-Cooperation Movement
   f. Dandi (Gujarat) - Civil Disobedience Movement

B. GEOGRAPHY (Outline Political Map of India)

Chapter 1: Resources and Development (Identification only)

   a. Major soil Types

Chapter 3: Water Resources (Locating and Labelling)

Dams:

a.	Salal	b.	Bhakra Nangal
c.	Tehri	d.	Rana Pratap Sagar
e.	Sardar Sarovar	f.	Hirakud
g.	Nagarjuna Sagar	h.	Tungabhadra

Note: The theoretical aspect of chapter 'Water Resources' to be assessed in the Periodic Tests only and will not be evaluated in Board Examination. However, the map items of this chapter as listed above will be evaluated in Board Examination.

Chapter 4: Agriculture (Identification only)

a. Major areas of Rice and Wheat

b. Largest / Major producer states of Sugarcane, Tea, Coffee, Rubber, Cotton and Jute

Chapter 5: Minerals and Energy Resources

Minerals (Identification only)

a. Iron Ore mines

- Mayurbhanj
- Bellary
- Durg
- Kudremukh
- Bailadila

b. Coal Mines

- Raniganj
- Neyveli
- Bokaro
- Talcher

c. Oil Fields

- Digboi
- Bassien
- Naharkatia
- Kalol
- Mumbai High
- Ankaleshwar

Power Plants

(Locating and Labelling only)

a. Thermal

- Namrup
- Singrauli
- Ramagundam

b. Nuclear

- Narora
- Kalpakkam
- Kakrapara
- Tarapur

Chapter 6: Manufacturing Industries (Locating and Labelling Only)

Cotton Textile Industries:

a. Mumbai
b. Indore
c. Surat
d. Kanpur
e. Coimbatore

Iron and Steel Plants:

a. Durgapur
b. Bokaro
c. Jamshedpur
d. Bhilai
e. Vijaynagar
f. Salem

Software Technology Parks:

a.	Noida	b.	Gandhinagar	c.	Mumbai
d.	Pune	e.	Hyderabad	f.	Bengaluru
g.	Chennai	h.	Thiruvananthapuram		

Chapter 7: Lifelines of National Economy

Major Ports: (Locating and Labelling)

a.	Kandla	b.	Mumbai	c.	Marmagao
d.	New Mangalore	e.	Kochi	f.	Tuticorin
g.	Chennai	h.	Vishakhapatnam	i.	Paradip
j.	Haldia				

International Airports:

a. Amritsar (Raja Sansi)

b. Delhi (Indira Gandhi International)

c. Mumbai (Chhatrapati Shivaji)

d. Chennai (Meenam Bakkam)

e. Kolkata (Netaji Subhash Chandra Bose)

f. Hyderabad (Rajiv Gandhi)

Note: Items of Locating and Labelling may also be given for Identification.

Unit-I : HISTORY

The Rise of Nationalism in Europe

Summary

The Rise of Nationalism in Europe

- A series of four picture is portrayed by Fredric Sorrieu in 1948 which expressed the notion of ideal state.

- The imaginary manifestation of Fredric show the universal brotherhood.

- The Utopia showed the people of various country like USA, Switzerland, Germany, Canda, Englad and others have had same intention regarding freedom and liberty.

- The universal brotherhood was imagined by portrayer which was inspired with the democratic and social republics.

- According to him, universal fraternity in Europe could be obtained with Enlighten, Charter of rights for its citizen.

- The grass root changed took place in the political and mental arena of Europe due to emergence of Nationalism.

- Nationalism changed the multi national dynastic empires in the nation state.

The Age of Revolutions (1830-1848) and the Unification of Germany and Italy.

Emergence of Nationalism

- Revolutions broke out in the provinces of Ottoman empire, Ireland, Poland, in the reaction of the consolidation of power by conservative regimes.

- Revolutions were inspired by the liberalism and nationalism.

- Professors, commercial middle classes, elite of educated middle-class, clerks inspired with nationalism led the revolutions.

- Independence movement of Greek caused the decimation of feelings of nationalism in among peoples.

- Poets and artists raised the nationalist feeling among Greeks by shaping public opinion against Ottoman empire by praising ancient culture and civilization of Greece.

- Greece got independence as a nation in 1832 due to emergence of nationalism among its peoples.

- The feeling of nationalism or a nation was emerged with help arts, music and stories, folk lore etc.

- A cultural movement led by Romantic artists and poets tried to create a collective belongings with culture, tradition and pasts of a nation.

- The spirit of a German culture was popularized as a folk dance, folk songs and folk poetry. It is used to put the messages of modern nationalist to connects to a majority of peoples who were not able to read.

- Poland was divided by Austria Prussia and Russia, but national feeling was alive in peoples due to music and language.

- In Poland language played a major role in promotion of nationalist feelings against Russia,

- as Poland was occupied by Russia and Russian language was imposed.
- The armed opposition against Russia was failed in 1831, the Poland began to use Polish language as a symbol of opposition.

Hunger, Hardship and Popular Revolt

- The rise in population in Europe led the deplorable condition of peoples as employment was not hiked in the ratio of population.
- Slums were overcrowd with migrated peoples from rural area
- That time elites were enjoying and the peasants were struggling from the debt of feudal.
- In the same time food shortage occurred this paced the dissatisfaction of unemployed.
- Hungry and unemployed peoples came out from their home and forced Louis Phillippe to flee
- National assembly provided voting rights the age of 21 and above males and announce Europe as a Republic.
- Weavers in Silesia had driven a rebel against temporary workers who provided them crude material of weaving and gave them orders for products yet radically decreased their installments.

1848 Liberals' Revolution

- In a mid of unrest, The liberal Men and women of the Germany, Austria Poland, raised their demands for a constitution, freedom of press and freedom of forming groups.
- In Frankfurt the businessman, artisans and other middle class people gathered and 831 elected representatives were reached Church of St. Paul.
- Drafted a constitution for a German country to be headed by a government subject to a parliament.
- King of Prussia, Wilhelum IV, rejected it and opposed the elected assembly by joining other.
- The social base of parliament became ruined but the military and aristocracy became stronger.
- The middle classes dominated parliament lost is support by opposing the demands of artisans and workers.
- Women also formed organization and participated in revolutionaries movement but they failed to get voting rights in the election of assembly.
- The continuous oppose of liberals changed the

mind of monarchs, they started to respond over their demands and introduced the changes.

- The system of bonded labour and serfdom were abolished from Russia and Habsburg dominions.

Nation States – Unification of Italy, Germany and Britain

Germany

- The nationalist were trying to unite Germany from 1848 but the combined forces of the Jukers, military, and monarchs of Prussia always suppressed their movement.
- Otto van Bismark took the leadership of the unification of Germany.
- William I the king of Prussia became the emperor of unified Germany after three successful war with Austria, Denmark and France in the leadership of Vismark.
- Modernisation of Germany took place with the improvements in banking, legal, judicial system which became model for others.

Italy

- The only one Sardinia was ruled by an Italian princely house after division of Italy into seven part.
- A pope was head of centre, Spain was the ruler of south and Austrian Habsburgs was the head of north.
- Young Italy was founded for the unification of Italy by Mazzini but was failed to achieve its goal.
- Cavour was the new face to led the movement, Sardinia – Piedmont defeated Austria.
- Cavour and Mazzini together succeeded in muster support of peasants of Two Sicilies, against Spanish.
- They succeeded and Victor Emmanuel II become king of unified Italy.

Britain

- In Britain the arrangement of the country state was not the consequence of sudden change or unrest. It was the consequence of a long draw-out process.
- There was no British country preceding the eighteenth century. The essential characters of the general population who possessed the British thoughts were ethnic ones

- But as the English country relentlessly developed in riches, significance and influence, it could broaden its impact over alternate countries of the islands
- The English Parliament, which had seized control from the government in 1688 toward the finish of a secured conflict, was the instrument through which a country state with England at its focus, came to be produced.
- The Act of association (1707) amongst England and Scotland that brought about the development of the 'Joined together Kingdom of Great Britain' implied as a result, that England could force its effect on Scotland
- Ireland endured a comparative destiny. It was a nation profoundly separated amongst Catholics and Protestants. The English helped the Protestants of Ireland to force their strength over a generally catholic nation.
- Catholic rebels against British strength were severely smothered. After a fizzled revolt driven by Wolte Tone and his Joined Irishmen (1798). Ireland was persuasively consolidated into the assembled kingdom in 1801.
- Another 'English country' was produced through the spread of overwhelming English culture

Visualising the Nation – Nationalism and Imperialism

- From eighteenth centuries the artists started to represent nation as a Female.
- In France the nation was represented as a Christened Marianne, to connect the peoples with nation.
- German nation had allegory of Germania weared a crown of oak leaves to which show heroism.

Nationalism and Imperialism

- In the post nineteenth century nationalist groups had notion of dissatisfaction to each other, which is used by the European powers to diverted nationalist and extend their imperial .
- A large area of Balkan was controlled by Ottoman empire. Albania, Greece, Bosnia, Serbia, Macedonia, Croatia and many other countries were collectively termed as Balkan.
- After the disintegration of Ottoman empire, the condition of Balkan was very explosive as the idea of romantic nationalism was spreading.

- People were started to oppose in Balkan areas the ottoman empires tried to resolve this but was not successful.
- The Slavic Nationalist started to spread the history to create a sense of belongings to get rid from imperialism.
- Russia, Germany, England and Austria-Hungary both supreme power were also involves in acquiring power in Balkans.
- Rivalry of both supreme power for Balkan led to the series of wars which caused First world war.
- The anti-imperial movement was started by various colonial country of Europe, against imperial dominance.
- The movement was inspired by the collective national unity which changed the political shape of Europe and the idea of nation-states accepted.

Points to know

ABSOLUTIST

A form of the government centralised monarchial government ,had not any limit to exercise its power.

UTOPIA A imaginary state with universal brotherhood that is never going to be true.

PLEBISCITE A public related important issue is directly voted by its citizen.

ALLEGORY It's a illustration or expression of ideas, generally manifests by the things or person.

Zollverein To remove trade barrier in Prussia, it is formed in 1034.

DAS VOLK Common People in Germany

CARBONARI A secret society of Italy.

Important Personalities.

Fredric Sorrieu – Portrayer of Eutopia.

Napoleon – King of France.

Giuseppe Mazzini – Founder of Young Italy movement.

Meetternich – chancellor of Austria

Johannn Gotfrried Herder – German philosopher who encouraged Romantics to create nation feeling

Grimm brothers – Jacob and Wilhelm Grimm, collected the folk tales and published it.

Otto van Bismark – the chief minister of Prussia, known as architect of Italy

William I – King of Prussia, become emperor of unified Germany

Cavour – Chief minister of Italy, who led the movement to unify the Italy

Victor Emmanuel – King of unified Italy

Important Dates

1797 - Napoleon war begins.

1789 - French Revolution.

1804 - Napoleon code.

1814 - Napoleonic Wars, fail of Napoliean.

1815 - Vienna congress took place

1821 - Independence movement of Greek against the Ottoman Empire

1846 - Uprising in Greater Poland

1859 - 61 - Unification of Italy

1863 - Polish national revolt

1866 - 71 - Unification of led by Otto Von Bismarck

1867 - autonomy established in Hungary

1905 - Slav nationalism gathers force in the Habsburg and Ottoman Empire

PREVIOUS YEARS'
EXAMINATION QUESTIONS

▶ 1 Mark Questions

1. Which one of the following is not true about the female allegory of France?

   (*a*) She was named Marianne.

   (*b*) She took part in the French revolution.

   (*c*) She was a symbol of national unity

   (*d*) Her characteristics were drawn from those of Liberty and the Republic.

   [TERM 2, 2011]

2. Which one of the following states was ruled by an Italian princely house before unification of Italy?

   (*a*) Kingdom of Two Sicilies

   (*b*) Lombardy

   (*c*) Venetia

   (*d*) Sardinia-Piedmont

   [TERM 2, 2011]

3. Who, among the following formed a secret society, called 'Young Italy'?

   (*a*) Otto Van Bismark

   (*b*) Giuseppe Mazzini

   (*c*) Mettemich

   (*d*) Johann Gottfried Herder

   [TERM 2, 2011]

4. Which one of the following types of government was functioning in France before the revolution of 1789?

   (*a*) Dictatorship

   (*c*) Military

   (*c*) Body of French Citizen

   (*d*) Monarchy

   [TERM 2, 2012]

5. Where did the big European Powers meet in 1885 for dividing Africa?

   [TERM 2, 2013]

6. Identify the French artist from the following who prepared a series of four prints visualizing his dream of a world:

   (*a*) Kitagewa Utamaro

   (*b*) Richard M. Hoe

   (*c*) Voltaire

   (*d*) Frederic Sorreeu

   [MARKING SCHEME, TERM 2, 2013]

7. What was the main aim of the French revolutionaries?

   [TERM 2, 2015]

8. Who was proclaimed the King of United Italy in 1861?

   [TERM 2, 2011]

▶ 3 Mark Questions

9. Explain any three ways in which nationalist feelings were kept alive in Poland in the 18th and 19th centuries.

   [TERM 2, 2011]

10. Describe the process of unification of Germany.

    [TERM 2, 2012]

11. Explain the process of unification of Italy.

    [TERM 2, 2012]

12. "The decade of 1830 had brought great economic hardship in Europe." Support the statement with argument.

    [TERM 2, 2016]

13. Describe any three economic hardships faced by Europe in the 1830s.

    [TERM 2, 2017]

▶ 5 Mark Questions

14. Explain any four ideas of Liberal Nationalists in the economic sphere.

    [TERM 2, 2011]

15. "Napoleon had, no doubt, destroyed democracy in France, but in the administrative field he had incorporated revolutionary principles in order to make the whole system more rational and efficient." Support the statement.

[TERM 2, 2012]

16. How did culture play an important role in creating the idea of the 'nation' in Europe? Explain with examples.

[TERM 2, 2013]

17. How had revolutionaries spread their ideas in many European States after 1815? Explain with examples.

[TERM 2, 2014]

18. Describe any five steps taken by the French Revolutionaries to create a sense of collective identity among the French people.

[TERM 2, 2015]

19. "Napoleon had destroyed democracy in France but in the administrative field he had incorporated revolutionary principals in order to make the whole system more rational and efficient." Analyze the statement with arguments.

[TERM 2, 2016]

20. "The first clear expression of nationalism came with the 'French Revolution' in 1789." Examine the statement.

[TERM 2, 2017]

21. Describe the explosive conditions that prevailed in Balkans after 1871 in Europe.

[DELHI 2018]

🔑 Solutions

1. (b) She took part in the French revolution.   [1]
2. (d) Sardinia-Piedmont.   [1]
3. (b) Giuseppe Mazzini   [1]
4. (d) Monarchy   [1]
5. The big European Powers met in Berlin in 1885 for dividing Africa.   [1]
6. (d) Frederic Sorreeu   [1]
7. The main aim of the French revolutionaries was end of monarchy and establishing a formal constitution for the nation.   [1]

8. In 1861, Victor Emmanuel II was proclaimed king of united Italy.   [1]

9. Three ways in which nationalist feelings were kept alive in Poland in the 18th and 19th centuries are:

   (i) Folklore collection i.e. folk songs, folk poetry, and folk dances were emphasized just to keep the spirit of the nation alive. It was done just not to recover an ancient national spirit but also to carry the modern nationalist message to large audiences who were mostly illiterate.   [1]

   (ii) Language too played an important major role in developing the nationalist feelings. Language was used as a weapon of national resistance. Polish was used for Church and ceremonial gatherings. The use of Polish came to be seen as a symbol of the struggle against Russian dominance.   [1]

   (iii) Music and dance also acted as the nationalist symbols. For example: Karol Kurpinski celebrated the national struggle through his music and operas, turning folk dances like the Polonaise and Mazurka into nationalist symbols.   [1]

10. The process of unification of Germany, took place under the leadership of Prussia and can be described as:

    (i) Prussia took the initiative of nation-building after the failure of Frankfurt Parliament of 1848 due to the repression by monarchy and military.   [1]

    (ii) Otto Von Bismarck, the chief minister of Prussia being the architect of this process was with its army and bureaucracy.   [1]

    (iii) Prussia fought three wars with Denmark, Austria and France for over seven years that resulted in its victory and thus the unification of Germany. The Prussian king, William I was crowned as the German Emperor.   [1]

11. Italy was politically fragmented and unstable in the middle of 19th century.

    King Victor Emmanuel II from Sardinia-Piedmont was inspired to unify the Italian states after previous failure of revolutionary up springs.

    (i) Rome was declared the capital of Italy, and In 1861, Victor Emanuel II was declared as the first King of united Italy.   [1]

(ii) In 1860, the forces marched into South Italy and the Kingdom of Two Sicilies and drove out the Spanish rulers. [1]

(iii) Giuseppe Garibaldi headed a revolution against Austria in an alliance with France in 1859. [1]

12. Below are the points that justify the statement, "The decade of 1830 had brought great economic hardship in Europe."

    (i) There was an enormous increase in the population in the first half of the nineteenth century all over Europe. [1]

    (ii) Overpopulation resulted in migration of the population of rural area to the cities to live in overcrowded slums. [1]

    (iii) Due to the food shortage there was huge rise in food prices. A year of bad harvest resulted to poverty in the town and the country. [1]

13. Following are the hardships faced by Europe in the 1830s:

    (i) Due to cheap goods which were machine made, imported from England, small producers were facing tough competition. [1]

    (ii) A large number of job seekers but less employment. [1]

    (iii) The population was increasing at a large rate. [1]

14. The four ideas of Liberal Nationalists in the economic sphere are:

    (i) Freedom of markets and abolition of restrictions put up by the state on the movements of goods and capitals. [1]

    (ii) Formation of Zollverein in 1834 at the initiative of Prussia. That served as the cause for a unified economic territory. [1 + 1]

    (iii) Reducing currency disparity and allowing uniform weights and measures. [1]

    (iv) Creation of road and rail network to fuel mobility and also to connect economic interests to national unification. [1]

15. "Napoleon had, no doubt, destroyed democracy in France, but in the administrative field he had incorporated revolutionary principles in order to make the whole system more rational and efficient."

These principles are summarized as the Napoleonic Code of 1804. The following are some of the administrative measures of Napoleon:

(i) He established equality before law and secured the right to property. [1]

(ii) He simplified the administrative divisions. [1]

(iii) He freed peasants from serfdom and manorial dues. [1]

(iv) Transport and communication system was improved. [1]

(v) Uniform laws, standardized weights and measures and a common national currency facilitated the movement of goods and capital from one region to another. [1]

16. Culture played an important role in creating the idea of the 'nation' in Europe in the following ways:

    (i) Romanticism was a cultural movement which aimed at developing a particular form of nationalist sentiment. Romantic artists were against the idea of glorification of reason and Science and focused instead on emotions, institution and mystical feelings. Their aim was to create a sense of shared collective heritage, a common cultural past, as the basis of a nation. [1 + 1]

    (ii) Romantic artists felt, collection and recording forms of folk culture were essential to the project of nation-building. For example, Karol Kurpinski celebrated the national struggle through his operas and music, turning folk dances like the polonaise and mazurka into nationalist symbols. [1]

    (iii) Language too was used as a nationalist symbol. After Russian occupation, the Polish language was forced out of schools and the Russian language was imposed everywhere. The use of Polish was considered as a symbol of the struggle against Russian dominance. [1 + 1]

17. Following the years after 1815, many liberal-nationalists and revolutionaries went underground due to the fear of repression and to avoid arrest. [1]

    (i) They started forming secret societies in many European states to train people and

spread their ideas. An Italian revolutionary, Giuseppe Mazzini founded two underground societies in Marseilles and in Berne to unite the fragmented Italy. After that, other revolutionaries followed his footsteps and started setting up many secret societies in Germany, France, Switzerland and Poland. [1]

(ii) To spread the awareness about having a free society, revolutionaries started opposing monarchical forms of governments that were established after the Vienna Congress. They fought for liberty and freedom and thought the creation of nation-state as a necessary part of their struggle for freedom. [1]

(iii) The nationalists started a cultural movement called Romanticism. To inculcate the feeling of nationalist sentiment and to popularize the true spirit of the nation, they used folk songs, folk poetry and folk dances to celebrate the national struggle through operas and music and turn them into nationalist symbols. [1]

(iv) Liberalism and nationalism brought revolution in many regions of Europe like the provinces of Ottoman Empire, Ireland, Poland besides Italy and Germany. [1]

18. The steps taken by the French revolutionaries involved various measures and practices that could create a sense of collective identity amongst the French people. Five of them are given below:

(i) The ideas of the fatherland and the citizen emphasized the notion of a united community enjoying equal rights under a constitution. [1]

(ii) The tricolor, a new French flag, was chosen to replace the former royal standard. [1]

(iii) They declared that their mission is to liberate people of Europe from despotism. [1]

(iv) New oaths taken, hymns were composed, and martyrs commemorated all in the name of one nation. [1]

(v) A centralized administrative system was put in place and it formulated uniform laws for all citizens within its territory. [1]

(vi) All custom duties were abolished.

19. Below are the revolutionary principles that Napoleon incorporated in order to make the system more rational and efficient:

(i) All the privileges that were given on the base of birth were removed and this rule was given a civil code of 1804 and named as napoleon code.

(ii) In the administration, he published equity before the law and secured the right of property.

(iii) Guild or artist restriction was removed in the towns.

(iv) Transport and communication systems were improved.

20. France was under absolute monarchy before 1789. With the 'French Revolution', the monarch was dethroned and then a sovereign body of French citizens was established. France become the nation-state and many following changes were made: [1]

(i) The royal standard flag was replaced by tri-color new French flag. [1]

(ii) A body of French citizens elected the estate general and then renamed as General Assembly. [1]

(iii) They adopted the system of uniform weighing and measurement. [1]

(iv) They accepted French as the national language of France.

(v) They made changes in the constitution and equal rights were given to all citizens. [1]

21. Explosive condition of Balkans in 1871 were-

The Balkans was a region of geographical and ethnic variation comprising modern days Romania, Bulgaria, Albania, Greece and Macedonia whose inhabitants were broadly known as Slavs.

A large part of Balkans was under the control of the Ottoman Empire. [1]

The spread of ideas of Romantic Nationalism in the Balkans together with the disintegration of the Ottoman Empire made this region explosive. [1]

All throughout the 19th century the Ottoman Empire had sought to strengthen itself. [1]

The Balkan people based their claims for independence or political rights on nationality and used history for their claim. [1]

Balkan also became the scene of rivalry among big powers. [1]

MULTIPLE CHOICE QUESTIONS

1. Which French artist illustrated the feeling of nationalism?

    (a) Duke Metternich (b) Frédéric Sorrieu

    (c) John Locke (d) Zollverein

2. What was the major outcome of the French Revolution?

    (a) Formation of a constitutional monarchy

    (b) Reformation of monarchy

    (c) Reestablishment of feudalism

    (d) Establishment of a secular state

3. When did Napoleon introduce the Civil Code?

    (a) 1890 (b) 1840

    (c) 1817 (d) 1804

4. Who is known as the architect of German unification?

    (a) Napoleon (b) Otto von Bismarck

    (c) Giuseppe Mazzini (d) Kaiser William I

5. Which of these was used as an allegory of a nation state in France?

    (a) Statue of Liberty (b) Germania

    (c) Marianne (d) Both (b) and (c)

Answer Keys

1. (b)   2. (a)   3. (d)   4. (b)   5. (c)

FILL IN THE BLANKS

1. _______________ formed a secret society known as 'Young Italy'

2. Nationalism in Europe marked the beginning of _____________.

3. A political and social philosophy that promotes traditional social institutions in the context of culture and civilisation is called as _______________.

4. _______________ was the Chief Minister of Sardinia Piedmont.

5. _______________ is the policy of extending a country's power and influence through colonization, use of military force or other means

Solutions

1. Giuseppe Mazzini

2. Renaissance

3. Conservatism

4. Count Camillo de Cavour

5. Imperialism

TRUE OR FALSE

1. Monarchy form of government existed in France before the revolution of 1789.

2. The Treaty of Vienna signed in 1815 brought the conservative regimes back to power

3. Romanticism was a religious movement that aimed the purification of slaves.

4. Bismarck introduced the policy of 'Blood and Iron' for the unification of Germany.

5. Carl Welcker supported the idea of equal rights for women.

Solutions

1. True

2. True

3. False

4. True

5. False

CHAPTER 2

Nationalism in India

Summary

The First World War, Khilafat and Non-Cooperation Movement

- The first world war took place in 1914 and continued till 1918.

- To meet the expenses of war ,tax ,custom duties,were raised.

- Income tax was introduced to breach the economic needs during war time.

- To fulfil the requirement of soldiers, villagers were forced to join.

- Due to various reasons crop failed in 1920 that leads the shortage of food crops.

- In the same time diseases like influenza spread and caused death of peoples.

Khilafat and Non Cooperation Movement

- Disintegration of Ottoman empire was took place after the first world war.

- To uphold the status of Khilafat a movement was started by Muhammad Ali and Shaukat Ali.

- Ali brothers and other Muslim leaders formed a Khilafat committee in Bombay.

- They started Khilafat movement against British empire joining with mass movement started by Gandhiji.

- Gandhiji avails this golden opportunity to unite Hindu-Muslims for freedom struggle.

- In Congress session of Culcutta Gandhiji decide to launch nationwide movement in the support of Khilafat.

Non-Cooperation Movement

- The movement started with the notion of notion of not to cooperate Britishers in every sector.

- Students, teachers, left the educational institutions, foreign goods were boycotted.

- Except madras, the council elections were boycotted.

- Liquor shops picketed, peoples denied to use of foreign cloths.

- In Awadh peasants joined this movement to fulfil their demands i.e to reduce tax, abolish beggar and other social issues.

- They organized Nai dhobi bandh for landlords as a part of social boycott under the leadership of Baba Ramchandra.

- Peasants defined this movement as movement against tax.

- Thousands of plantation workers of Assam left the tea gardens and returned home to support the movement. They took this movement as the movement of land distribution among landless.

- Tribal peasants of accepted this movement as a movement against British policy against forests.

- During this movement the production of textile mills increased rapidly.

- In Awadh peasants expressed their anger on the house of Zamindars and Talukdars.

- The movement had a limited participation and alternatives of British institutions was not availabletherefore,movementdidnotattainitsgoal butcontributedindevelopingthesenseOfcommon people.

Civil Disobedience Movement

- After the failure of Simmon commission, Irwin offeredastatusofDominionstatusandroundtable discussion. Congress leaders didn't accepted it.

- The demand of Poorna Swarajya or complete independence raised by congress and on 26th of January accepted as Poorna Swarajya Day.

- Gandhiji opted salt to unite the Indian under the umbrella of nationalism to get the goal of freedom.

- Gandhiji gave a ultimatum of eleven demand to lord Irwin to fulfil by 11th of march 1930 and warned him if the government failed to respond he will launch a nation wide movement.

- Lord Irwin didn't responded, Gandhiji started Civil disobedience movement by Salt March.

- On 12th of march Gandhiji started march sabaramati ashram to dandi with his 78 followers.

- Gandhiji covered the Distance of 240 km in 24 day, travelling 24 km per day, by addressing thousands of peoples about Swaraj.

- The salt was defied on the morning of 6th April 1930, by making salt.

- Following Gandhiji, various place of India witnessed the breaking of salt under the leadership of famous freedom fighter.

- Peoples defied to pay taxes like chakidari tax, land tax and also refused to accept forest laws.

- Britisher government started to suppress this nationwide movement relentlessly.

- Brutual repression and peoples aggression compelled Gandhiji to think about the call off the movement and on 5th of march the famous Gandhi-Irwin pact was signed by both.

- According to the pact Gandhiji want to London but his travel to Round Table conference was not successful and he launched the movement again.

People Participation in the Movement

- The participation of all sector was not with the same goal they defined Swaraj as their own mindset.

- The Patidars of Gujarat and Jats of U.P joined this movement to reduce the land revenue but when the movement was stopped they lost their hope.

- The poor landless peasants participated in this movement to remove the land rents.

- The business class joined this movement against British policy regarding trade,as they wanted to earn benefits like during world war.

- G.D Birla and other members of FICCI supported the movement in financial term but with the failure of Round Table Conference they refused to support.

- The worker of Nagpur participated in this movement to oppose the low wages and poor working conditions.

- Thousand of woman took part in this movement by staging agitation, manufacturing salt, picketing foreign cloths but the congress had not clear aspects regarding women.

- This movement had some limits however it was successful in creating a strong sense of Nationalism.

Sense of Collective Belonging

- When the peoples started to identify themselves or all to be part of one nation, than it is said the nationalism is spreading.

- The experience, came from united struggles, created a sense of collective belongings.

- The folklore, folk tales ,popular prints, songs, symbols, history and fiction contributed to create a sense of one or Nationalism.

- To unit people, painters started to visualize India as a mother and a image of mother were portrayed with iron, that invoke peoples to fight against freedom of mother.

- The image of Bharat Mata first created by Bankim Chandra Chattopadhyay later he composed Vande Matram. The song was used in procession or protest against Britishers.

- The reverence for Bharat image is considered as the sign of nationalism and patriotism.
- Folk lore sung by bards in village also relates peoples with the sacrifice and brave heros of freedom movement, which invoke peoples to be a part of freedom movement.
- Images and symbols also contributed in the development of nationalism and create a bond of one nation among peoples.
- Tricolour flag designed in Bengal and flag designed by Gandhiji was example of unifying India by symbols.
- Revival and reinterpretations of history connected peoples with the ancient glory of India and inspired to attain it again by driving out Britishers from India
- These icons, image, history was related with Hindus it also create a sense of alienation among different religions.

Points to know

Nationalism – Notion towards nation.

Forced recruitment – to fulfil the needs of workers or soldiers a imperialist force to join the colonizers.

Satyagraha – Request for truth. Gandhiji used it as a weapon against British empire.

Picket – Blockage of the door to preventing the use of shop or factories by workers or peoples.

Gudem Rebel – A Guerrilla warfare took place in Andhra Pradesh against British empire to achieve swaraj.

Important Personalities

General Dyer – commander of British of army in Amritsar, attacked on the procession of Jaliawala Bagh.

Ali Brothers – Muhammad Ali and Shaukat Ali both brothers organized a committee to oppose the minimization of power of Khilafat.

Baba Ramchandra – Led the peasant revolt in Awadh.

Alluri Sitaram Raju – known as incarnation of god, encouraged the non cooperation movement.

C R Das – founder of Swaraj party.

Muhhamad Ali Zinnah – prominent leader of Muslim League, demanded for the nation of Muslims Or separation of India.

Abanindranath Tagore – famous painter, designed the image of Bharat Mata.

Mahatma Gandhi – started non cooperation, civil disobedience movements based on Satyagraha. He brought Indian under the umbrella of Nationalism to fight against Britishers.

Important Dates

1918-19 – Crops failed in India

1915 – Mahatma Gandhi returned from south Africa in January.

1919 – The Jaliawala Bagh massacre took place on 13th April.

1919 – In march, Khilafat committee was formed.

1909 – Hind swaraj written by Gandhiji was published.

1923 – Non cooperation movement was launched.

1927 – FICCI was formed

1928 – Simon commission was arrived.

1929 – Round table conference took place.

1930 – On 13 march 1930 Gandhiji started salt march.

1931 – 2nd round table conference was held in London.

1931 – Civil disobedience movement was launched.

PREVIOUS YEARS'
EXAMINATION QUESTIONS

▶ 1 Mark Questions

1. Which one of the following statements is not related to the Gandhi-Irwin Pact?

   (a) Gandhiji agreed not to launch any further mass agitations against the British.

   (b) Gandhiji agreed to participate in the Round Table Conference.

(c) Gandhiji decided to call off the Civil Disobedience Movement.

(d) The British agreed to release the political prisoners.

[TERM 2, 2011]

2. Why did Nationalists in India tour villages to gather folk songs and legends? Choose the most appropriate reason from the following:

(a) Nationalists wanted to study their own culture.

(b) Nationalists wanted to publish it and earn money.

(c) Nationalists did it because it gave a true picture of traditional culture.

(d) Nationalists wanted to keep folk culture intact.

[TERM 2, 2011]

3: In which of the following years Mahatma Gandhi inspired the peasants of Champaran district of Bihar to struggle against the oppressive plantation system:

(a) 1916   (b) 1917

(c) 1918   (d) 1919

[TERM 2, 2012]

4: In which one of the following Indian National Congress Sessions, the idea of 'Non-Cooperation Movement' was accepted?

(a) Lahore Session

(b) Nagpur Session

(c) Calcutta (Kolkata) Session

(d) Madras (Chennai) Session

[TERM 2, 2012]

5. The Non-Cooperation Movement began during

(a) January 1921

(b) November 1921

(c) December 1921

(d) May 1921

[TERM 2, 2013]

6. Name the writer of the book 'Hind Swaraj'.

[TERM 2, 2017]

7. What was the main aim of the popular movement of April 2006, in Nepal?

[TERM 2, 2015]

▶ 2 Mark Questions

8. Two features (1) and (2) are marked in the given political outline map of India. Identify these features with the help of the help of the following information and write their correct names on the lines marked in the map:

(1) The place, where the Indian National Congress Session of September 1920 was held.

(2) The place, where the movement of Indigo Planters took place.

[TERM 2, 2011]

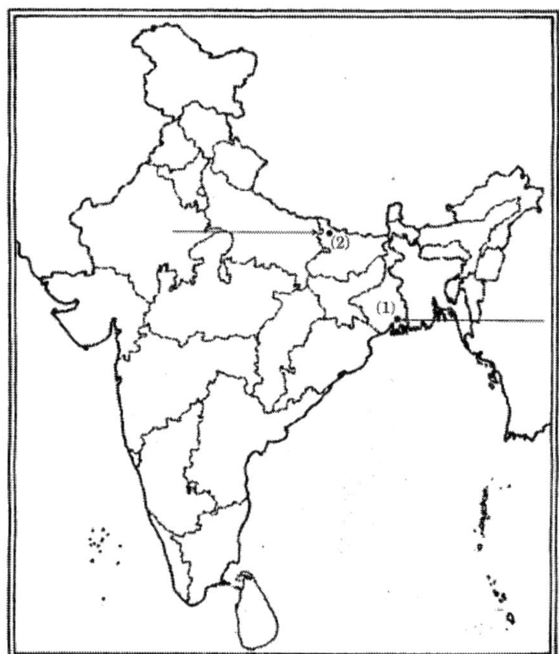

9. Locate and label the following features with appropriate symbols on the same political outline map of India:

(i) Amritsar: The place of Jallianwala Bagh incident.

(ii) Bardoli: The place where no tax campaign was held.

[TERM 2, 2011]

10. Two features - A and B are marked in the given political outline map of

India. Identify these features with the help of the following information and write their correct names on the lines marked in the map

(A) The place where Indian National Congress Session was held in September 1920.

(B) The place where the Peasant Satyagraha was held in Gujarat.

[TERM 2, 2012]

11. Locate and label the following items with appropriate symbols on the same map:

(*i*) Chauri-Chaura - The place of calling off the Non-Cooperation Movement (N.C.M.)

(*ii*) Amritsar - The place where Jallian Wala Bagh incident took place.

[TERM 2, 2012]

▷ 3 Mark Questions

12. Explain any three effects of the Non Co-operation Movement on the economy of India.

[TERM 2, 2011]

13. Why did Non-Cooperation Movement gradually slowdown in cities?

Explain any three reasons.

[TERM 2, 2012]

14. How had the First World War created a new economic situation in India? Explain with three examples.

[TERM 2, 2013]

15. How was the Rowlatt Act opposed by the people in India? Explain with examples.

[TERM 2, 2013]

16. Describe the main features of 'Poona Pact'.

[TERM 2, 2015]

17. How did 'Salt March' become an effective tool of resistance against colonialism? Explain.

[TERM 2, 2015]

18. Three features A, B and C are marked on the given political outline map of India (on page 9). Identify these features with the help of the following information and write their correct names on the lines marked in the map:

A. The place where the Indian National Congress Session was held.

B. The place associated with the Peasant's Satyagraha.

C. The place related to calling off the Non-Cooperation Movement.

[TERM 2, 2015]

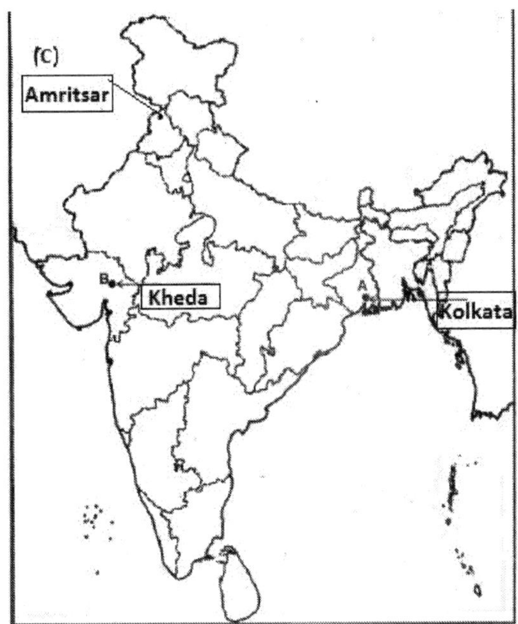

19. (*a*) Name the place where the Indian National Congress Session was held in December 1920.

(*b*) Name the place associated with the movement of Indigo Planters.

(*c*) Name the place related to the Satyagraha of peasants in Gujarat.

[TERM 2, 2015]

20. What type of flag was designed during the 'Swadeshi' Movement' in Bengal? Explain its main features.

[TERM 2, 2016]

21. "The plantation workers in Assam had their own understanding of Mahatma Gandhi and the notion of Swaraj". Support the statement with arguments.

[TERM 2, 2016]

22. Three features A, B and C are marked on the given political outline map of India. Identify these features with the help of the following information and write their correct names on the lines marked in the map:

A. The place where cotton mill workers organized Satyagraha.

B. The place related to the calling off the Non-cooperation Movement.

C. The place where the Indian National Congress Session was held.

[TERM 2, 2016]

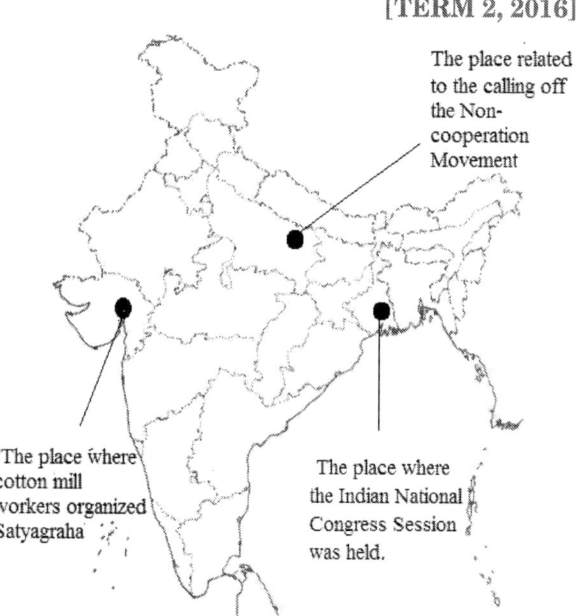

23. Why did Gandhi ji decide to withdraw the 'Non-Cooperation Movement' in February 1922? Explain any three reasons.

[TERM 2, 2017]

24. Evaluate the role of business classes in the 'Civil Disobedience Movement'.

[TERM 2, 2017]

25. Three features A, B and C are marked on the given political outline map of India. Identify these features with the help of the following information and write their correct names on the lines marked on the map:

A. The city associated with the Jallianwala Bagh incident.

B. The place where the Indian National Congress session was held.

C. The place where Gandhiji violated the Salt Law.

[TERM 2, 2017]

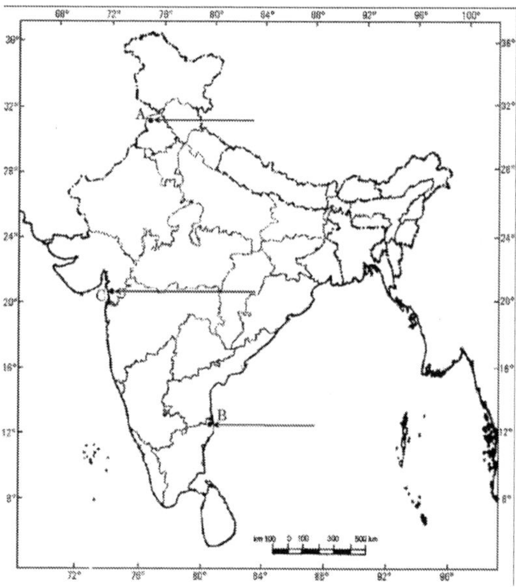

▶ 4 Mark Questions

26. Explain four points about Gandhi ji's idea of 'Satyagraha'.

[TERM 2, 2011]

27. How did people and the colonial government react to the Civil Disobedience Movement? Explain.

[TERM 2, 2012]

▶ 5 Mark Questions

28. Explain the attitude of the Indian merchants and the industrialists towards the 'Civil Disobedience Movement'.

[TERM 2, 2015]

29. How did the Civil Disobedience Movement come into force in various parts of the country? Explain with examples.

[TERM 2, 2016]

30. How did the Colonial Government repress the 'Civil Disobedience Movement'? Explain.

[TERM 2, 2017]

31. Why was Congress reluctant to allow women to hold any position of authority within the organization? How did women participate in Civil Disobedience Movement? Explain.

[DELHI 2018]

🔑 Solutions

1. Gandhiji agreed not to launch any further mass agitations against the British.   [1]

2. Nationalists did it because it gave a true picture of traditional culture.   [1]

3. 1917 [1]

4. Calcutta (Kolkata) Session [1]

5. May 1921 [1]

6. Hind Swaraj is written by Mahatma Gandhi.[1]

7. Restoration of democracy was the popular movement of April 2006 in Nepal. [1]

8. The features identified are as:

(1) Calcutta [1]

(2) Champaran(Bihar) [1]

9. Political outline map of India

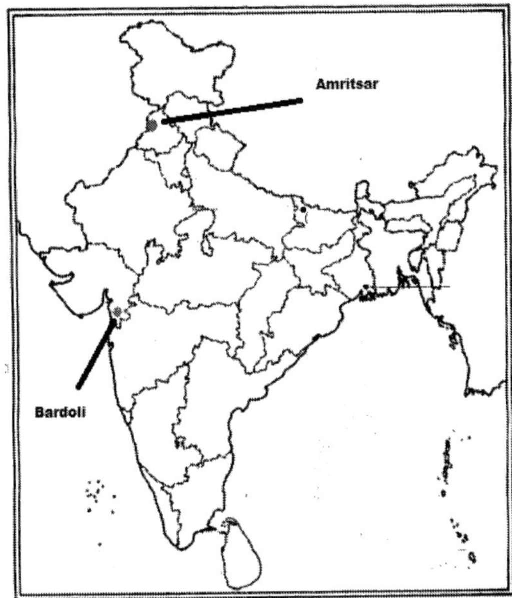

[1 + 1]

10.

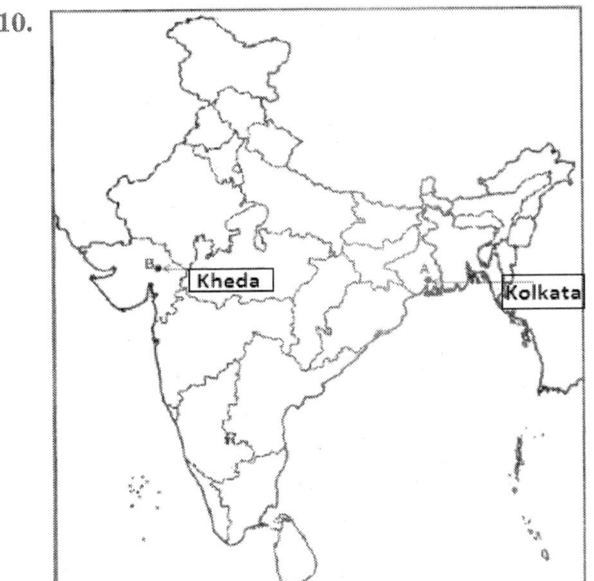

[1 + 1]

11.

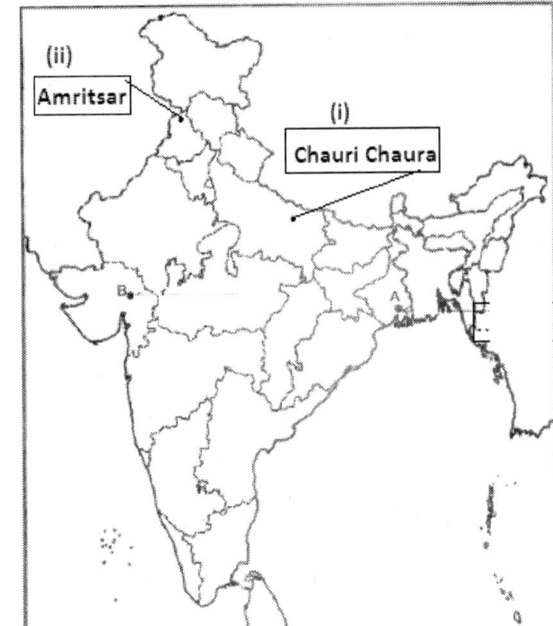

12. The following are the effects of the Non Co-operation Movement on the Indian economy:

(i) Rejection of foreign goods. Liquor shops were picketed and huge bonfires of foreign clothes were burnt. [1]

(ii) Between 1921 and 1922, import of foreign clothes halved with its value dropping from Rs. 102 crore to Rs. 57 crore. Many merchants and traders denied to finance the foreign trade and to trade in foreign goods. [1]

(iii) Indian textile mills and handlooms increased as the people started wearing Indian clothes and rejected the imported ones. [1]

13. The following reasons explains the slowing down of Non-Cooperation Movement in cities:

(i) Khadi clothes were more expensive than the mass-produced mill cloth, hence people could not afford them. [1]

(ii) Disruption of the functioning of public institutions caused problems to people as the process of setting up Indian institutions was very slow. [1]

(iii) Lack of alternate Indian institutions that could replace the British institutions forced the students to go back to their colleges and the lawyers to return back to work in courts thus quitting the Non-Cooperation Movement. [1]

14. The First World War had created huge impact on the economic situation in India.

    (*i*) It led to a huge increase in defence expenditure of British Raj which increased various taxes. [1]

    (*ii*) As Indian industrialists started manufacturing war materials to send to Britain the process of industrialization intensified. [1]

    (*iii*) A demand for industrial goods such as Jute, Bags, Cloth, Rails, etc. increased and it caused a decline of imports from other countries to India and increase in employment in India. [1]

15. The Rowlatt Act of 1919 was opposed in many different ways.

    (*i*) Workers working in railway workshops went on strike. [1]

    (*ii*) All commercial establishments were closed down. [1]

    (*iii*) In different cities rallies were organized.

    (*iv*) The infamous Jallianwala Bagh massacre took place because people had gathered in opposition to the Rowlatt act. [1]

    (*v*) Open fire was ordered by General Dyer, on innocent civilians who gathered outside the city of Amritsar to attend a peaceful meeting.

16. The main attributes of 'Poona Pact' are as follows:

    1. The seats were reserved in provincial and central legislative councils for Schedule Castes but they were to be voted in by the general electorate. [1]

    2. Poona Pact came into acceptance as Gandhiji began a fast unto death. [1]

    3. Ambedkar also accepted Gandhiji's position and Poona pact was announced on September 1932. [1]

17. Salt is a crucial part of food. The dictatorial face of British rule was exposed by the monopoly of tax, salt and government over the salt production. Under this movement, Gandhiji asked for swaraj from Britishers. Mahatma Gandhi started his famous salt march taking 78 of his trusted volunteers along. The march was undertaken from Sabarmati(Gandhiji's ashram) to the coastal town of Gujarat (Dandi) which was over 240 miles. This led to the widespread resistance against British rule. [1 + 1 + 1]

18. (*a*) Kolkata [1]

    (*b*) kheda [1]

    (*c*) Amritsar [1]

19. (*a*) Kolkata [1]

    (*b*) Champaran [1]

    (*c*) Ahmedabad [1]

20. During the Swadeshi movement in Bengal, Flag had become a symbol of defiance. A tricolor flag (red, green, yellow) had been designed. It had eight lotuses symbolizing eight provinces of British India, and a crescent moon, representing Hindus and Muslims. In the meantime by 1921, Gandhiji had designed the Swaraj Flag. It was a tri-color flag (red, green and white) having a spinning wheel in centre, representing the Gandhian Ideal of self help. [1 + 1 + 1]

21. The plantation workers in Assam had their own understanding of Swaraj.

    (*i*) For them freedom meant the right to move freely in and out from their horizons. [1]

    (*ii*) For them it was retaining again to their villages from where they belonged as Under the Inland Emigration act of 1859, they were not allowed to leave tea gardens without permission. [1]

    (*iii*) Thousands of workers left the plantations and headed homes defying the authorities and government of then. [1]

    (*iv*) According to them Gandhi Raj was emerging and their sufferings and troubles would be eliminated. .

22. A. Ahmedabad is the place where cotton mill workers organized Satyagraha. [1]

    B. Chaura Chauri is the place related to the calling off of the Non-cooperation Movement. [1]

    C. Calcutta is the place where the Indian National Congress Session was held. [1]

23. Gandhi ji decided to withdraw the 'Non-Cooperation Movement' in February 1922 due to following reasons: [1]

    (*i*) The Movement was meant to be a peaceful movement but Satyagrahis were turning violent so he felt that Staygrahis needed to be trained properly for mass agitation. [1]

   (*ii*) Congress leaders wanted to contest elections, so they did not want any mass-struggle. [1]

24. Following are the roles of business class in the 'Civil Disobedience Movement':

   (*i*) 'Indian Industrial and Commercial Congress' was formed by the business class in 1920 and the 'Federation of the Indian Chamber of Commerce' and Industries in 1927 to organize business interest. [1]

   (*ii*) Finances were being provided by business class for the movement. [1]

   (*iii*) They refused to sell and buy imported good. [1]

25. 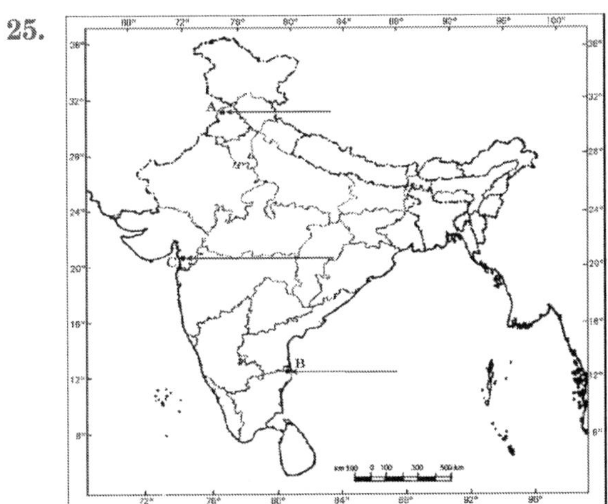

(A) Amritsar [1]

(B) Madras [1]

(C) Dandi [1]

26. The idea of Gandhi ji's Satyagraha can be abstracted as follows:

   (1) It highlights the Power of Truth and the need to search for it. [1]

   (2) It puts forward that if the motive is true and the fight is against the injustice, then physical force is not necessary. [1]

   (3) A Satyagrahi could win the battle through non-violence without being agitated or being aggressive by appealing to the conscience of the oppressors. People need to see and accept the truth, instead of being forced to accept it through the use of violence. [1]

   (4) Gandhi ji believed that truth was bound to ultimately triumph and that 'Dharma' of non-violence was enough to unite all the Indians. [1]

27. People and the colonial government reacted to the Civil Disobedience Movement in the following ways:

Reaction of the people Civil disobedience movement consisted of the people from all castes and classes of the society. [0.5]

   (*i*) Thousands of people from different parts of the country broke the salt law by manufacturing salt and demonstrating in front of the government salt factories. [0.5]

   (*ii*) People boycotted foreign cloth, and protested in front of the liquor shops. [0.5]

   (*iii*) Peasants refused to pay the chaukidari taxes and revenues. Many of the village officials resigned and the forest laws were violated by the forest people by entering the Reserved Forests to collect wood and graze cattle. [0.5]

Reaction of the government The colonial government reacted brtually to stop the Civil disobedience movement by arresting the Congress leaders one by one, Abdul Ghaffar Khan (a staunch follower of Mahatma Gandhi) being one of them. [0.5]

   (*i*) Many were killed by the police firing and the angry crowd had to face the armoured cars. [0.5]

   (*ii*) The government responded with brutal aggression when the industrial workers of Sholapur attacked police posts protesting against Gandhi's imprisonment. [0.5]

   (*iii*) Satyagrahis protesting peacefully were attacked and over 100,000 people were arrested. [0.5]

28. The attitude of the Indian merchants and the industrialists towards the 'Civil Disobedience Movement' can be described as follows:

   (*i*) Indian industrialists believed that the colonial policies were restricting their business as they made huge profits during the First World War. [1]

   (*ii*) They refused to buy or sell any imported goods. [1]

   (*iii*) They were against all the trade barriers and wanted to expand their business at their own. [1]

(iv) The organization FICCI (Federation of the Indian chamber of commerce) was organized in 1927, to look after their business interests. [1]

(v) They wanted protection against imports of foreign goods and therefore, they were an active participant in the 'Civil Disobedience Movement'. [1]

29. Answer: The Civil Disobedience Movement came into force in various parts of the country as:

(i) Gandhiji led the Salt March from Sabarmati Ashram to Dandi with his followers starting the Civil Disobedience Movement. Salt law was broken by most of the people from the different parts of the country. The salt was produced and demonstrated in front of the factories by the people. [1]

(ii) The rich Patidars of Gujarat and Jats of Uttar Pradesh in the countryside actively participated in the movement. Many communities were led by these rich peasants, and sometimes they forced the members who were unwilling to participate in the movement. They considered this fight for Swaraj against high revenues. [1]

(ii) The industrial working class of Nagpur region participated in the movement. Railway workers, dock workers, coal mine workers took part in the protest rallies and boycott crusade. [1]

(iv) Large number of Women also actively participated in the movement. Many came out of their houses, took part in the protest marches and also manufactured salt. [1]

(v) Industrialists led by Purshottamdas Thakurdas and G D Birla supported the Civil Disobedience Movement. [1]

30. The Colonial Government took following brutal steps to repress the 'Civil Disobedience Movement':

(i) The Congress leaders were arrested by the government one by one. This led to violence in many places of the country. [1]

(ii) In April 1930, it arrested Abdul Ghaffar Khan who was a devout disciple of Mahatma Gandhi. [1]

(iii) The government arrested Gandhi ji also. [1]

(iv) Police fired on an angry crowd in the streets of Peshawar and killed many people. [1]

(v) They beat women and children and attacked Satyagrahis. [1]

(vi) They arrested about 100 000 people. [1]

31. Congress was reluctant in participation of women-

(i) Congress was keen only on the symbolic presence of women within the organization. [1]

(ii) Gandhi ji believed that role of women was to look after home and hearth so as being good mothers and good wives. [1]

Participation of women in Civil Disobedience Movement

(i) During Gandhiji's Salt March, lots of women came out to participate in protest marches. [0.5]

(ii) They manufactured salt and picketed liquor shops. [0.5]

(iii) They boycotted foreign goods. [0.5]

(iv) Women from high caste families and from rich peasant households participated. [0.5]

(v) Moved by Gandhiji's call, they began to see service to nation as a sacred duty of women.

MULTIPLE CHOICE QUESTIONS

1. Mahatma Gandhi travelled to Champaran in Bihar to...........
   (a) Understand the geographical extent of India
   (b) To encourage people to support Indian goods
   (c) Inspire the peasants to struggle against the oppressive plantation system
   (d) All of the above

2. Which act gave enormous powers to the British Government to repress political activities?
   (a) Irwin Pact
   (b) Simon Act
   (c) Indian Emigration Act
   (d) Rowlatt Act

3. The Simon Commission was not well received in India because......

(a) It did not constitute of any Indian representative

(b) It did not constitute of any women representative

(c) The Indians were not aware of the arrival of the commission

(d) It gave the British absolute cultural rights over India

4. The Salt March or Dandi March was started by Gandhiji on?

(a) 12th March 1936   (b) 12th March 1930

(c) 12th May 1930   (d) 12th March 1931

5. Why did Gandhiji withdraw the Non-Cooperation Movement?

(a) Gandhiji realized that British was more powerful and could not be defeated

(b) Some Congress leaders wanted to participate in elections to Provincial Councils

(c) Some Congress leaders wanted to lead the movement

(d) Gandhiji felt the movement was turning violent in many places

Answer Keys

1. (c)   2. (d)   3. (a)   4. (b)   5. (d)

Solutions

1. Inspire the peasants to struggle against the oppressive plantation system

2. Rowlatt Act

3. It did not constitute of any Indian representative

4. 12th March 1930

5. Gandhiji felt the movement was turning violent in many places

FILL IN THE BLANKS

1. The Khilafat movement was initiated by _____________ and __________.

2. During _______________ movement, the people refused to buy/support British goods.

3. The Jallianwala Bagh incident took place on ___________.

4. The ____________ gave Depressed Classes (later to be known as Scheduled Caste) reserved seats in provincial and central legislative councils.

5. This image of Bharat Mata was created by _______________.

Solutions

1. Muhammad Ali and Shaukat Ali

2. Civil Disobedience

3. 13th April 1919

4. Poona Pact

5. Abanindranath Tagore

TRUE OR FALSE

1. Depressed Classes Association was established by Ali brothers.

2. During the "Swadeshi Movement" in Bengal the flag designed was a Tricolour Flag.

3. The idea of Satyagraha emphasized on achieving independence through violence.

4. The resolution of Purna Swaraj was adopted at Lahore Session of 1929.

5. The Civil Disobedience Movement did not witness women participation.

Solutions

1. False

2. True

3. False

4. True

5. False

CHAPTER 3

The Making of a Global World

Summary

The Pre modern World and the Nineteenth Century (Global Economy and Colonialism)

- Globalisation is a process of integration by sharing ideas, technology, culture and tradition.

- Trade with other countries and migration enabled the Globalisation.

- Money, skills, goods, ideas travelled a long distance with religious person, traders.

- We had some specific routes for trade, which enabled the access of knowledge, food products, skill and germs from one place to another. These routes were known as silk routes.

- Silk routes connects the Asia, Europe and Northern Africa.

- Food materials travelled with the traders and food produced in many part of the world, like the spaghetti of Italy was travelled from china. In china it was noodles.

- Some food materials like soya, ground nuts, potatoes, chillies, tomatoes travelled in Europe and Asia after discovery of America.

- European conquest American colonies with the help of small pox.

Nineteenth Century (Global Economy and Colonialism)

- In 19th century the society improved rapidly due to intermingle of, cultural, social and technological factors.

- Three types of movements took place in the economical context of the world in 19th century.

- First one was the hike in the trade of cloths and wheat. Second was the migration of people in search of job and third was the investment of money at small or large scale.

Global Economy

- In Britain the population was increasing but not the land. The government banned the import of corn to satisfy the landed group.

- Industrialist and urban dwellers were unhappy with the high food price and mounted pressure to lift the banned from corn laws.

- Consumption of food material increased but not the price. British farmers were not able to compete with markets they started to migrate.

- The purchasing power of peoples in England increased by faster industrial growth, Now the Eastern Europe, Australia, America started to cultivate to meet the demands of Britain.

- Agricultural regions needed to connect with ports or other centre for trade therefore infrastructural development took place like setup of Railways and making of Harbours.

- All development work and agriculture needed work force, that was fulfilled by the migrated labours of America and Australia

- Britishers developed canal to irrigate the land for growing cotton, to meet the demands of industries.

- The important inventions also paced the globalization of economies,especially means of transportation made easier to trade of perishable goods like meat. Now the meat is transported from America, Australia to Europe.

Colonialism

- The freedom of some countries was captured by developed ones, to meet the demands. It was the dark face of globalization.

- European powers to capture the geographical part to meet the demands they divided Africa for their means.

- In 1885 the European powers met in Berlin to divide Africa legally.

- The Belgium and Germany, Britain and France captured the geographical areas and became colonial powers.

- The colonies were used to fulfil the need of masters. The social economical exploitation placed the colonies in miserable conditions.

The Inter War and Post War Economy

- The first world war was continued more than four year, it was the industrial war.

- Technology, weapons, guns were used at large scale in this war. A millions of soldiers were recruited. 20 million soldiers injured.

- To meet the demands of war the industries were re-structured. Women started to do the work of men as men were involved in war.

- Britain took high amount of money from US to meet his war expenses.

- War changed the status of US from borrower to lender.

- The post war economy changed the economical scenario of the world.

- The condition of Britain was deplorable after the war. It was very tough to gain its status again.

- Britain lost his dominance in Indian market and was not able to compete with Japan.

- During war the production was increased due to high demand but after war production went down and unemployment increased.

- End of war created unemployment at large scale in Britain.

- After the war the production of wheat increased in Canada, Australia and America while decreased in Eastern Europe. The condition of agricultural economies were worsened after the war.

- After the war price of grains were fallen, incomes became declined.

- After war the economy of US went up due to mass production.

- Henry Ford, owner of Ford cars, used conveyer belt for mass production which was later followed by Europe.

- After the war the great depression was faced by many countries like US, India.

- After the world war, over production, fall of price of products, collapse of banks in US, fall in trade were the major reason of the Great Depression

Points to know

Biological war – a war in which germs, bacteria or other microorganism is used to defeat the enemy.

Dissenter – who is not going to accept the beliefs and practices, prevailing in society.

Indentured labour – a labour, bonded with a contract to work for employer for a frame time after that he can return his home. They termed as Girmitiya majdoor.

Exchange rate – for the purpose of international trade, the value of money is fix, to change it from other, national currencies.

Silk routes – a route which connected the Asia to its various regions also from Europe and Africa.

El Dorado – city of Gold

Important Personalities

Shikaripuri shroffs and **Nattukottai Chettiars** – were made a group of bankers to provide economical assistance in trade and agriculture.

Henery ford – owner of ford motors, who started the use of conveyer belt for production.

Important Dates

1890 – US become colonial power

1890 – Cattle plague and Rinderpest in Africa.

1800 – Indian cotton decline at 15%

1929 – The great depression

1928-34 – Price of wheat fall by 50 %

1944 – Bretton wood conference took place

PREVIOUS YEARS'
EXAMINATION QUESTIONS

▶ 1 Mark Questions

1. People's livelihoods and local economy of which one of the following was badly affected by the disease named 'Rinderpest'?

    (a) Asia

    (b) Europe

    (c) Africa

    (d) South America

    [TERM 1, 2011]

2. Which one of the following powerful weapons was used by the Spanish conquerors to colonise America during the mid seventeenth century?

    (a) Conventional Military Weapons

    (b) Modern Military Weapons

    (c) Biological Weapons (Germs of small pox)

    (d) Nuclear Weapons

    [TERM 1, 2011]

3. From where did most of the Indian Indentured Workers come from?

    [TERM 1, 2015]

4. Why did big European powers meet in Berlin in 1885?

    [DELHI 2018]

▶ 3 Mark Questions

5. Give three examples to show that the world changed with the discovery of new sea routes to America.

    [TERM 1, 2011]

6. What were Corn Laws? Why were these laws abolished? What were its results?

    [TERM 1, 2012]

7. Why did MNCs began to shift their production centres to Asian countries? What were its effects?

    [TERM 1, 2013]

8. Explain the impact of the First World War on the British economy.

    [TERM 1, 2014]

9. Explain the three types of "flows" within the international economic exchanges.

    [TERM 1, 2014]

10. Explain any three effects of the Great Depression of 1929 in the United States.

    [TERM 1, 2015]

11. "19th century indenture had been described as a new system of slavery". Explain the statement briefly.   [TERM 1, 2015]

12. State three reasons why did Europeans flee to America in 19th century.

    [TERM 1, 2016]

13. Describe the impact of 'Rinderpest' on people's livelihoods and local economy in Africa in the 1890s.

    [DELHI 2018]

▶ 4 Mark Questions

14. Describe the causes of Great Depression.

    [TERM 1, 2011]

15. Explain any four features of primitive subsistence agriculture in India.

    [TERM 1, 2011]

▶ 5 Mark Questions

16. What attracted the Europeans to Africa? Mention any three methods used to recruit and retain the African laborers.

    [TERM 1, 2014]

17. Describe the effects of the Great Depression on the US.

[TERM 1, 2012]

🔑 Solutions

1. (c) Africa [1]

2. (c) Biological Weapons (Germs of small pox) [1]

3. Most of the Indian Indentured Workers came from the regions of eastern Uttar Pradesh, Bihar, Central India and the dry districts of Tamilnadu. [1]

4. European powers met in Berlin in 1885 to decide the sharing of Africa among them. [1]

5. The world changed in the following ways with the discovery of new sea routes to America:

    (i) Many common foods were introduced to Europe from America e.g. Soya, Tomatoes, Potatoes, Maize, etc. Potato became the food for poor people. They began to eat better and live longer in England. [1]

    (ii) Europe started using Silver, a precious metal to enhance its wealth and finance its trade. These silver mines are located in present day Peru. [1]

    (iii) Europe started slave trades. Slaves were captured by European traders and taken to America. These slaves worked on plantations. Europe soon became the centre of the world trade. [1]

6. The restrictions of tariff and trade on the import of corn were Corn Laws. These were imposed between 1815 and 1846 by the British government in Great Britain. [1]

    Because of the unhappiness of the industrialists and urban dweller due to hike in food prices, these laws were terminated as the price of grains was very high. [1]

    The abolition of the Corn Laws resulted in free trade in Britain. Food could be imported into Britain at cheaper rates as a result, since agriculture was not able to compete with imports. This resulted in migration of farmers to urban areas in search of employment. [1]

7. MNCs began to shift their production centres to Asian countries because of the following reasons:

    (i) Cheap labor and low wages. [1]

    (ii) Availability of raw materials and a large market. [1]

    It simulated world trade and also flow of capital. Countries like India, China and Brazil underwent rapid economic transformation. It generated employment opportunities and introduced competition in the domestics markets. [1]

8. The First World War had a very bad impact on the British economy. Some of the effects are as follows:

    (i) 15-25% part of their stockpiled wealth was spent on the war, and after the war they had to suffer massive debts, especially from US. [1]

    (ii) Britain had many buyers before the war. But after the war, it realized that its many buyers did not need to buy goods from Britain anymore as they had set up their own industries. It was because it could not provide goods for its foreign buyers during the war. [1]

    (iii) The farmers also suffered because of the war as they had to produce more crops in the period of war but when the war ended, they had excess stock of the crops. As a result of it, prices declined and farmers had to face a great loses. [1]

    (iv) In the period of war, many industries failed to modernize.

9. The three flows within the international economic exchanges were flow of trade, flow of labour and flow of capital.

    (i) Flow of Trade: The trade in goods like cotton, wheat etc. is referred as the flow of trade. In the beginning, the weavers of India used to produce cotton cloth and export it to European countries. [1]

    (ii) Flow of Labour: In order to find the employment, people used to migrate and this migration is referred to as flow of labour. Many Indians migrated from India to Africa and other countries in search of employment in the 19th century.   [1]

(*iii*) Flow of Capital: The movement of capital for long or short term investments over long distances is referred as the flow of capital.   [1]

10. (*i*) The great depression began around 1929 and lasted till the mid-1930s. During this period most parts of the world experienced disastrous declines in production, employment, incomes and trade.   [1]

(*ii*) The depression directly affected the Indian trade. India's exports and imports nearly cut down by 50% between 1928 and 1934.   [1]

(*iii*) As international prices crashed, prices in India also got imported.

(*iv*) Peasants and farmers suffered more than urban residents. They got trapped in indebtedness.   [1]

(*v*) The jute producers of Bengal were hard hit by this depression.

(*vi*) The price of raw jute fell by 60 % and as a result, the jute growers fell deeper and deeper in debt.

11. (*i*) Agents attracted the poor people by giving incorrect facts about the nature of work, place of work, living and working conditions, means of travel, etc. The living and working conditions were harsh for the people.   [1]

(*ii*) Less willing workers were at time forcibly kidnapped by the agents. Workers had few legal rights.   [1]

(*iii*) On arrival at the plantations, when laborers found conditions to be different, many of them escaped into the wilds. If they were caught, they were severely punished.   [1]

12. (*i*) Economic crisis, increased poverty and hunger compelled people to leave Europe.   [1]

(*ii*) Cities were crowded and deadly diseases were widespread.   [1]

(*iii*) Religious conflicts were common and religious dissenters were persecuted.   [1]

13. Impact of Rinderpest on Africa-

(*i*) 90% of cattle were killed by Rinderpest.[1]

(*ii*) Livelihood was destroyed due to loss of cattle.   [1]

(*iii*) People were forced into labour market. [1]

(*iv*) European colonizers were able to conquer and subdue Africa when they got control over the cattle resources.

14. The causes of Great Depression are as follows:

(*i*) There was an immense industrial expansion due to the increased demand of goods supplied to the army, during the period of the First World War. After the war, the demand for these goods suddenly dropped and so, there was no demand in many industries. There was also a large fall in the agricultural prices due to reduced demand.   [1]

(*ii*) In the mid-1920s, many countries financed their investments through loans from the USA. While it was often very easy to raise loans in the USA during the boom period, lenders in the USA panicked at the first sign of trouble. Countries that depended crucially on US loans, now faced an acute crisis.   [1]

(*iii*) Agricultural over production was another major factor responsible for the depression. This was made worse by falling agricultural prices. As prices slumped and agricultural incomes declined, the farmers tried to increase the production and bring a larger volume of produce to the market to maintain their overall income. This worsened the situation by pushing down the prices of farm produce further.   [1]

(*iv*) Large-scale unemployment: Farmers could not sell their harvests and businesses collapsed. As a result, large scale unemployment occurred.   [1]

15. The following points explain the attributes of primitive subsistence agriculture in India:

(i) This type of farming is performed on small land areas.The primitive tools such as hoe, Dao and digging sticks are used with the help of family/community. [1]

(ii) In primitive subsistence agriculture, land availability per hectare is very low. [1]

(iii) It is dependent upon the natural conditions such as monsoon, natural soil fertility and also other suitable environmental conditions, which are responsible for the growth of the crops. [1]

(iv) This type of agriculture is done for self-consumption by the farmers. [1]

16. The Europeans got attracted to Africa due to the following reasons:

(i) The Europeans were in search of the precious minerals like coal, silver and gold etc. [1]

(ii) Africa had enormous resources of land. [1]

(iii) They hoped to start mines and plantations in Africa. [1]

The three methods used to recruit and retain the African laborers were:

(i) Due to the imposition of heavy taxes by The Colonial government, the African laborers were forced to work for wages on plantations and mines. [1]

(ii) The peasants were also displaced from the land because of the change in the Inheritance laws. According to this law, only one family member could inherit the land and as a result of it, others were forced to work in the labour market. [1]

(iii) Minors were not allowed to move out and they were enclosed at the workplace.

17. The great depression was an economic crisis that started in 1929 and ended in mid 1930s. The effect of the Great Depression on the US was:

(i) US experienced decline in production, demand, employment, trade and incomes. [1]

(ii) Mass migration was experienced in major cities of USA and there was increase in crime rate, alcoholism and suicide. [1]

(iii) Because of unemployment workers opted theft for food and survival and alcohol and suicide to escape from despair. [1]

(iv) There was a huge decrease of enrolment in education sector and demographic system was also affected. Birth rate and divorce rate dropped and marriages were delayed. [1]

(v) Banking system in US collapsed and banks ran out of money. [1]

MULTIPLE CHOICE QUESTIONS

1. The laws allowing the British Government to restrict the import of corn were known as:
   (a) Corn Laws
   (b) Indentured labour
   (c) Cowrie
   (d) Dissenter

2. Why did the wheat price fall down by 50 per cent between 1928 and 1934?
   (a) Droughts
   (b) Due to less production
   (c) Due to floods
   (d) Due to the Great Depression

3. The network of routes connecting Asia with Europe and Northern Africa is called as......?
   (a) Sea Route   *(b)* Silk Route
   (c) Panama Islands   *(d)* Atlantic Drift

4. Which of these was a well-known Pioneer of mass production?
   (a) Ratan Tata   *(b)* Wright Brothers
   (c) Henry Ford   *(d)* Albert Einstein

5. What does G-77 stands for?
   (a) It refers to the seventy seven developing countries that did not benefit from the fast growth western economies experienced in 1950s and 1960s.
   (b) It refers to the seventy seven developed countries
   (c) It refers to a group of 77 intellectual people
   (d) Both *(a)* and *(c)*

Answer Keys

1. *(a)*   2. *(d)*   3. *(b)*   4. *(c)*   5. *(a)*

FILL IN THE BLANKS

1. Most Indian indentured workers came from _______________.

2. _____________ is referred to as the Bretton Woods twins.

3. In 1890, a fast spreading disease of _________ had a terrifying impact on people's livelihoods in Africa.

4. The Great Depression occurred in the year_________.

5. _______________ is an imaginary city of gold situated in South America

🔑 Solutions

1. Eastern Uttar Pradesh
2. The International Monetary Fund (IME) and the World Bank
3. Rinderpest
4. 1929
5. El Dorado

TRUE OR FALSE

1. Indian exports and imports nearly halved between1928-1934.

2. Europeans were attracted to Africa due to availability of milk.

3. When the disease destroyed the potato crop, Ireland's, poor peasants died of starvation.

4. Christopher Columbus discovered the African continent

5. The United Nations Monetary and Financial Conference held at San Francisco in 1944.

🔑 Solutions

1. True
2. False
3. True
4. False
5. False

CHAPTER 4

The Age of Industrialization

Summary

Industrialization in India

- Silk and finer varieties of cotton of India had a larger demand in international market before the uses of machines.

- Goods were taken from Punjab by Persian and Armenian trader, had sent in Afghanistan and central Asia.

- There was a trade link between many countries through Hooghly port, Surat port, and financing production importing goods was done by various Indian merchants, capitalist and bankers.

- Network of trade relating with various countries was controlled by the Indians merchant and traders.

- But taking grants and monopoly from local courts and kings the European countries, slowly controlled over the trade. This led the declination of Indian traders and bankers.

- European traders replaced the ports from Surat and Hooghly to Calcutta and Bombay.

- The entrance of east India company changed the manual weaving industries, economic assistance started to provide as a loan to weavers to manufacture cloths and entire manufacturing activity was supervised by Gomasthas.

- The situation led the migration of weavers as they were not able to survive.

- The development of cotton industries, led the britishers to sell cotton in Indian market, the Indian weavers could not compete with the machine products of England.

- There was a huge decline in the cotton industries of due to European cotton.

Factories in India

- In Bombay the first cotton mill was set up in 1854.

- In Bengal first jute mill was set up in 1855, the eligin mill was started in Kanpur and first spinning and weaving mills were setup in Madras.

- Some of Indian traders were involved in trade with china and earned huge profit.

- In Bengal the Dwarakanath Tagore setup six joint stock company to trade with china.

- In Bombay Dinshaw petit and Jamset ji tata established huge business empire in India and were involved in trade with China.

- Hukumchand and G.D birla also setup the industries in India after making huge profit from trade with China.

- The merchant, bankers and trader who were involved in carrying goods and supply within countries also setup industries in India after earning huge profit.

- The setup of industries changed the social scenario as the workers were employed by the jobbers at large scale.

Industrialization in Britain

* England had a huge production of products before the age of machine that age is termed as proto industrialisation in England.

* Merchants started to connect with workers in village and offered economical assistance for production of goods

* Due to increase in world trade, merchants were not able to produce goods with urban crafts therefore they moved towards village and offered work to poor peasants.

* By using the working capacities of all family the peasants were able to fulfil the demands of merchants and by manufacturing goods they raised their income.

* A network was developed by merchants before the age of machines strengthened the relationship between town and villages.

* By 1730, factories came up in England after that a number of factories were setup by the late eighteenth centuries.

* Cotton was the symbol of new age ,the increase of the production changed the status of England

* A series of inventions took place for the development of cotton industries.

* With the help of technology production process like carding, twisting, spinning and rolling, were improved. The Richard Arkwright made a cotton mill.

* With high production rate factories became lifeline of England. It was the leading sector of England.

* The demand of iron and steel went up after the development of Railway.

* A large part production was taking place outside the factories, it was not possible to displace traditional industries.

* The worker of mid nineteenth century was a manual worker not the machine operator.

* The demand for labour in industries was seasonal, in season based industries there was a manual (hand working) labour. Industries of England had a wide range of products made by hand.

* The upper class was the main user of hand made products therefore the products of machine was exported in colonies.

* The machine was used in production where the availability of labours was less.

* The job opportunities was affected by the large number of availability of labours,

Points to know

Stapler – a person who sorts wool according to its fibres.

Carding – a process of preparing Fibres.

Bourgeoise – the upper middle class.

Gomastha – a agent or paid servant under the britishers to play a role of middle man between weavers and merchants.

Trade guilds – association of producers.

Important Personalities

Richard Arkwright – created cotton mill.

James Watt – improved the steam engine.

Mathew Bolten – manufactured the new model of steam engines.

Jamest Ji Tata – Founder of TATA.

Important Dates

1854 - in India the First cotton mill was set up

1730 - in England the Earliest factory was set up

1760 - 2.5 millions pounds of raw materials was imported by Britain

1840 - Expansion of cotton in England

1860 - Expansion of railway in England

1764 - Spinning Jenny was Invented.

1750 - breaking down of Indian merchant network

1855 - in Bengal First Jute mill was established

1733 - Flying shuttle invented

1779 - Invention of mules

PREVIOUS YEARS'
EXAMINATION QUESTIONS

▶ 1 Mark Questions

1. Which of the following mechanical devices was used for weaving with ropes and pullies, which helped to weave wide pieces of cloth?

    (*a*) Handloom   (*b*) Power loom

    (*c*) Fly shuttle   (*d*) Spinning Jenny

    [TERM 1, 2011]

2. Which of the following were the Pre-Colonial ports of India?

    (*a*) Surat and Masulipatam

    (*b*) Madras and Hoogly

    (*c*) Madras and Bombay

    (*d*) Bombay and Hoogly

    [TERM 1, 2011]

3. Where was the first Indian Jute Mill set up?

    [TERM 1, 2013]

4. In which year did the first cotton mill in Bombay(Mumbai) come up?

    [TERM 1, 2015]

5. Who adopted the assembly line production of cars?

    [TERM 1, 2016]

6. Which was the first country to undergo industrial revolution?

    [TERM 1, 2016]

7. Between which place the first section of the underground railway in the world was opened?

    [TERM 1, 2016]

8. Why did merchants from towns in Europe begin to move to countryside in seventeenth and eighteenth centuries?

    [DELHI 2018]

▶ 3 Mark Questions

9. What technique of advertisement did Manchester industrialists use to entice the Indian consumers?

    [TERM 1, 2011]

10: Why were Jobbers employed by Indian industrialists?

    [TERM 1, 2012, 2015]

11. Why did women workers in Britain attack the Spinning Jenny? Give any reasons.

    [TERM 1, 2013]

12. Describe the condition of the workers in nineteenth century in England?

    [TERM 1, 2014]

13: What were guilds? How did they make it difficult for new merchants to set business in towns of England? Explain.

    [TERM 1, 2014]

14. Describe the contributions of Dwarakanath Tagore as an entrepreneur of Bengal.

    [TERM 1, 2015]

15. What is meant by "Trade Surplus"? Why did Britain have a trade surplus with India?

    [TERM 1, 2016]

16. "Although wages increased somewhat in the nineteenth century yet they could not improve the welfare of the workers," How do you agree with this statement? Explain any three points?

    [TERM 1, 2016]

17. "The old ports of Surat and Hoogly declined by the end of the 18th century". Why? Explain any three reasons.

    [TERM 1, 2016]

18. Describe any three major problems faced by Indian cotton weavers in nineteenth century.

    [DELHI 2018]

▶ 4 Mark Questions

19. How did the East India Company procure regular supplies of cotton and silk textiles from Indian weavers?

    [TERM 1, 2011]

▶ 5 Mark Questions

20. What problems did the cotton weavers face in India?

    [TERM 1, 2012]

21. 'Bombay was a Prime city of India." Justify by giving examples.

    [TERM 1, 2012]

22. "The modern Industrialization could not marginalize the traditional industries in England." Justify the statement with any four suitable arguments.

    [TERM 1, 2013]

23. Explain the process of industrialization in Britain during the nineteenth century.

[TERM 1, 2014]

24. "In the eighteenth century Europe, the peasants and artisans in the countryside readily agreed to work for the merchants." Explain any three reasons.   [TERM 1, 2015]

🔑 Solutions

1. (c) Fly shuttle   [1]

2. (a) Surat and Masulipatam   [1]

3. The first jute mill was set up at Rishra, on the River Hooghly near Calcutta.   [1]

4. In 1854, "The Bombay Spinning Mill", was the first cotton mill in Bombay.   [1]

5. Henry Ford installed the first moving assembly line for the mass production of an entire automobile.   [1]

6. Britain was the first country to undergo industrial revolution.   [1]

7. On 10th January 1863, the first section of the underground railway in the world was opened between Paddington and Farrington Street in London.   [1]

8. Merchants began to move to countryside in the 17th & 18th centuries because

    (i)   They could not expand production within towns.   [0.5]

    (ii) The trade guilds restricted the entry of new people into the trade in towns.   [0.5]

9. Following techniques were used by Manchester industrialists to entice the Indian consumers:

    (i)   These industrialists took advantage of people's religious values. The products were produced with pictures of god and goddess printed on it. This was done to attract people towards their products.   [1]

    (ii) As these goods were machine made, they sold it at cheap rates that attracted Indian consumer because they were purchasing handmade goods at very high prices.   [1]

    (iii) They spent large amount of money in the advertisement. There were posters of their products everywhere.   [1]

10. Jobbers were employed by Indian industrialists:

    (i)   To get new recruits as they were very often an old and trusted worker. As the mills multiplied, the demand of workers went up.   [1]

    (ii) They got jobs for people and helped them settle in cities and in crisis.   [1]

    (iii) They became powerful and started demanding money and gifts for their favours and also started controlling the lives of the workers.   [1]

11. The women workers in Britain attacked the Spinning Jenny because:

    (i)   The spinning wheel was able to spin many spindles with one wheel. This led to decrease in employment of women for spinning. [1]

    (ii) The women opposed the new technology because of the fear of unemployment.   [1]

12: In the mid-nineteenth century, the workers in England were wrong in very bad conditions. However after 1840, their condition got better due to urbanization. But they had to suffer a lot till 1840. It can be understood as follows:

    (i)   The employment of the workers was dependent on their social networks. The workers who had good connections in the factories or had friends and relatives there could get work easily. So it was difficult for those who had no connections in the factories.   [1]

    (ii) The employment was seasonal. The workers had to stay unemployed once the busy period was over. Most of the workers wanted to have odd jobs but it was quite difficult to find at that time.   [1]

    (iii) The workers had a fear of unemployment due to the introduction of new technology.   [1]

    (iv) In the early nineteenth century, the wages rate was increased somehow but the prices were also increased and as a result, that increment got nullified.

13. The associations of merchants or artisans who controlled their craft practices and trade in any distinct city were known as guilds. The rulers granted them monopoly rights to produce and trade in some particular products so they were very powerful. They used to train the people

themselves and regulated the competition. The entry of new people in the trade was also restricted by them. Therefore new merchants faced difficulty in setting up business in the towns of England.   [1 + 1 + 1]

14. (*i*) Dwarakanath Tagore was in favour of the fact that by westernization and industrialization, India would develop. [1]

(*ii*) He made huge investments in banking, shipping, mining, plantations and in insurance.   [1]

(*iii*) Dwarakanath Tagore made industrial investments and set up six Joint Stock Companies between 1830s and 1840s. He also made a fortune in China.   [1]

15. When the value of exports is higher than the value of imports, then this difference is called the trade surplus.   [1]

Britain had a trade surplus with India because of:

(*i*) British colonialism in India and their economic policies.   [1]

(*ii*) The higher value of British exports to India than the Indian exports to Britain.   [1]

Britain used this trade surplus to balance their trade deficits. Britain's trade surplus also helped it to pay private remittance back to Britain by British officials and traders, interest payment of India's external debt and business of British officials in India.

16. (*i*) The prices of different commodities rose sharply during the prolonged Napoleonic war, and even with the increased in wages the workers could only buy fewer things.   [1]

(*ii*) The workers did not get employment everyday and their average daily income was determined by the number of days they worked.   [1]

(*iii*) In 1830s, the proportion of unemployment went up to between 35 and 75 per cent in different regions.   [1]

17. The old ports of Surat and Hoogly declined by the end of the 18th century because:

(*i*) The European companies slowly gained power, by first taking a huge amount of concessions from the local courts and then having the monopoly on the trade rights. [1]

(*ii*) Exports from these ports started to fall suddenly. The credit that was given earlier began to become less and the local bankers gradually started to go bankrupt.   [1]

(*iii*) In the last years of the 17th century, the gross value of trade that passed through Surat decreased to Rs.16 million. Thre was a shift in European companies towards Bombay and Calcutta, which caused the decline of old ports.   [1]

18. Major problems faced by the Indian cotton weavers-

(*i*) Their export market collapsed.   [0.5]

(*ii*) The local market shrunk and was glutted with Manchester products .   [0.5]

(*iii*) There was increase in price of raw cotton. [0.5]

(*iv*) There was shortage of cotton.   [0.5]

(*v*) It was difficult for weavers to compete with the imported machine made cheaper cotton products.   [0.5]

(*vi*) Factories in India also began making cheaper machine made goods with which our weavers could not compete.   [0.5]

19. The following are the various steps adopted by the East India Company to ensure regular supplies of cotton and silk textiles.

(*i*) They established political power to assert monopoly right to trade.   [1]

(*ii*) They developed a system of 'managing and control' to eliminate any competition, control cost and ensure regular supply of cotton and silk goods.   [1]

(*iii*) They eliminated the existing traders as well as the broker that had any link with cloth and made direct links with the weaver.   [1]

(*iv*) They appointed paid servants and called them 'gomasthas' in order to supervise weavers, examine the quality of the cloth and collect supplies.   [1]

(*v*) Weavers were not allowed to contact other buyers. Weavers were given advances and were offered loans to buy raw material. Those who took advance or loan could not contact any other trader.

(*vi*) The weavers had to sell at a price dictated by the Company. By giving loan the Company tied the weavers with them.

20. Problems faced by cotton weaver in India were as follows:

    (*i*) There was long decline in export of textile in India. [1]

    (*ii*) There was not sufficient supply of good quality raw cotton. [1]

    (*iii*) Cheap machine made cotton goods was imported and the weavers were not able to easily compete with that. [1]

    (*iv*) Since there was not sufficient supply of good quality raw cotton, so weavers had to buy raw cotton at a very high price. [1]

    (*v*) By the end of 19th century textile factories were set up in India flooding the market with machine made goods, which made situation difficult for the weavers to survive. [1]

21. 'Bombay was a Prime city of India' because of the following reasons:

    (*i*) In the 17th century Bombay was under Portuguese control and it was a group of seven islands. [1]

    (*ii*) Control of Bombay was passed into the hands of British after the marriage of Portuguese princess with King of Britain. [1]

    (*iii*) The East India Company quickly shifted its principal western port from Surat to Bombay. [1]

    (*iv*) By the beginning of 19th century, Bombay was functioning as a port through which huge quantities of raw material such as cotton and opium would pass. [1]

    (*v*) Bombay slowly became one of the most important administrative centre of Western India. [1]

    (*vi*) By the end of 19th century, Bombay becomes a major industrial centre.

22. The modern industrialization could not marginalize the traditional industry in England because:-

    (*i*) Less than 20% of total workforce was employed in technologically advanced industrial sectors even at the end of the 19th Century. Textiles was a dynamic sector but a large portion of the output was produced within domestic units. [1 + 1]

    (*ii*) Small and ordinary innovations were the basis of growth in many non-mechanized sectors such as construction, pottery, glass work, tanning, furniture making, food-processing and making of tools. [1]

    (*iii*) Technological changes occurred slowly. New technology was expensive and the merchants and industrialists were cautious about using it. [1]

    (*iv*) The machines often broke down and their repair was costly. [1]

23. The process of industrialization in Britain during the 19th century was as follows:

    (*i*) The process of industrialization began with the installment of the major industries like cotton and metal. After that the iron and steel industries were also established and these industries started increasing rapidly as the railways were expanded in England and its colonies. So Britain started exporting steel and iron and their cost was double of the cost of cotton export. [1]

    (*ii*) The conventional industries could not easily be replaced by the new technologies. The workforce employed in the advanced industries was very low. Though the textile industry was a major one, still most of the output was produced in the domestic units. [1]

    (*iii*) In some of the non-mechanized sectors like building, glass work, food processing, pottery, furniture making etc. small inventions like steam powered cotton industries built the base of the growth. [1]

    (*iv*) The efficiency of the production process was increased by the new inventions. The cotton mill was established by Richard Arkwright. [1]

The rate of execution of the technology was very low. New machineries were very costly so they could not spread rapidly. Also the repairing of the machines was expensive if they broke down. They were not found as effective as they were supposed to be. [1]

24. In the eighteenth century Europe, the peasants and artisans in the countryside readily agreed to work for the merchants due to the following reasons: [1]

(*i*) The poor peasants were dependent on an open field and common lands for their firewood, vegetables, straws and hay which were disappearing. [1]

(*ii*) Peasants were not able to provide work for all the members of the family due to tiny owned plots which are not sufficient for all of them. [1]

(*iii*) They were offered advances by merchants to produce goods for them. With this, the peasants could cultivate their small lands and could stay in the countryside. [1]

(*iv*) Peasants and artisans could supplement their agricultural income with that of the income from the merchants' work. [1]

MULTIPLE CHOICE QUESTIONS

1. Which machine was invented by James Hargreaves in 1764?
   (*a*) Spinning Jenny
   (*b*) Fully automatic machine
   (*c*) Steam Iron
   (*d*) Car polishing

2. Steam Engine was patented by?
   (*a*) Henry Ford
   (*b*) Richard Arkwright
   (*c*) James Watt
   (*d*) James Hargreaves

3. The first cotton mill in India was set up at?
   (*a*) Madras   (*b*) Gujarat
   (*c*) Punjab   (*d*) Bombay

4. A person employed by the industrialists to get new recruits for the mills was called as....
   (*a*) Dyer   (*b*) Jobber
   (*c*) Sepoy   (*d*) Vagrant

5. Whom did the British government appoint to supervise weavers collect supplies and to examine the quality of cloth?
   (*a*) Entrepreneur   (*b*) Sepoy
   (*c*) Policeman   (*d*) Gomastha

Answer Keys

1. (*a*)   2. (*c*)   3. (*d*)   4. (*b*)   5. (*d*)

FILL IN THE BLANKS

1. _____________, an Indian port lost its importance during colonial rule

2. New technology like_____________________ helped in increased the handloom cloth production in the early 20th century.

3. The early phase of industrialisation was known as________________.

4. The first spinning and weaving mill set up in 1874 at _______________.

5. ____________ produced a music book in 1900.

Solutions

1. Surat
2. looms with fly shuttle
3. proto-industrialisation
4. Madras
5. E.T. Paull

TRUE OR FALSE

1. Industrialisation gave rise to imperialism.
2. The workers in England were overwhelmed with the coming up of machines and new technology.
3. Guild was an association of Indian workers employed by the East India Company.
4. The nationalists spread the message of Swadeshi through advertisements.
5. Advertisements like images of gods and goddesses frequently appeared on the labels of the cloth.

Solutions

1. True
2. False
3. False
4. True
5. True

Print Culture and the Modern World

Summary

History of Printing in Europe

- Macro Polo bring the technology of woodblock printing from China .

- Books started publishing with woodblocks by Italians and the technology of printing books spread rapidly in Europe.

- The cheaper printed copies were started to read by students of the university and Merchants

- Booksellers, hired the Scribes and skilled hand writers to meet the demands for books.

- One bookseller usually hired More than 50 scribes for publishing the books.

- The publication of manuscripts was time consuming process as it took a lot of time and labour in copying books

- Manuscripts were delicate, cumbersome to deal with, and couldn't be conveyed or perused effortlessly. Their course along these lines stayed constrained. Henceforth woodblock printing continuously turned out to be increasingly prominent.

- There was a need of rapid mechanism for preparing book, it was possible only by mechanical process.

- Gutenberg fulfilled the need of mechanical process by inventing printing press in Germany.

- Bible was the first book printed by Guntenberg, Later he printed 180 copies.

- Printing press were setup in the countries of Europe between 1450-1550, the print workers of Germany moved in other European countries for job, they helped in the development of press.

Impact of Print Revolution

- Reduction of costs created a new reading section as it was feasible to purchase.

- In market a number of books were available due to low cost, which enabled the access of books in large reading sections.

- For a specific section of reader, folk tales, ballads were started to print with illustration. A new oral reading culture emerged as the listening was more joyful by reading.

- The circulation of books containing ideas, knowledge and logic crated a world of discussion and debates.

- The questions were raised against authorities and sensitive issues by book readers or writers.

- It was a major arm to circulate the idea and to create a sense of questioning among the readers.

- Many were afraid due to circulation of books as their status was questioned .

- Roman Catholic church was criticized by Martin Luther in his Ninety Five Theses.

- He challenged the dogma and working of church by his writings and a great impact created among common people.

- The writings of Luther created a division in church and paved the way for Protestant Reformation.

Growth of Press in 19th century in India

- Portugese missionaries brought printing press in Goa.
- Several texts in Konkani, were printed by Jesuit priests.
- In 1579 the first Tamil book printed by catholic priest in madras.
- 32 Tamil texts were printed by Dutch Protestants.
- The Bengal Gazette a weekly magazine edited by James Augustus Hickey from 1780.
- Hickey wrote about misdeeds of the officers of East India company, after that Hastings started the official newspaper in order to maintain the image of company.
- Bengal Gazette edited by Gangadhar Bhattacharya was the first Indian newspaper.
- The Sambad Kaumudi written by Raja Ram Mohan Roy in 1821 on various social issues.
- Jam I Jahan Nama and Shamsul Akhbar wriiten in Persian from 1822.
- The Deoband society published thousands of Fatwas relating with the social conduct of Muslims.
- Ramcharitmanas of Tulsidas was printed in 1810 from Calcutta.
- In vernacular a number or religious texts were published from Lucknow by Naval Kishore Press.
- Religious texts and stories created a sense of discussion among common people regarding social issues.
- New literary forms emerged in the reading world like lyrics,short stories,essays and social issues.
- Women also started writing books and novels
- A lady of Bengal, Rashsunndari Devi wrote her autobiography Amar-Jivan.
- Pandit Rama Bai and Tara Bai Shinde of Maharashtra wrote about the miserable life of upper caste women and widows.
- In Istri Dharm Vichar was published by Ramchandra.
- With the help of books and pamphlets, writers tried to create a sense of nationalism among Indians.
- Vernacular newspaper generally published by nationalists to create a spark against British empire.
- The law was enacted in 1878 for proper monitoring of press.

Points to know

Calligraphy – Art of writing beautifully

Anthology – poetry and song, collected from literature.

Mechanical Press – A press for printing which is operated by machine.

Manuscripts Book or document written by hand

Ballad – Sentimental song with repeated melody; poem or song in short stanzas narrating a popular story.

New Testament – Part of Bible concerned with teachings of Christ and his earliest followers.

Protestant Reformation movement – A movement of protest against the corrupt practices of the Catholic Church. The movement was led by Martin Luther, a German monk.

Chapbooks – Cheap pocket size books available at roadside shops of books.

Vernacular Language – Language or dialect of the country, language spoken by a particular clan or group.

Despotism – A system of governance in which absolute power is exercised by an individual, unregulated by legal and constitutional checks.

Ulemas – Legal scholars of Islam.

Important Personalities

Marcopolo – traveller of Italy, brought print technology.

Jotiba phule – social reformer or thinker, who raised voiced against caste system.

James augustus hickey – edited Bengal Gazzete, critised the east India company.

Guntenberg – invented printing press in Germany, printed bible

Bal gangadhar Tilak – prominent nationalist, published Maratha, Keshri,

Important Dates

594 - Books in china were printed by rubber paper.

868 - Buddhist Diamond Sutra was printed

1448 - Gutenberg published bible

1517 - Ninety Five Theses written by Mratin Luther wrote.

1558 - Church maintained index of prohibited books.

1812 - Traditional folk tales were compiled

1780 - James Augustus Hickey began to edit the Bengal Gazette.

1821 - sambad kaumudi was published by Raja Ram Mohan

1878 - varnacular press act was passed

PREVIOUS YEARS'
EXAMINATION QUESTIONS

▶ 1 Mark Questions

1. Who said 'Printing is the ultimate gift of God and the Greatest one'?

   (a) E.V. Ramaswamy Naickar

   (b) Bal Gangadhar Tilak

   (c) Martin Luther

   (d) Erasmus　　　　　　　　　　[TERM 1, 2011]

2. Which one of the following statement is true?

   (a) A children press, devoted to literature for children alone, was set up in France in 1757.

   (b) Penny magazines were especially meant for men.

   (c) Lending libraries had been in existence from the Seventeenth century onwards.

   (d) None of the above.

   　　　　　　　　　　　　　　[TERM 1, 2011]

3. Who wrote about the injustice of the caste system in 'Gulamgiri'?

   　　　　　　　　　　　　　　[TERM 1, 2014]

4. Name a religious reformer who criticized the practices of the Roman Catholic Church?

   　　　　　　　　　　　　　　[TERM 1, 2014]

5. When did the first printing press come to India?

   　　　　　　　　　　　　　　[TERM 1, 2014]

6. Which previous knowledge did Gutenberg drew to design his innovation in the form of a printing press?

   　　　　　　　　　　　　　　[TERM 1, 2017]

7. Name the book by Kashi Baba that had detailed the experiences of poor workers in India.

   　　　　　　　　　　　　　　[TERM 1, 2017]

8. Why did the Roman Catholic Church impose control over publishers and booksellers?

   　　　　　　　　　　　　　　[DELHI 2018]

▶ 3 Mark Questions

9. What was the impact of Print culture on the poor people of India during the 19th century? Explain.

   　　　　　　　　　　　　　　[TERM 1, 2011]

10. Why did people in the eighteenth century Europe think that print culture would bring enlightenment and end despotism?

    　　　　　　　　　　　　　　[TERM 1, 2011]

11. What were the main features of the Gutenberg Press?

    　　　　　　　　　　　　[TERM 1, 2011, 2015]

12. How did print culture affect women in the 19th century?

    　　　　　　　　　　　　　　[TERM 1, 2012]

13. Explain any three factors responsible for the invention of new printing techniques.

    　　　　　　　　　　　　　　[TERM 1, 2013]

14. What is manuscript? Mention any two limitations of it, during nineteenth century.

    　　　　　　　　　　　　　　[TERM 1, 2013]

15. Highlight any three circumstances that led to the intermingling of the hearing culture and the reading culture.

    　　　　　　　　　　　　[TERM 1, 2014, 2015]

16. Explain the contribution of print to the spread of knowledge.

    　　　　　　　　　　　　　　[TERM 1, 2015]

17. "The 'Print Revolution' had transformed the lives of people changing their relationship to information and knowledge." Analyse the statement.

    　　　　　　　　　　　　　　[DELHI 2018]

▶ 5 Mark Questions

18. Explain the different stages of development of printing technology in China?

    　　　　　　　　　　　　　　[TERM 1, 2014]

19. What was the contribution of print culture in the growth of nationalism in India? How did the British attempt to check them?

    　　　　　　　　　　　　　　[TERM 1, 2014]

20. Explain any five efforts made to popularize reading of books in Europe.

    　　　　　　　　　　　　　　[TERM 1, 2014]

 Solutions

1. (c) Martin Luther　　　　　　　　　　　[1]

2. (*c*) Lending libraries had been in existence from the Seventeenth century onwards. [1]

3. Jyotiba Phule wrote about the injustice of the caste system in 'Gulamgiri'. [1]

4. Martin Luther criticized the practices of the Roman Catholic Church. [1]

5. The first printing press come to India as early as 1670 by the Parsi businessman Bhimjee Parikh. [1]

6. Gutenberg drew his previous knowledge to design his innovation in the form of printing press from his previous experiences. He had seen olive and wine presses in his childhood, he also learnt the art of polishing stones, became a master goldsmith and also had expertise in creating lead moulds. [1]

7. Chhote Aur Bade Ka Sawal was the book written by Kashi Baba in 1938 that has detailed the experiences of poor workers in India. [1]

8. A restriction was imposed on publishers and booksellers by Roman Catholic churchs for it was dreaded that without control over what was printed and read, rebellious and irreligious thoughts would start to spread amongst people. [1]

9. 1. Small books were sold at very cheap cost in crossroads of Madras so as to make them affordable to poor people. [1]

   2. To increase the accessibility of books, public libraries were set up. [1]

   3. Chhote Aur Bade Ka Sawal was written by a mill worker Kashibaba to demonstrate the links between class exploitation and the caste system. [1]

   4. Libraries were set up by the cotton mill workers of Bangalore to educate themselves, which was then followed by the Bombay workers.

10. Print culture made the availability of books at cheaper rates. It helped to increase the number of readers and hence, improved the lives of people by increasing knowledge and information. It helped to understand popular perceptions and helped open new ways to perceive things and ideologies. Also, cheaper books helped a lot to spread revolutionary ideas among large section of people in more efficient ways. [1 + 1 + 1]

11. The following were the features of Gutenberg's press:

    (*i*) It was the first printing press of the world. [1]

    (*ii*) Borders were drawn with hand.

    (*iii*) Every purchaser could choose the design of his choice. [1]

    (*iv*) The books printed in the press looked like the written manuscripts. [1]

12. The print culture affected women in the 19th century in the following ways:

    (*i*) Women became important as readers as well as writers. [1]

    (*ii*) Many journals began carrying writing by women and explained why women should be educated, defining a new type of woman- a person with will, strength and determination. [1]

    (*iii*) Penny magazines changed the lifestyle of women teaching them proper behavior and housekeeping. [1]

13. Three factors responsible for the invention of new printing techniques were:

    (*i*) The increasing demand of the books which the handwritten scripts could not meet. [1]

    (*ii*) Need for a faster and cheaper way of printing texts, though woodblock printing was popular at that time. [1]

    (*iii*) To find an alternative for expensive, time consuming and a strenuous task of copying the texts. [1]

14. Manuscript is a hand-written document which is very fragile and is passed on from one generation to another. Two limitations of manuscript during nineteenth century were: [1]

    (*i*) Being handwritten and not printed, it was quite difficult and almost next to impossible to reach the public. [1]

    (*ii*) They were difficult to carry as well as to read so they were not widely used by people in their daily lives. [1]

15. The circumstances that led to the intermingling of the hearing culture and the reading culture are as follows:

(*i*)   The literacy rate was very low until the end of the 20th century. In order to interest people towards books, the printers started printing popular poems and folktales with a lot of images. [1]

(*ii*) Such books were narrated at gatherings and it attracted listeners. [1]

(*iii*) The oral culture combined with the reading culture as the oral culture was printed and then orally transmitted. [1]

16. Print media is one of the powerful ways to spread knowledge. With the help of print media, ideas of a scientist like Newton could be spread throughout the globe and researchers could work on it. With the help of print media ancient and medieval scientific texts were compiled and published and maps and scientific diagrams were widely printed . [1 + 1]

Self-teaching could be possible for gaining knowledge. This was not possible at the time of oral culture as earlier people had to look for someone to teach them. [1]

17. Transformation due to Print Revolution-

(*i*)   People's perceptions were influenced & that opened up new ways of looking at things. [1]

(*ii*) A new reading public emerged and the number gradually increased. [1]

(*iii*) Intermingling of hearing and reading public

(*iv*) Created the possibility of wide circulation of ideas. [1]

(*v*)   Introduced a new world of debate and discussion.

18. The different stages of development of printing technology in China are as follows:

(*i*)   Chinese started to print by rubbing paper after 594 AD using the inked surface of woodblocks. [1]

(*ii*) For quite a long time, China was the major producer of printed material. China recruited its personnel through civil service examinations. [1]

(*iii*) The number of examination candidates increased after the sixteenth century, which further expanded print technology. [1]

(*iv*) Urban culture was at a boom in China during the seventeenth century. Merchants started using print technology in their daily lives, in the trade information they collected. Reading started becoming a leisure activity. [1]

(*v*)   In the late nineteenth century, mechanical presses were imported as various outposts were established in China by the Western powers. Shanghai became the hub of the new print culture, and many Western-style schools were also opened there. Now, there was a gradual shift from hand printing to mechanical printing. [1]

19. The print culture played an important role in the growth of nationalism in India. It can be understood as follows:

(*i*)   Most of the newspapers started publishing in vernacular languages by the end of nineteenth century. [1]

(*ii*) The articles which were written by the leaders started publishing in the newspapers and as a result of it, people were able to get the ideas transmitted through these newspapers. [1]

(*iii*) The print media was able to connect the people which were from various communities and places. [1]

(*iv*) The feeling of nationalism started arising in the people as the colonial misrules were exposed through the newspapers. [1]

Because of the development of print media and the availability of newspapers in vernacular languages, a sense of nationalism was developed in the people of India. So specific regulations were passed from the Calcutta Supreme Court in order to control the freedom of press and only the newspapers which demonstrated the British rule were encouraged to publish. The colonial government started keeping an eye all the printed books and newspapers which were publishing in India and also took steps to control the press. [1]

20. The following efforts were made in Europe to popularize the reading of books:

(*i*)   A new approach was adopted by the publishers and printers of Europe in order to increase the selling of their products.

Episodic novels were started in Europe which got famous and readers started waiting eagerly for the coming editions of the novels. [1]

(ii) They lowered the prices of the novels and books so that people from all the sections could afford them. [1]

(iii) Different types of novels and journals were published like fairy tales, history, romance etc in order to popularize reading. [1]

(iv) Some magazines and manuals for women started publishing which became very popular. [1]

(v) Some novels, journals and books were very popular as they covered social problems like pollution, poverty and inequality etc. [1]

MULTIPLE CHOICE QUESTIONS

1. Which was the first book printed by Gutenberg?
   (a) My story
   (b) The Bible
   (c) Diamond Sutra
   (d) History of Paper

2. Who brought the knowledge of producing books with woodblocks to Europe from China?
   (a) Marco Polo
   (b) Christopher Columbus
   (c) The Roman Church
   (d) Johann Gutenberg

3. What piece of work written by Martin Luther criticised many of the practices and rituals of the Roman Catholic Church
   (a) The Roman church ill practices
   (b) Twenty five Theses
   (c) The Roman Church
   (d) Ninety Five Theses

4. Which Indian weekly magazine was edited by James August Hickey?
   (a) Bengal Gazette
   (b) Indian nationalism
   (c) Sambad Kaumud
   (d) Kesari

5. A book or document written by hand is called as.....
   (a) Novel   (b) Newspaper
   (c) Manuscript   (d) Theses

Answer Keys

   1. (b)   2. (a)   3. (d)   4. (a)   5. (c)

FILL IN THE BLANKS

1. ____________ method of hand-printing was developed in China.

2. ____________ wrote the autobiography 'Amar Jiban' Published in 1876.

3. The newspaper started by Bal Gangadher Tilak in India in 19th Century was called as __________

4. The Roman Catholic Church maintained an ______________.

5. In ancient India __________ material was used for writing manuscripts.

🔑 Solutions

1. Woodblock printing
2. Rashsundari Debi
3. Kesari
4. Index of prohibited books from 1558
5. Palm Leaves

TRUE OR FALSE

1. Vellum is a parchment made from wood pulp.

2. E.V. Ramaswamy Naicker was popularly known as Periyar

3. The print culture had a significant impact on the growth of nationalism in India.

4. Calligraphy is a modern writing technique using steep edged pens to create artistic lettering using thick and thin lines depending on the direction of the stroke.

5. The French Revolution occurred as printing helped in spreading the ideas of liberty, freedom and nationalism.

🔑 Solutions

1. False
2. True
3. True
4. False
5. True

Unit-II : GEOGRAPHY

Resources and Development

Summary

Resources; Type and Planning

Classification of resources

Basis of origin – (*i*) Biotic (*ii*) Abiotic,

Basis of exhaustibility – (*i*) Renewable (*ii*) Non-Renewable

Basis of ownership – (*i*) Individual (*ii*) community (*iii*) national (*iv*) international

On the basis of status of development – (*i*) potential (*ii*) developed (*iii*) stock and (*iv*) reserve.

Planning

- The availability of resources is necessary condition for the development of any regions but it is not equally distributed.
- Identification and inventory of resources across the regions of the country by surveying, mapping and qualitative estimation.
- Evolving a planning structure endowed with appropriate technology.
- Matching the resource development plans with overall national development plans.
- India has taken concrete action to achieve the goal of resource planning from first five year plan 1952.
- India having unequal distribution of resources.
- Some regions have ample amount of specific type of resources but are deficient in other resources.
- Chattisgarh and Madhya Pradessh rich in minerals and coals.

- Arunachal Pradesh has a abundant amount of water resources but lack in infrastructure
- Rajasthan is doing well in solar and wind energy but lack in water resources.
- This unequal distribution of resources needed balanced resources planning at the national, state

And regional level.

Land and soil as a resource

- Land is an important assets.
- Land provide natural vegetation, shelter and other for human survival.
- India has variety of relief feature about 43 percent of land area is plain,30 percent of land area is Mountain and 27 percent of land area is plateau.
- Total geographical area of India is 3.28 sq km.
- Land use is available only for 93% of the total area due to not proper estimation of land in Assam.
- Some area of Jammu & Kashmir occupied by Pakistan and china have also not surveyed.
- The land under permanent pasture has also decreased.
- The national forest policy implemented in 1952, according to it 33 percent forest is desirable in India.
- The pattern of net sown area vary from one state to another.

- 80 percent total net sown area in Punjab and Haryana and less than 10 percent in Arunachal Pradesh.
- Continuous use of land over a long period of time without maintaining its fertility, leads to land degradation.
- Over irrigation, mining, over grazing, deforestation are factors which affect the land fertility adversely.

Soil

- Surface layer of earth crust, including weathered rocks, organic materials.
- It is a medium of plant growth and support different types of living organism.
- **Alluvial soil** is a deposit of three rivers, forms the northern plain.
- Its very fertile soil therefore regions of this soil are intensively cultivated and densely populated.
- Black soil is known as Regur soil, made up of lawa flows.
- Its ideal for growing cotton that is why it is known as cotton soil.
- Latrerite soil develops in area with high temperature and heavy rainfall.
- It is useful for growing Tea and Coffee, in Tamilnadu, A.P and Kerala.
- Red and Yellow soil found in the part of Orrisa, Chattisgarh and along the piedmont zone of the Western ghats.
- It have low water holding capacity which are not suited for agriculture. Agriculture can be practiced in red and yellow soils with proper application of **fertilizers and manure.**
- **Arid soils** generally in sandy in texture and saline in nature.

  In some area the salt content is very high and common salt is obtained by evaporation of water.
- **Forest soil** found in the hilly area is acidic with low humus content.

  The soil found in the lower part of the valley particularly on the river terrace and alluvial fans are fertile.

  Human activities, deforestation, over grazing, construction and mining disturbs the natural balance of the soil.

Points to know

EEZ

An **exclusive economic zone (EEZ)** is an area which is beyond, and is adjacent to, a given country's territorial seas, and extends not more than 200 nautical miles (370 kilometers) out from a country's own coastlines

Sustainable Development

Development without damaging environment

BANGAR

Old alluvial soil having higher concentration of Kanker nodules.

KHADAR

New alluvial soil

PREVIOUS YEARS'
EXAMINATION QUESTIONS

▶ 1 Mark Questions

1. Which relief feature of Indian has 30 percent of the total surface area of the country?

   [TERM 1, 2013]

2. Which states have mostly laterite soil?

   [TERM 1, 2013]

3. Classify resources on the basis of origin.

   [DELHI 2018]

▶ 3 Mark Questions

4. Suggest any three measures of soil conservation.

   [TERM 1, 2011]

5. What is the total geographical area of India? What are its relief features?

   [TERM 1, 2012]

6. Distinguish between potential and developed resources.

   [TERM 1, 2012]

7. What are the three stages of resource planning in India?

   [TERM 1, 2013, 2014]

8. "India's vast and diverse size is the most important resource". Support the statement.

   [TERM 1, 2013]

9. "Indiscriminate use of resources has led to numerous problems." Justify the statement.

   [TERM 1, 2013, 2017]

10. Give three main features of the soil found in the river deltas of the Indian coast?

    [TERM 1, 2013]

11. Describe alluvial soil under the following heads:

    (a) Formation,

    (b) Distribution,

    (c) Classification.

    [TERM 1, 2013]

12. Distinguish between individual resources and community owned resources. Give any three differences.

    [TERM 1, 2014]

13. Explain any three human activities responsible for land degradation in India.

    [TERM 1, 2014]

14. "The future generation may not have sufficient resources as compared to the present generation". Support the statement.

    [TERM 1, 2017]

▶ 5 Mark Questions

15. Explain the two types of soil erosion mostly observed in India. Mention different human activities responsible for soil erosion.

    [TERM 1, 2013]

16. Explain any five factors responsible for the formation of soil.

    [TERM 1, 2016]

Solutions

1. Mountains account for of the total surface area of India. [1]

2. States which have mostly laterite soil are Gujarat, Madhya Pradesh, Maharashtra, Tamil Nadu, Andhra Pradesh and Karnataka. [1]

3. On the basis of origin, resources are of two types- biotic & abiotic. [1]

4. Soil can be conserved by the following measures:

    (i) Terrace farming: This type of farming is carried out in hilly areas. It helps to hold the top soil and prevents its erosion. [1]

    (ii) Over grazing of fields by animals can be avoided. [1]

    (iii) By ensuring afforestation, planting as many trees possible and preventing deforestation. [1]

5. The total geographical area of India is 3,287,263 square kilometers. [1]

    The relief features of India can be divided into 6 divisions:

    (i) The Himalayas: The Himalaya lies from the Northern borders of India to the Eastern hilly regions. [0.5]

    (ii) The Indo-Gangetic Plain: They are large alluvial plains located in the southern part of the Himalayan region. [0.5]

    (iii) The Peninsular Plateau: This is the table land surrounded by sea on three sides. [0.5]

    (iv) The Coastal Plains: They are the southern part of the peninsular plateau. [0.5]

    (v) The Desert: The Thar Desert is located on the leeward side of Aravalis.

    (vi) The Islands: The two major Island formations are, The Lakshadweep and the Andaman and Nicobar Islands.

6. **Potential Resources:** These resources are present in the environment but have not been utilized because of lack of adequate technologies or lack of capital. For example- Uranium in Ladakh is a potential resource. [1 + 0.5]

    Developed Resources: They are the actual resources for which quality or quantity have been determined for use and are readily used at the present time depending on their feasibility. The overall quantity of these resources is known. For example- Coal and Petroleum. [1 + 0.5]

7. The stages of resource planning are:

    (i) First we have to prepare inventory of resources which involves surveying, mapping and measurement of characteristic properties of resources. [1]

    (ii) Secondly we have to measure in terms of availability for development i.e. examining resources from the points of view of technology, economy and need. [1]

    (iii) At last we have to plan for exploitation of resources which involves action-oriented planning where the main emphasis is on use and reuse of there sources. [1]

8. "India's vast and diverse size is the most important resource".

    India has been blessed with the following:

    (i) Relief features like mountains, islands, plateaus. [1]

    (ii) Plains provide apt resources to set up industries and undergo agricultural practices. [1]

    (iii) Perennial system of rivers that facilitate cultivation of crops and promote tourism. [1]

(*iv*) Abundance of minerals, forests and fossil fuels.

9. Indiscriminate use of resources has led to numerous problems like :-

(*i*) Depletion of resources for satisfying the interests of a few people. [1]

(*ii*) Division of society into rich and poor by accumulation of resources in the hands of a few individuals. [1]

(*iii*) Global ecological crisis like global warming, depletion of ozone layer, environmental pollution and land degradation. [1]

10. The three main features of the soil found in the river deltas of the Indian coast are :-

(*i*) The alluvial soils are more common in the piedmont plains or plains at the foothills such as Duars, Chos and Terai. [1]

(*ii*) The soil has been transported by the rivers to its current location, so it is also called transported soil. [1]

(*iii*) The soil can also be described on the basis of age. The older alluvial soil is farther away from the rivers known as Bangar, whereas the newer soil near the rivers is known as Khadar. Water holding capacity is ample in this soil,therefore it is good for agriculture. [1]

11. Alluvial soil can be described as follows:

(*a*) **Formation:** Alluvial soil consists of silt, sand and clay. Alluvial soil is deposited by three important Himalayan river-systems the Indus, the Ganga and the Brahmaputra. It is bigger and coarser in the upper region of the river and becomes finer as the river flows down. [1]

(*b*) **Distribution:** Alluvial soil is mostly found in the river valleys of the Northern plains (Indus, Ganga,Brahmaputra), parts in Gujarat and Rajasthan, and also in the Eastern coastal plains in the deltas of rivers of the Peninsular plateaus. [1]

(*c*) **Classification:** Based on their age, alluvial soils can be classified as old alluvial (Bangar) and (new alluvial) Khadar. [1]

12. The three differences between individual resources and community owned resources are as follows:

	Individual resources	Community owned resources
1.	The resources owned by a person or any individual.	These are resources owned by a group of people or any community. [1]
2.	No other person can use this type of resources except the one who own it.	This type of resource can be used by any person. [1]
3.	Permission from the owner is necessary to use this type of resources. e.g. a car owned by a person	There is no need to take permission to use these resources. e.g. public park [1]

13. The three human activities which are responsible for land degradation in India are as follows:

(*i*) The most responsible activity for land degradation is mining. It has been seen that severe land degradation is caused by deforestation which is due to mining in some states like Chhattisgarh, Jharkhand, Orissa and Madhya Pradesh. [1]

(*ii*) The other main reason of land degradation is overgrazing which has been seen in some states like Rajasthan, Gujarat, Maharashtra and Madhya Pradesh. [1]

(*iii*) Over irrigation is another activity responsible for land degradation. It has been seen in states like Haryana, western UP and Punjab. [1]

14. We can say this statement because there is a lot of deforestation due to which trees are reducing. If there aren't many trees there will be a deficiency of both soil and water as trees hold both water and soil which are necessary for the agriculture. Water is our life if water won't be there we can't live. If lots of trees are being cut there is a great chance of draught. The amount of these resources is decreasing rapidly and the recycling and regeneration process is very slow. [1 + 1 + 1]

15. Two types of soil erosion observed in India are Gully erosion and sheet erosion. [1]

(*i*) Gullies cut the clayey soils into deep creeps and the land becomes unfit for cultivation and popularly known as badlands. [1]

(*ii*) Sheet erosion washes away top soils over a large areas hence reducing the productivity. [1]

Different human activities responsible for soil erosion are:-

(*i*) Deforestation

(*ii*) Mining activities

(*iii*) Excessive use of fertilizer [2]

16. Factors responsible for the formation of soil are:-

(*i*) Parent Material: Soil carries the features of its parent material which is mineral or organic material from which the soil is formed. These features include colour, texture, structure, mineral composition and so on. [1]

(*ii*) Climate: Climatic factors which affect the formation of soil are temperature and precipitation. This has a major affect on soil formation. [1]

(*iii*) Time: Time plays a crucial role in soil formation. It takes years to form soil. As the soil ages more organic material is added, it is exposed to moisture and other environmental factors that may change its parental features. [1]

(*iv*) Topography: It is considered as a passive factor to modify the effects of climate because it affects soil processes, soil distribution and the type of vegetation. [1]

(*v*) Organisms: The source and richness of organic matter depends on the living beings (plants and animals) that live on and in the soils. Plants provide lots of vegetative residue that are added to soils. [1]

MULTIPLE CHOICE QUESTIONS

1. The term sustainable development means:

   (*a*) Focus on developing the present

   (*b*) Development that takes place without compromising the present needs and also keeping in mind the needs of future generation

   (*c*) Focus on meeting the needs of future generation

   (*d*) Conservation of resources available

2. Solar energy is an example of:

   (*a*) Non-renewable resource

   (*b*) Individual resource

   (*c*) National resource

   (*d*) Renewable resource

3. Which one of the following is the main cause of land degradation in Punjab?

   (*a*) HYV cultivation   (*b*) Over irrigation

   (*c*) Excess water   (*d*) Overgrazing

4. Red soil is found in.....

   (*a*) Odisha

   (*b*) Karnataka

   (*c*) Kerala

   (*d*) Jammu & Kashmir

5. Which one of the following methods is ideal for controlling land degradation in coastal areas and in deserts?

   (*a*) Strip cropping

   (*b*) Contour plough

   (*c*) Planting of shelter belts

   (*d*) Plugging of gullies

Answer Keys

1. (*b*)   2. (*d*)   3. (*b*)   4. (*a*)   5. (*c*)

FILL IN THE BLANKS

1. Resources on the basis of origin are classified as ____________ and ____________

2. ____________ is a technique of proper utilization of resources

3. Human activities that caused degradation of land in India are________, ____________ and _________.

4. Alluvial soil is classified as ______________ and______________

5. The denudation and subsequent washing down of top soil cover by agents of nature e.g. wind, water, glacier and air is called______________

Solutions

1. Biotic & Abiotic

2. Resource Planning

3. Deforestation , Overgrazing and Mining and quarrying

4. Khadar (new alluvial) and Bangar (old alluvial)

5. Soil Erosion

TRUE OR FALSE

1. Various forces of nature such as actions of running water, wind and glaciers, activities of decomposers, etc., contribute to the formation of soil.

2. Laterite soil develops in areas with low temperature and scanty rainfall.

3. Deforestation can help to solve the problem of land degradation in India.

4. Human beings transform material available in our environment into resources and use them.

5. The area brought under cultivation in a year is called as Gross sown area

Solutions

1. True
2. False
3. False
4. True
5. False

CHAPTER 2

Forest and Wildlife

Summary

- This entire habitat that we live in has immense biodiversity. We humans along with all living organisms form a complex web of ecological system in which we are only a part and very much dependent on each other for our own existence.

- India is one of the world's richest countries in terms of its vast array of biological diversity.

- There are various categories of existing plants and animal species. Based on the International Union for Conservation of Nature and Natural Resources (IUCN), we can classify as follows:

  a) Normal Species: Species whose population levels are considered to be normal for their survival, such as cattle, pine etc.

  b) Endangered Species: These are species which are in danger of extinction if the negative factors that have led to a decline in their population continue to operate. The examples of such species are black buck, Indian rhino etc.

  c) Vulnerable Species: These are species whose population has declined to levels from where it is likely to move into the endangered category in the near future if the negative factors continue to operate. The examples of such species are blue sheep, Asiatic elephant, etc.

  d) Rare Species: These are species with small population. Example; The Himalayan brown bear, wild Asiatic buffalo etc.

  e) Extinct Species: These are species which are not found after searches of known or likely areas where they may occur.

- The world's fastest land mammal, the cheetah, is a unique and specialised member of the cat family and can move at the speed of 112 km./hr. Today, the Asian cheetah is nearly extinct due to a decline of available habitat and prey.

- Habitat destruction, hunting, poaching, over-exploitation, environmental pollution, poisoning and forest fires are factors, which have led to the decline in India's biodiversity.

- Conservation in the background of rapid decline in wildlife population and forestry has become essential.

- Tiger is one of the key wildlife species in the faunal web. In 1973, the authorities realised that the tiger population had decreased to 1,827 from an estimated 55,000 at the turn of the century. The major threats to tiger population are numerous, such as poaching for trade, shrinking habitat, depletion of prey base species, etc.

- "Project Tiger", one of the well publicised wildlife campaigns in the world, was launched in 1973. Tiger conservation has been viewed not only as an effort to save an endangered species, but with equal importance as a means of preserving biotypes of sizeable magnitude.

- Corbett National Park in Uttarakhand, Sunderbans National Park in West Bengal, Bandhavgarh National Park in Madhya Pradesh, Sariska Wildlife Sanctuary in Rajasthan, Manas Tiger Reserve in Assam and Periyar Tiger Reserve in Kerala are some of the tiger reserves of India.

Biodiversity or Biological Diversity

PREVIOUS YEARS'
EXAMINATION QUESTIONS

▶ Very Short Answer Type Questions

1. What is the main reason for the depletion of flora and fauna?

   [Board Term I, 2015 DDE Set – E]

2. Name an endangered species.

   [Board Term I, NCT – 2014

▶ Short Answer Type Questions

3. "Large-scale development projects have also contributed significantly to the loss of forests." Justify this statement with relevant examples.

   [Board Term I, DDE 2015 Set-M]

4. Distinguish between endangered species and vulnerable species of wild animals. Give one example of each.

   [Board Term I, DDE - 2014]

5. How have human activities affected the depletion of flora and fauna? Example.

   [NCERT]
   [Board Term I, 2012, 2011, 2010]

6. What is Himalayan Yew? Why is it under great threat at present ?

   [Board Term I, 2012 (35)]

🔑 Solutions

1. Insensitivity to our environment   [1]

2. Black buck, Indian rhino, crocodile, Indian wild ass.

   (Any one)   [1]

3. (*i*) Since 1951, over 500 sq km forest was cleared for riven valley projects.

   (*ii*) Clearing of forests is still continuing with projects like the Narmada Sager Project in Madhya Pradesh which would inundate 40,000 hectares of forest.

   (*iii*) Mining is another important factor behind deforestation.

   [1 × 3 = 3]

4.

	Endangered Species	Vulnerable Species
(i)	These are the species which are in danger of extinction.	These are the species whose population has decreased over a period of time and in danger of extinction.
(ii)	The survival of these species in difficult if the negative factors that have led to a decline in their population are not checked in time.	A vulnerable species is a step short of an endangered species, which in turn in a step short of an extinct species.
(iii)	**Example :**Black buck.	**Example :**Gangetic dolphin.

[1 × 3 = 3]

5. (*a*) Habitat destructions agricultural expansion has resulted in destruction of habitat.

   (*b*) Hunting is carried out illegally, thereby, decreasing the number of animals

   (*c*) Poaching is done and parts of animals are sold for profit.

   (*d*) Overexploitation of resources, cutting of trees for profit motive without replanting and conserving.

   (*e*) Environmental pollution caused by industries destroys soil and water.

   (*f*) Poisoning the forest.

   (Any three)

   (CBSE Marking Scheme, 2012(35)]

6. It is a medicinal plant.

   (*a*) Over-exploitation of the tree has led to drying up of many yew trees in Himachal Pradesh and Arunachal Pradesh.

   (*b*) The biggest selling anti-cancer drug in the world, taxol, is extracted from it to treat cancers.

   (CBSE Marking Scheme, 2012) [1 + 1 = 3]

Conservation of Forest and Wildlife in India

PREVIOUS YEARS' EXAMINATION QUESTIONS

▶ Very Short Answer Type Questions

1. Name a few tees that are considered sacred in India?

2. What was the aim of Chipko Movement?

3. Name the state in which Corbett National Park in located.

4. When was Project Tiger launched?

5. Write the full form of JFM.

▶ Short Answer Type Questions

6. What is joint Forest Management Programme ? Which was the first state to adopt this programme ?

[Board Term I, 2015 Set-6AP67LB]

7. What efforts or steps were taken by the government to project forests and wildlife of the country ?

[Board Term I, NCT-2014]

OR

Write a note on good practices towards conserving forest and wildlife.

[NCERT]

OR

Explain any three measures taken by the India government to project wildlife.

[Board Term I, 2011 (580014,43) 43) 2010 (B1)]

8. Why do we need to conserve our forests and wildlife? Explain any two steps taken by the government to project forests and wildlife resources.

[Board Term I, DDE-2019]

9. "Forests play a key role in the ecological system" Highlight the value of forest in our life.

[Board Term I, 2013 (3K)]

🔑 Solutions

1. Peepal, Banyan and Mango.   [1]
2. Forest conservation.   [1]
3. Uttarakhand.   [1]
4. In 1973.   [1]
5. Joint Forest Management.   [1]

6. (*i*) A programme which involves local communities in the management and restoration of degraded forests. It involves local communities and land managed by forest department.

(*ii*) The Programme was first passed in 1988 by the state of Odisha.

(CBSR Marking Scheme 2015) [1½ + 1½ = 3]

7. Measures taken by the Indian government to protect wildlife are :

(*a*) The Indian Wildlife Projection Act was implemented in 1972 with various provisions for protecting habitats.

(*b*) An all-India list of protected species was also published.

(*c*) To protect the remaining population of certain endangered species government has banned hunting, given legal protection of the habitats of those species and restricted trade in wildlife.

(*d*) Central and many state government have established national parks and wildlife sanctuaries.

(Any three)   **[1 × 3 = 3]**

8. (*a*) We need to conserve our forests and wildlife because :

(*i*) Conservation preserves the ecological diversity and our life support system – air, water and soil.

(*ii*) Conservation also preserves the genetic diversity of plants and animals for better growth of species and breeding.

(*iii*) It makes the planet Earth safe.

(Any one)

(*b*) Steps taken by the government of protect forests and wildlife resources :

(*ii*) The Indian Wildlife Protection Act was implements in 1972 with various provisions for protecting habitats.

(*iii*) Central and many state government have established national parks and wildlife sanctuaries.   **[1 + 2 = 3]**

9. We need to save the biodiversity of our planet because:

(*a*) Human beings along with all living organisms form a complex web of ecological system in which they are only a part and are very much dependent on this system for their existence.

(b) The plants, animals and micro-organisms recreate the quality of the air we breathe, the water we drink and the soil that produces our food without which we cannot survive (c) Forests play a key role in the ecological system as these are also the primary producers on which all other living beings depend.

(CBSE Marking Scheme, 2013)

$[1 \times 3 = 3]$

MULTIPLE CHOICE QUESTIONS

1. Which of these is an endangered species?
   (a) Elephants
   (b) Deer
   (c) Australian Kangaroo
   (d) Indian rhino

2. How many species of flora are found in our country?
   (a) 74,000
   (b) 47,000
   (c) 25,000
   (d) 81,000

3. The aim of Chipko Movement was
   (a) Removal of unwanted trees
   (b) Preservation of wildlife
   (c) Forest Conservation
   (d) All of the above

4. Project Tiger was launched in......
   (a) 1973   (b) 1975
   (c) 1983   (d) 2007

5. Sundarban National Park is located in which state
   (a) Assam
   (b) West Bengal
   (c) Gujarat
   (d) Uttarakhand

Answer Keys

1. (d)   2. (b)   3. (c)   4. (a)   5. (b)

FILL IN THE BLANKS

1. Gangetic dolphin is an example of ___________

2. ___________________ has classified existing plants and animal species of the world.

3. Himalayan Yew is an example of ___________ plant

4. Corbett National Park is located in ______________

5. People of _____________ are fighting against mining.

🔑 Solutions

1. Vulnerable Species
2. International Union for Conservation of National and Nature Resources (IUCN).
3. Medicinal
4. Uttarakhand
5. Sariska Tiger Reserve

TRUE OR FALSE

1. Conservation preserves the ecological diversity and our life support system - air, water and soil.
2. The Indian Wildlife Protection Act was implemented in 1972.
3. Joint Forest Management Programme was passed by the state of Madhya Pradesh.
4. Asiatic cheetah is a protected species.
5. Hornbill is an example of rare species.

🔑 Solutions

1. True
2. True
3. False
4. False
5. True

CHAPTER 3

Water Resources

Summary

Water scarcity and water conservation

- Only 2.5 percent water is present as fresh water.
- The non availability of water is to fulfil basic needs is known as water scarcity.
- It is outcome of large and growing population and consequent greater demands for water.
- Large population means more water not for domestic use but also to produce more food.
- To facilitate higher food grain production, water resources are over exploited.
- Intensive industrialization and urbanization on post independent India also led the water scarcity.
- The development of industries also based on water, which also contributes in water scarcity.
- Bad quality of water, polluted by domestic and industrial water is major causes of water scarcity.
- Indiscriminate use of pesticide, fertilizers, chemicals also unbalanced the quality of fresh water.

Need of Water conservation

- We need to conserve our water as it is in meagre amount.
- To safeguard against health hazards.
- To ensure food security.
- To prevent degradation of our natural ecosystem.
- To prevent ecological crisis.

Multi purpose river projects

- Dams were traditionally built to impound rivers and rainwater.
- In first century B.C water harvesting system channelling the flood water of Ganga.
- In 11th century the largest Bhopal lake was built.
- Dams built for irrigation.
- For electricity generation.
- For electricity generation for industrial water supply.
- For fish breeding.

Disadvantage

- Regulating and damming of rivers cause poor sediments flow and excessive sedimentation.
- Excessive sedimentation caused the poor habitats for aquatic life.
- Reservoirs submerge the existing vegetation.
- Made difficult to aquatic Fauna to migrate to fragmentation of rivers.
- It caused conflicts between state for use of water.
- People have to give up their lands for projects but their condition is not raked up.
- It induced earthquakes caused water borne disease and pollution.

Rain water harvesting

- In India there was extra ordinary tradition of rain water harvesting.
- Guls or Kuls diversion channel were built for agriculture in western Himalaya.

- People developed inundation channels to irrigate their fields, in the flood plains of Bengal.
- To store drinking water, in Rajasthan Rooftop rain water harvesting was commonly practised.
- In arid and semi arid regions, agricultural fields were converted into rain fed storage structures that allowed the water to stand and moisten the soil like the 'khadins' in Jaisalmer and 'Johads' in other parts of Rajasthan.
- Tankas – underground tanks or tankas for storing drinking water.
- In Bikaner, phalodi and Barmer. The tanks could be as large as a big room.
- Many houses constructed underground rooms adjoining the 'tankas' to beat the summer heat as it would keep the room cool.

Points to know

BAMBOO DRIP IRRIGATION

It is 200 years old system to irrigate the betel leaf or black pepper crops with the help of bamboo pipes in Meghalaya.

PALAR PANI

In arid regions of Rajasthan, rain water which is considered as the purest form of natural water is known as **Palar pani.**

PREVIOUS YEARS'
EXAMINATION QUESTIONS

▶ 1 Mark Questions

1. Rooftop rainwater harvesting is a technique to recharge:
   - (*a*) Sea water
   - (*b*) Groundwater
   - (*c*) Lake water
   - (*d*) River water

   [TERM 1, 2011]

2. Name the largest artificial lake built in 11th century?

   [TERM 1, 2014]

3. How much percent of the total volume of world's water is estimated to exist as freshwater?

   [TERM 1, 2014]

4. What is the technical term used for diversion channels of the Western Himalayan?

   [TERM 1, 2016]

▶ 3 Mark Questions

5. Define rain water harvesting. State its main objective.

   [TERM 1, 2011]

6. Jawaharlal Nehru proudly proclaimed the dams as the 'temples of modern India'. Give reasons.

   [TERM 1, 2012, 2013]

7. Why is it essential to conserve and manage our water resources? Explain any three reasons.

   [TERM 1, 2013]

8. What is bamboo drip irrigation? Mention any two features of it.

   [TERM 1, 2013]

9. How multipurpose river projects failed to achieve the purposes for which they were built? Explain.

   [TERM 1, 2014]

10. Explain any three methods of rainwater harvesting?

    [TERM 1, 2015]

11. How has irrigation changed the cropping pattern in many regions of India? Explain with the help of examples.

    [TERM 1, 2015]

12. How has the ever increasing number of industries in India made the position worse by exerting pressure on existing fresh water resources? Explain.

    [DELHI 2018]

▶ 5 Mark Questions

13. How does urbanization and urban life style lead to overexploitation of water resources?

    [TERM 1, 2013]

14. Describe any five traditional methods of rain water harvesting adopted in different parts on India.

    [TERM 1, 2014]

🔑 Solutions

1. (*b*) Groundwater   [1]

2. The largest artificial lake built in 11th century was Bhopal Lake.   [1]

3. 2.5% water of the total volume of world's water is estimated to exist as fresh water, out of which only 0.3% is found in liquid state.   [1]

4. Kuls or Guls is the technical term used for diversion channels of the Western Himalayan. [1]

5. The storing and saving of rain water for different purposes is called rain water harvesting. It is useful in drought prone areas. [1]

   Rain water harvesting has the following objectives:

   (*i*) It reduces water runoff. [0.5]

   (*ii*) The stored water can be used in different purposes like washing of clothes, roads and houses. [0.5]

   (*iii*) It may avoid flooding of roads. [0.5]

   (*iv*) Helps to maintain ground water level.[0.5]

6. Jawaharlal Nehru proudly proclaimed the dams as the 'temples of modern India' as the dams were multipurpose river projects and it was felt that the construction of dams would solve many problems in India which included:

   (*i*) Power generation as electricity is important for agriculture and industries. [1]

   (*ii*) Regulating flow of water to control floods.[1]

   (*iii*) Providing water to the areas that suffer from water scarcity. [1]

   (*iv*) Irrigation of agricultural fields during dry seasons.

   (*v*) Fish breeding and Recreational Facilities.

   Water dams intregates development of agriculture and village economy with industrial sector that leads to economic growth.

7. It is necessary to conserve and manage our water resources because:

   (*i*) Water is important for sustainability of life. We use it for drinking and other household chores. [1]

   (*ii*) Water is required for irrigation purposes for the cultivation of crops. It is also used as a solvent, coolant or a raw material for many industries. [1]

   (*iii*) Water is key component of our ecosystem. Conserving water would prevent the ecosystem from degrading. [1]

   The presence of useful water resource is in a fixed amount, there is a need of judicious management and proper conservation to ensure its presence for future needs.

8. Bamboo drip irrigation is a very old system of tapping spring water and transporting it with the help of a bamboo pipe from higher grounds to lower levels. It is done in Meghalaya. [1]

   Here are the features of Bamboo drip irrigation:

   (*i*) Deflecting perennial springs is done with the help of bamboo pipes on to the top of hilltops with the help of gravity. [1]

   (*ii*) The channel sections are made of bamboo which deflect water to the plant site where it is sectioned into branches. 20-80 drops of water is received at the plant site which was carried hundreds of meters through the bamboo pipe system. It ensures adequate amount of water for irrigation, especially for Betel leaf or Black peeper. [1]

9. "Multipurpose river projects have failed to achieve the purposes for which they were built". It can be understood by these three facts:

   (*i*) The main purpose behind the construction of these dams was to control floods. But they could not fulfill this purpose completely as they instead prompted floods because of the sedimentation in the reservoir. [1]

   (*ii*) During heavy rainfall, the big dams have mostly failed in flood control. [1]

   (*iii*) At the time of excessive rainfall, authorities are forced to release water as well. [1]

   (*iv*) Multi purpose projects also induced earthquakes .

10. (*i*) 'Gul' or 'Kul' are built in western Himalayas for agriculture as these are hilly or mountainous regions. [1]

    (*ii*) In Rajasthan, to store drinking water, roof top rain water harvesting is commonly implemented. [1]

    (*iii*) People develop backlog channels to irrigate their fields in the lands of West Bengal, [1]

    (*iv*) In semi-arid regions agricultural fields a converted into rain fed storage structures called Khadins and Johads that allow the water to stand and moisten the soil.

11. Irrigation has transformed the social landscape. It changed the agriculture pattern, from

subsistence farming to intensive farming . For irrigation many multipurpose projects have been introduced. The aim of these projects is to manage the scarcity of water. The availability of water in ample amount ensures proper irrigation facilitiy for growing crops like sugarcane, cotton, banana etc. This shifted the traditional cropping to commercial cropping , ensuring profitable income of farmers. [1 + 1]

Shifting to water intensive and commercial crops is done by many farmers due to the irrigation facilities. For example, regardless of low rainfall a developed irrigation system enables Punjab to be a major producer of rice. [1]

12. Increasing number of industries is exerting pressure on fresh water resources-

    (i) Industries are heavy users of water. [1]

    (ii) Demand of hydroelectric power has increased. [1]

    (iii) Industrial wastes and effluent are discharged into rivers causing water pollution. [1]

    (iv) Multiplying urban centres, due to industries has increased usage and has caused pressure on water resources.

13. Rapid urbanization means rapid growth in the number of industries, houses, buildings, etc. which lead to the pressure on existing water sources around the cities. Over exploitation of water resources is disturbing the environment in many ways:

    (i) Over population leads to over utilization of water resources [1]

    (ii) Urbanization adds to water pollution. [1]

    (iii) Lack of rain water harvesting structures like ponds, lakes etc. [1]

    (iv) Poor waste management. [1]

    (v) Industries require electricity which often comes from hydroelectric power. [1]

14. Water plays a crucial role in the life of every living organism on the earth. But the amount of fresh water on the earth is very low and hence it has become necessary to save water. Rain water harvesting is therefore a very necessary and effective way to save water. In different parts of India, many types of methods are used for rain water harvesting. Some of them are as follows:

    (i) In Rajasthan, people use roof-top rain water harvesting so that the drinking water can be stored. This is the most common practice in Rajasthan. [1]

    (ii) In the hill stations, diversion channels like 'kul' or 'gul' are built by the people for rain water harvesting. This is mostly practiced for agriculture in the Western Himalayas. [1]

    (iii) In order to allow the water to stand and maintain the moisture in the soil, the agricultural fields a transformed to rain fed storage structures in semi-arid regions. These storage structures are called Khadins and Johads. [1]

    (iv) In order to irrigate the fields in West Bengal, people have started to develop irrigation channels. [1]

    (v) Tanks are also used to store drinking water in some places like Bikaner, Phalodi and Barmer. In these places, all the houses have tanks so that they can store water. [1]

MULTIPLE CHOICE QUESTIONS

1. Which of these is a cause of water scarcity in India?

    (a) Washing clothes

    (b) Manufacturing drinks that require water

    (c) Over exploitation of water

    (d) Less number of rivers

2. Multi-purpose river projects help in:

    (a) Reducing chances of a natural disaster

    (b) Power generation

    (c) Avoid waterborne diseases

    (d) displacement of local communities.

3. Which river valley project which has significantly contributed to the loss of forests?

    (a) Sardar Sarovar Dam

    (b) Chamera Dam

    (c) Bhakra Nangal Dam

    (d) None of these

4. Which water is recharged by rooftop rainwater harvesting technique?

    (a) Sea Water

    (b) River water

    (c) Ocean water

    (d) Ground water

5. Which of these is the largest artificial lake built in the 11ᵗʰ century?

   (*a*) Bhopal lake   (*b*) Chilika Lake

   (*c*) Dal Lake   (*d*) Wular Lake

Answer Keys

  1. (*c*)   2. (*b*)   3. (*a*)   4. (*d*)   5. (*a*)

FILL IN THE BLANKS

1. ___________ or ________ diversion channels were built for agriculture in western Himalaya.

2. Bamboo drip irrigation is prevalent in ___________

3. In West Bengal, people develop ___________ to irrigate their fields.

4. Nagarjunakonda in ___________, has evidence of irrigation structures.

5. In the cities, every housing society or colony is exploiting groundwater for daily use with the help of___________.

Solutions

1. Guls' or 'Kuls

2. Meghalaya

3. Inundation channels

4. Andhra Pradesh

5. Pumping devises

TRUE OR FALSE

1. B.R. Ambedkar proclaimed the dams as the "temples of modern India"

2. Multi-purpose river projects are the main source of irrigation and also help in conserving soil.

3. Rainwater harvesting system is viable alternative both socio-economically and environmentally

4. Underground tanks are not beneficial to the people of Rajasthan

5. Increasing number of industries are exerting pressure on freshwater resources

Solutions

1. False

2. True

3. True

4. False

5. True

CHAPTER 4

Agriculture

Summary

Type of Farming, cropping pattern and major crops

Primitive Subsistence Farming

- This ancient method of farming is still practised in some region of India.
- In this type of farming the members of a family or a small community cultivate food crops on a small piece of land using primitive tools like hoe, dao, digging sticks etc. for self consumption.
- This type of farming entirely depends on nature for water and fertility.

Intensive Subsistence Farming

It is a type of farming where more number of people are engaged in cultivating a small piece of land.

It is generally practised in thickly populated regions.

Farmers use more of chemical fertilizers to get the maximum yield.

This type of farming is prevalent in many parts of India due to the growing population and the 'right of inheritance' which has led to decrease in the size of land holding.

Main crop grown in this type of farming is rice.

Commercial Farming

- It is a type of farming where crops are grown on a large scale for selling them in the market.
- Modern inputs like HYV seeds, fertilizers, insecticides and pesticides are used to maximise the yield.

Cropping pattern

- **Cropping pattern** means the proportion of area under various crops at a point of time. This is, however, a dynamic concept as it changes over space and time.
- There are three distinct crop seasons in the northern and interior parts of country, namely kharif, rabi and zaid.
- The **kharif** season largely coincides with **Southwest Monsoon** under which the cultivation of **tropical crops** such as rice, cotton, jute, jowar, bajra and tur is possible. It is harvested in **September- october**.
- The **rabi** season begins with the **onset of winter** in October-November **and ends in April-June**. The **low temperature** conditions during this season facilitate the cultivation of **temperate and subtropical** crops such as **wheat, gram** and **mustard**.
- **Zaid** is a **short duration summer** cropping season beginning after harvesting of rabi crops, the cultivation of **watermelons, cucumbers, vegetables and fodder** crops during this season is done **on irrigated lands**.

Major crops

RICE:

It is the most important **Kharif crop** and **staple food**.

It grows in **hot and humid conditions**.

The ideal temperature is 250°C and rainfall is 100 cm.

Grown in the plains of north and north eastern India.

WHEAT

* Wheat is the second most important food crop of India sown in the beginning of winter and harvested in the beginning of summer.
* It is a Rabi or winter crop. It is sown in Normally (in north India) the sowing of wheat begins in the month of October-November and harvesting is done in the month of March-April.
* Rainfall 50 to 75 cm is needed.
* The largest wheat producing states are U.P, Punjab and Madhya Pradesh. Other than that the main regions of wheat production in India are Haryana, Rajasthan, Gujarat, and Maharashtra.

MILLETS

* Millets are short duration warm weather crops.
* Jowar, bajra, and ragi are important millet crops of India.
* Crops have very high nutritional value.
* Ragi is rich in iron, calcium,
* Jowar is the third most important food crop.
* Maharastra is the largest producer of Jowar
* Bajra grows in the sandy and shallow black soil. Rajasthan is the largest producer.

Maize

* It is a crop which is used both as food and fodder.
* It is a kharif crop which requires temperature between 21°C to 27°C and grows well in old alluvial soil.
* In some states like Bihar maize is grown in rabi season also. It is used both as food and fodder.
* Use of modern inputs such as HYV seeds, fertilisers and irrigation have contributed to the increasing production of maize.
* Major maize-producing states are Andhra Pradesh, Karnataka, Maharashtra, Uttar Pradesh, Bihar, Telangana and Madhya Pradesh.

PULSES

* India is the largest producer as well as the consumer of pulses in the world.
* These are the major source of protein in a vegetarian diet. Pulses need less moisture and survive even in dry conditions. Being leguminous crops,
* All these crops except arhar (pigeon pea) helps in restoring soil fertility by fixing nitrogen from the air.
* Most of these are green manure crops too. Major pulse producing states in India are Madhya Pradesh, Rajasthan, Maharashtra, Uttar Pradesh and Karnataka.

Technological and Institutional reform.

* A comprehensive land development programs was initiated.
* Provision of crop insurance against drought, floods, cyclone, fire and disease was introduced.
* Cooperative societies, Gramin banks and banks for providing loan to the farmers at lower rates of interest were established.
* Kissan Credit Card (KCC) was introduced.
* Accident Insurance Scheme (PAIS) was introduced.
* The government announced Minimum Support Price, remunerative and procurement prices to reduce exploitation.

Technological Reforms

* HYV seeds / Chemical Fertilizer/ Pesticides were provided.
* Methods of irrigation got modernized.
* The latest agricultural equipment were introduced.
* Special weather bulletins and agricultural programs were telecast on radio and television.

Points to know

SLASH AND BURN

Type of primitive agriculture in which farmers clear a patch of land and produce cereals

And other food crops to sustain their family.

BLOOD LESS REVOLUTION

The Bhoodan–Gramdam movement initiated by Vinoba Bhave is known as Blood Less Revolution.

FOOD SECURITY

To ensure the availability of food to all sections of society, a proper system as buffer stock and PDS is developed by the government.

PREVIOUS YEARS'
EXAMINATION QUESTIONS

▷ 1 Mark Questions

1. Which of the following crops is grown in the black soil?

    (*a*) Rice

    (*b*) Wheat

    (*c*) Cotton

    (*d*) Tea

    [TERM 1, 2011]

2. Which are the two main beverage crops produced in India?

    (*a*) Sugar cane and oilseeds

    (*b*) Tea and coffee

    (*c*) Jowar and bajra

    (*d*) Rice and wheat

    [TERM 1, 2011]

3. Who initiated the Bhoodan - Gramdaan movement?

    [TERM 1, 2014]

4. Crops, which are grown with the onset of monsoons and are harvested in the months of September – October are known as?

    [TERM 1, 2016]

▷ 3 Mark Questions

5. Explain any three features of primitive subsistence agriculture in India?

    [TERM 1, 2014]

6. Mention the main features of "Bhoodan – Gramdan" movement started by Vinoba Bhave?

    [TERM 1, 2014]

7. (*a*) One item A is shown in the given political outline map of India. Identify this item with the help of following information and write its correct name on the line marked on the map.

    (*a*) Type of soil

    (*b*) On the same political outline map of India, locate and label the following items with appropriate symbols

    (*c*) Periyar Tiger Reserve

    (*d*) Salal Dam

    [TERM 1, 2014]

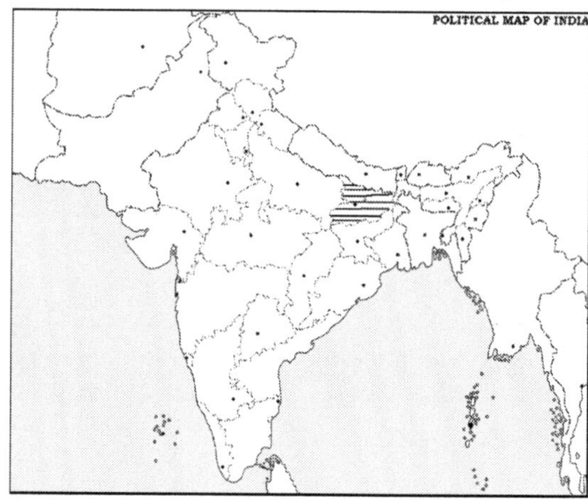

8. Explain Rubber Cultivation in India under the following heads:

    (*i*) Importance

    (*ii*) Geographical conditions

    (*iii*) Producing states.

    [TERM 1, 2015]

▷ 4 Mark Questions

9. Identify the two features A & B marked on the political outline map of India and write their correct answers.

    A. A multipurpose dam

    B. Type of soil

    AND

    Locate and label the following with appropriate symbols on the same map:

    1. Corbett National park

    2. Major tea producing area

    [TERM 1, 2012]

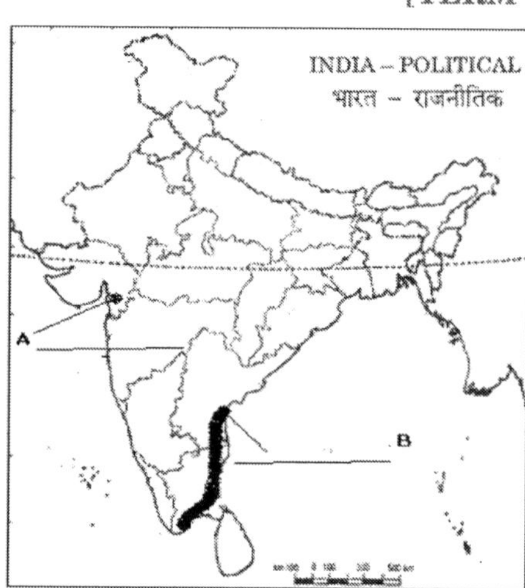

▶ 5 Mark Questions

10. Which is the second staple crop of India? What are the conditions required for its growth?

[TERM 1, 2012]

11. "The Government of India has introduced various institutional and technological reforms to improve agriculture in the 1980s and 1990s." Support this statement with examples.

[DELHI 2018]

12. Compare 'intensive subsistence farming' with 'commercial farming' practiced in India.

[DELHI 2018]

🔑 Solutions

1. (c) Cotton [1]

2. (b) Tea and Coffee [1]

3. The Bhoodan – Gramdaan movement was initiated by Acharya Vinoba Bhave. [1]

4. Kharif crops are grown with the onset of monsoons and are harvested in the months of September – October. [1]

5. Here are three features of primitive subsistence agriculture in India –

   (i) Primitive tools like dao, hoe and digging sticks are used for this type of farming which is done over a small area of land with the help of community or family. [1]

   (ii) Primitve subsistence farming depends on the natural conditions like natural fertility of soil, monsoon etc. [1]

   (iii) The production is basically for self-consumption of the farmers and the land availability per hectare is low. [1]

6. The "Bhoodan – Gramdan" movement is also called Land Gift Movement. It was initiated by Vinoba Bhave, a spiritual heir of Mahatma Gandhi. This voluntary land reform movement was started in 1951 at Pochampally of Telangana. The purpose of this movement was to assure the people of India to think about the reformation of the landless and poor villages. To fulfill the purpose of this movement, Vinoba Bhave started padyatra and reached to the people of the entire country with the messages of Mahatma Gandhi. As the result of his efforts, this movement got started and 80 acres of land was offered and distributed among 80 landless villagers by Sri Ram Chandra. This act was called as Bhoodan. Because of the land ceiling act (Gramdan), some land owners distributed some of their lands to the poor and landless villages. This whole movement was also known as Bloodless Revolution. [1 + 1 + 1]

7. (A) Alluvial [1]

   (b) (1) Periyar Tiger Reserve and (2)Salal Dam are shown in the following map [1 + 1]

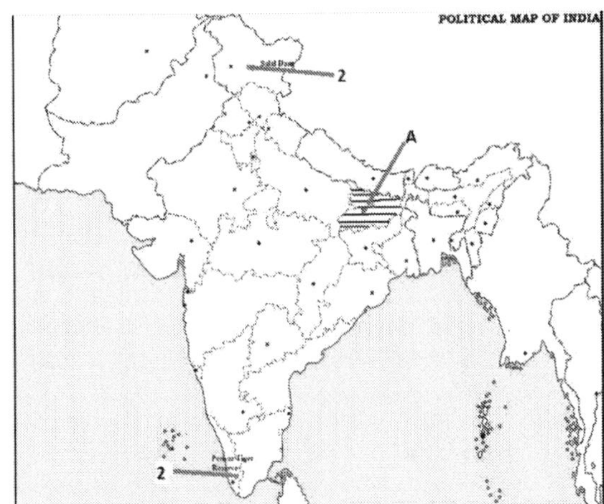

8. (a) Importance: Many industries depend upon the production of Rubber as their raw material. It includes transport industry and auto-mobile industry. [1]

   (b) Geographical conditions:

   (i) Rubber is an equatorial crop, that can also be grown in tropical and sub-tropical areas.

   (ii) Rubber requires moist and humid climate with rainfall of more than 200 cm and temperature above 25°C. [1]

   (c) Producing states: Kerala, Karnataka, Tamil-nadu, Andaman and Nicobar Islands and Garo hills of Meghalaya. [1]

9. The areas shaded in gray are the major tea producing parts in India. [1 + 1 + 1 + 1]

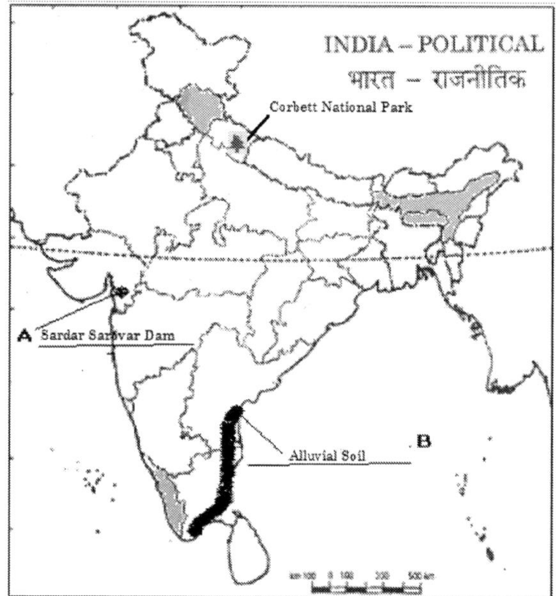

10. Second staple crop of India is rice. It mainly grows in the plains of north and north-east India, coastal areas and deltaic regions. It is a kharif crop. To grow rice the temperature is about $16°C – 27°C$ and ideal rainfall of 100 cm to 200 cm. Alluvial soil or the fertile river basin soils are ideal for cultivation of rice. Generally rice grows on plain lands or land with gentle slopes which are suitable for the production of rice. The second largest producer of rice in the world is India after China.   [1 + 1 + 1 + 1]

11. Institutional and technological reforms to improve agriculture in the 1980's and 1990's by the Government of India- **Institutional Reforms:**

(*i*) A comprehensive land development program was initiated.   [0.5]

(*ii*) Provision of crop insurance against drought, floods, cyclone, fire and disease was introduced.   [0.5]

(*iii*) Cooperative societies, Gramin banks and banks for providing loan to the farmers at lower rates of interest were established. [0.5]

(*iv*) Kissan Credit Card (KCC) was introduced.   [0.5]

(*v*) Accident Insurance Scheme (PAIS) was introduced.   [0.5]

(*vi*) The government announced Minimum Support Price, remunerative and procurement prices to reduce exploitation.   [0.5]

Technological Reforms

(*i*) HYV seeds / Chemical Fertilizer/ Pesticides were provided.   [0.5]

(*ii*) Methods of irrigation got modernized. [0.5]

(*iii*) Latest agricultural equipment were introduced.   [0.5]

(*iv*) Special weather bulletins and agricultural programs were telecast on radio and television.   [0.5]

12.

intensive subsistence farming	commercial farming
In intensive subsistence **pressure of population on land is high**.	In commercial farming population **pressure is low**. [1]
In intensive subsistence **farming labour intensive farming is used**.	In commercial **farming mechanized form of farming is used**. [1]
In intensive subsistence **farming there is low capital investment**	In commercial farming **high capital investment is seen**. [1]
In intensive subsistence farming **farmers produce for their own consumption**	In commercial **farming production is mainly for the market**. [1]
In intensive subsistence farming **processing industries are not associated with farms**	In commercial farming **processing industries are associated with plantations**. [1]
In intensive subsistence **farming multiple cropping is practiced**	In commercial farming **single cropping is practiced**.
In intensive subsistence farming **land holdings are small**	In commercial farming **land holdings are large**.

MULTIPLE CHOICE QUESTIONS

1. What type of farming is practiced in areas of high population?

(*a*) Primitive Subsistence Farming:

(*b*) Commercial Farming

(*c*) Intensive Subsistence Farming

(*d*) Both (*a*) & (*c*)

2. What is the other name for Sericulture?

   (a) Silk Farming

   (b) Crop Rotation

   (c) Jhumming

   (d) Horticulture

3. Which of these is a rubber producing state?

   (a) Jammu& Kashmir   (b) Assam

   (c) Punjab   (d) Tamil Nadu

4. The Government of India made concerted efforts to modernise agriculture by establishing the......

   (a) Food Corporation of India

   (b) Buffer stock

   (c) Indian Council of Agricultural Research (ICAR)

   (d) None of these

5. The National Jute policy was introduced in:

   (a) 2010   (b) 1998

   (c) 1965   (d) 2005

Answer Keys

1. (c)   2. (a)   3. (d)   4. (c)   5. (d)

FILL IN THE BLANKS

1. _____________ avoids or largely excludes the use of synthetically compounded and fertilisers, pesticides.

2. _____________ procures food grains from the farmers at the government announced minimum support price

3. The coarse grains which have very high nutritional value are called as __________

4. Grouping of small land holding into a bigger one is called as __________

5. _____________ and _____________ are the two other schemes introduced by the Government of India for the benefit of the farmers.

Solutions

1. Organic Farming

2. Food Corporation of India

3. Millets

4. Consolidation of land holding

5. Kisan Credit Card (KCC) , Personal Accident Insurance Scheme (PAIS)

TRUE OR FALSE

1. Rice is a commercial crop in Haryana and Punjab .

2. Bhoodan-Gramdan Movement was initiated by Vinoba Bhave

3. Rabi crops are sown with the onset of monsoon in different parts of the country and harvested in September-October.

4. Sugarcane does not need standing water to increase juice content in it ..

5. Rajasthan is the largest producer of groundnut in India .

Solutions

1. True

2. True

3. False

4. True

5. False

Minerals and Energy Resources

Summary

Minerals and mode of their occurrence.

- Naturally occurring homogenous substance with a definable internal structure.
- Minerals are usually found in Ores

Occurrence

- In the cracks of Igneous and metamorphic rocks
- The smaller occurrence is Lodes, and larger is Veins.
- Major metallic minerals like tin, copper, zinc and lead are obtained from loads and veins.
- In the bed or layers of sedimentary rocks, minerals like coal, gypsum, potash etc. are found.
- It is formed as a result of deposition, accumulation and concentration in horizontal strata.
- Another mode of formation involves the decomposition of surface rocks and the removal of soluble Constituents. Bauxite is formed by this way.
- In the placer deposits of sands minerals like gold, silver, tin and platinum are found.
- Common salt, magnesium and bromine are derived from the bed of oceans.

Ferrous and Non ferrous minerals and their conservation

- Three fourth of the total value of the production of metallic minerals
- India exports substantial quantities of ferrous minerals after his domestic use.

Ferrous

Orissa Jharkand Belt

- In Orissa high grade hematite ore is found in Badampahar mines in the Mayurbhanj and Kendujhar
- Gua and Noamundi of Jharkhand having haematite iron ore.
- **Durg - Bastar - Chandrapur belt -** Lies in chattisgarh and Maharashtra **high grade hematitis** are found in Bailadila range of hills in Chatisgarh.
- Bellavy Chitradurga - Chikmaglur - Tumkur Belt – In Karnataka has large reserves of iron ore. Kudermuch mines located in western Ghats of Karnataka and known to be one of the largest.
- Maharashtra - Goa Belt - Goa and Ratnagir district of Maharashtra have ample amount of ore. It is not of very high quality yet they are efficiently exploited.
- For manufacturing of steel and ferro-manganese alloy, manganese is obtained from Orrisa, the largest producer of it.

Non Ferrous

- **Copper** – The Balaghat mines of M.P produces **52 percent copper** of total production. Khetri and Singhbhum of Jharkhand is important producer.
- It is used in electrical industries.

  Bauxite - Amarkantank plateau, Maikal hill and the region of Bilaspur–Katni have a ample amount of it.
- **Orrisa** produce 45 percent bauxite of total production. **Panchpatmali of koraput** is important producer.

Conservation

- Minerals required millions of years to be created and concentrated.
- The total workable minerals deposit is one percent of the earth crust, and are rapidly consuming.
- The geological processes of mineral formation are slower than the rate of replenishment.
- The present rate of consumption of finite and non renewable minerals is high.
- To extract the minerals from depth is become expensive.
- To ensure the availability of minerals resources in future, need to accept planned and sustainable use.
- Recycling of metals using scraps metal and other substitute are steps in conserving minerals resources for future.

Conventional sources of Energy

Coal-occurs mainly in west Bengal-Jharkhand, and Godavari, Mahanadi, Son, Wardha valley and Assam, Arunachal Pradesh.

Lignite is low grade iron ,major reserve are in Neyveli in Tamilnadu, is used for generating electricity.

- Bituminous coal is used in blast furnace for smelting iron and other commercial purpose.
- Anthracite is the highest quality of coal .

Petrolium - occurrence in India are associated with anticlines and fault traps in the rock formation of tertiary age.

- About 63 percent of India's is from Mumbai high and 16 percent from Assam.

- In Gujarat Ankeleshwar is the most important field. Digboi, Naharkatiya are the oil field of Assam.
- For synthetic textile, fertilizer and other chemical industries,it acts as a Nodal industry.

Natural gas - reserves found in the Krishna–Godavari basin, along the west coast of Mumbai high and Andaman-Nicobar islands.

The power and fertilizers industries are key users of natural gas.

Electricity - generated by fast flowing water of various multi- purpose river projects.

- electricity is also generated by the use of coal. There are over 310 thermal power plants in India.
- nuclear energy is also use for generation electricity. Uranium of Aravali and Jharkhand region is used to generate electricity.

Non conventional sources of Energy

Solar energy - the photovoltaic technology converts sunlight directly into electricity. It becomes very popular in remote and rural areas.

- Madhupur near Bhuj is the largest solar plant in India. it is used to sterilise milk cans.

Wind power - India rank as a wind super power in the world.

The largest wind farm cluster is located from Nagarcoli to Madurai of Tamilnadu.

Biogas - It is obtained by decomposition of organic materials as shrubs, farm waste, animal and human waste.

- The gobar gas plants provide twin benefits to the farmer in the form of energy and improved quality of manure.
- Tidal energy-oceanic tides is used to generate electricity.
- The gulf of kuchchh provides ideal condition for utilizing tidal energy. 900 MW tidal energy power plant is set up by National Hydro power .

Geo thermal energy – electricity is generated by the internal heat of the earth.

- Paravati valley near Manikarn in Himachal Pradesh and Puga valley of Ladakh is two experimental projects set up by the government to generate electricity.

Points to know

RAT HOLE MINING

In tribal area of north east India, especially in Meghalaya digging pits ranging from five to 100 m² into the ground to reach the coal seam by tribals to obtain coal.

PREVIOUS YEARS'
EXAMINATION QUESTIONS

▶ 1 Mark Questions

1. Which one of the following minerals is a fossil fuel?

    (*a*) Barium

    (*b*) Coal

    (*c*) Zircon

    (*d*) Uranium

    [TERM 2, 2011]

2. Orissa is the leading producer of which one of the following minerals?

    (*a*) Copper

    (*b*) Iron ore

    (*c*) Manganese ore

    (*d*) Mica

    [TERM 2, 2011]

3. Kodarma Gaya-Hazaribagh belt of Jharkhand is the leading producer of which one of the following minerals?

    (*a*) Copper

    (*b*) Bauxite

    (*c*) Iron-ore

    (*d*) Mica

    [TERM 2, 2012]

4. Which one of the following fuels is considered environment friendly?

    (*a*) Coal   (*b*) Petroleum

    (*c*) Natural gas   (*d*) Firewood

    [TERM 2, 2012]

5. How do minerals occur in sedimentary rocks?

    [TERM 2, 2015]

6. Why has aluminum metal great importance?

    [TERM 2, 2016]

▶ 3 Mark Questions

7. Make a distinction between hydroelectricity and thermal electricity stating the three points of distinction.

    [TERM 2, 2011]

8. Mention any three major iron-ore belts of India. Write any three characteristics of the southernmost iron-ore belt.

    [TERM 2, 2012]

9. Three features - A, B and C are marked in the given political outline map of India. Identify these features with the help of the following information and write their correct names on the lines marked in the map:

    (*a*) Iron-ore mine

    (*b*) Oil field

    (*c*) Terminal Station of NH. 7

    [TERM 2, 2012]

10. Differentiate between metallic and non-metallic minerals with examples.

    [TERM 2, 2013]

11. Which state is the largest producer of manganese in India? Mention any four uses of manganese.

    [TERM 2, 2013]

12. On the same political outline map of India, locate and label the following with appropriate symbols:

    (*i*) Narora – a nuclear power plant

    (*ii*) Rourkela – an iron and steel plant

    (*iii*) Kandla – a major sea port

    [TERM 2, 2014]

13. How can solar energy solve the energy problem to some extent in India? Give your opinion.

    [TERM 2, 2015]

14. (*i*) Two features A and B are marked on the given political outline map of India. Identify these features with the help of the following information and write their correct names on the lines marked in the map:

    A.   Iron-ore mines

    B.   Terminal Station of East-West Corridor

    (*ii*) On the same political outline map of India, locate and label the following:

    Vishakhapatnam – Software Technology Park   **[TERM 2, 2015]**

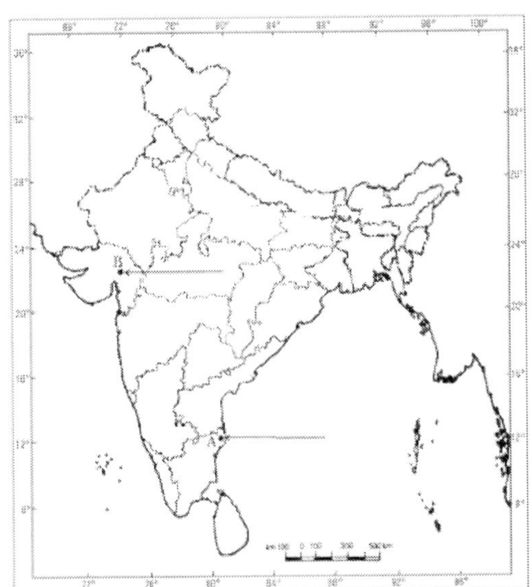

15. (*a*) In which state are Bailadila Iron-ore mines located ?

(*b*) Name the Western Terminal Station of East-West Corridor.

(*c*) Name the well-known Software Technology Park located in Karnataka State

[TERM 2, 2015]

16. 'Consumption of energy in all forms has been rising all over the country. There is an urgent need to develop a sustainable path of energy development and energy saving'. Suggest and explain any three measures to solve this burning problem.

[TERM 2, 2016]

17. On a given political map of India, locate and label the following with appropriate symbols:

A. Oil Field- Digboi

B. Iron and Steel Plant – Bhilai

C. Major Sea Port-Kochi.

Locate and label Rihand. On the same political map of India.

[TERM 2, 2014]

18. Describe any three characteristics of the Durg-Bastar-Chandrapur Iron-ore belt in India.

[TERM 2, 2017]

19. On the given political outline map of India locate and label the following features with appropriate symbols:

A. Naraura – Nuclear Power Plant

B. Tuticorin – Major Sea Port

C. Bhilai – Iron and Steel Plant

[TERM 2, 2017]

▶ 5 Mark Questions

20. Three features (*a*), (*b*), (*c*) are marked in the given political outline map of India. Identify these features with the help of the following information and write their correct names on the lines marked in the map:

(*a*) Coal mine

(*b*) Silk Industry

(*c*) International Airport

AND

Locate and label the following items on the same political outline map of India with appropriate symbols:

(*i*) Kanpur – Cotton Textile Industry

(*ii*) Bhadravati- Iron and Steel Plant

(*iii*) Kandla- Sea Port

[TERM 2, 2011]

21. Why is there a pressing need for using renewable energy sources in India? Explain any five reasons.

[TERM 2, 2014]

22. Which is the most abundantly available fossil fuel in India? Assess the importance of its different forms.

[TERM 2, 2015]

23. Why is it necessary to conserve mineral resources? Explain any four ways to conserve mineral resources.

[TERM 2, 2017]

🔑 Solutions

1. (*b*) Coal   [1]

2. (*c*) Manganese ore   [1]

3. (*d*) Mica   [1]

4. (*c*) Natural ga   [1]

5. Mineral occurs in beds or layers in sedimentary rocks.   [1]

6. Aluminum is an important metal because it combines the strength of metals such as iron, with extreme lightness and also with good conductivity and great malleability.   [1]

7. Electricity generated mainly in two ways can be recognized as Hydroelectricity and Thermal electricity.

Hydroelectricity is generated by hydropower that is water falling on turbines or fast flowing water. The sources are renewable that is inexhaustible.

It causes no pollution and is cheaper. Many multi-purpose projects are there in India, like Bhakra Nangal, Damodar Valley whereas Thermal Electricity is generated from petroleum (oil) or coal. Its source is non-renewable or exhaustible. Burning of coal and oil causes pollution and it is expensive. The number of Thermal Power Plants in India is more than 310.   [0.5 + 0.5 + 0.5 + 0.5 + 0.5 + 0.5]

8. The three major iron ore belts of India are: Orissa-Jharkhand belt, Durg-Bastar- Chandrapur belt lying in Chhattisgarh and Maharashtra and the Bellary-Chitradurga- Chikmaglur-Tumkur belt in Karnataka.   [1.5]

   The three characteristics of the southernmost iron-ore belt i.e. Bellary-Chitradurga-Chikmaglur-Tumkur belt in Karnataka are:

   (i)   The Kudremukh mines are located in the Western Ghats of Karnataka and their entire produce is exported.

   (ii) The Kudremukh deposits are one of the largest deposits of iron ore in the world.

   (iii) Through a pipeline ore is transported as slurry to a port in Mangalore.   [1.5]

9.   [1 + 1]

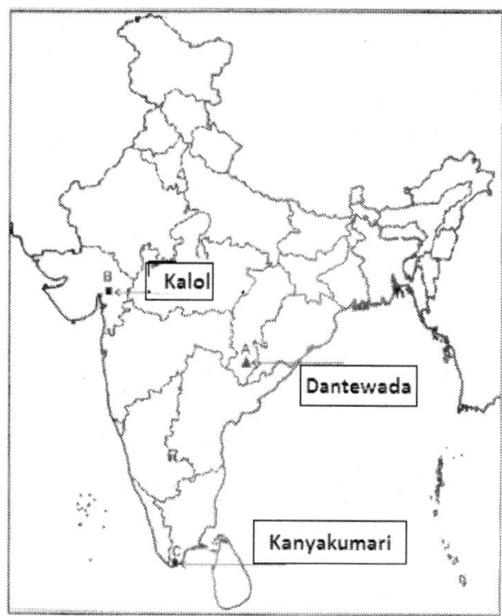

10.

Metallic Minerals	Non Metallic Minerals
They contain **metals in raw form**.	They **do not contain metals**. [1]
Metallic minerals have **higher boiling point and melting point**.	Non Metallic minerals have **lower boiling point and melting point**. [1]

Act as **good reducing agents**	Act as **good oxidizing agents** [1]
They are **lustrous, malleable and ductile**.	They are **brittle**.
Examples: Iron ore, Bauxite, Zinc and Lead	Examples: Limestone, Mica, Gypsum.

11. Odisha is the largest producer of manganese in India. Being a leading producer of manganese ore with a share of 22.62 % in India during 2010-11, it accounts for country's 44% of manganese ore.   [1]

   Uses of manganese are:

   (i)   Mostly required in glass industry.   [1]

   (ii) Helps in manufacturing bleaching powder in chemical industry.   [1]

   (iii) Used to manufacture good quality steel.

   (iv) Used for manufacturing alloys, pesticides and insecticides.

12.

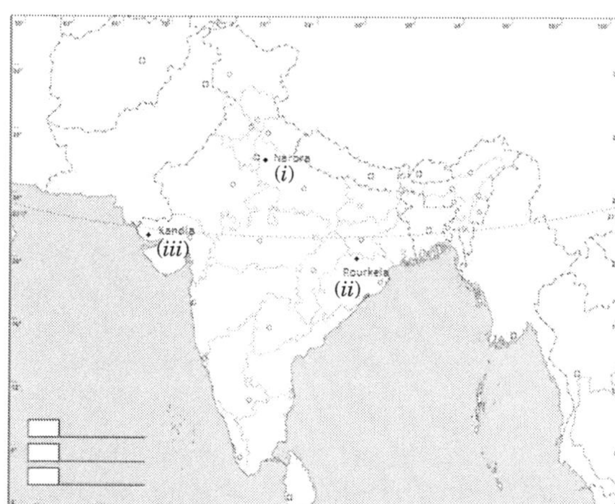

13. As India has enormous possibilities of tapping solar energy so it is known as a tropical country.   [1]

   Sunlight can be converted into electricity directly using the Photovoltaic technology.   [1]

   Solar energy is getting popular among rural areas. Some big solar power plants are being are established in different part of India which will minimize the dependence of rural households on firewood and dung cakes.   [1]

14. (i)

   A.   Iron-ore mines – Bellary   [1]

   B.   Terminal Station of East-West Corridor - Porbandar   [1] (*ii*) Vishakhapatnam – Software Technology Park has been labeled in the map as follows: [1]

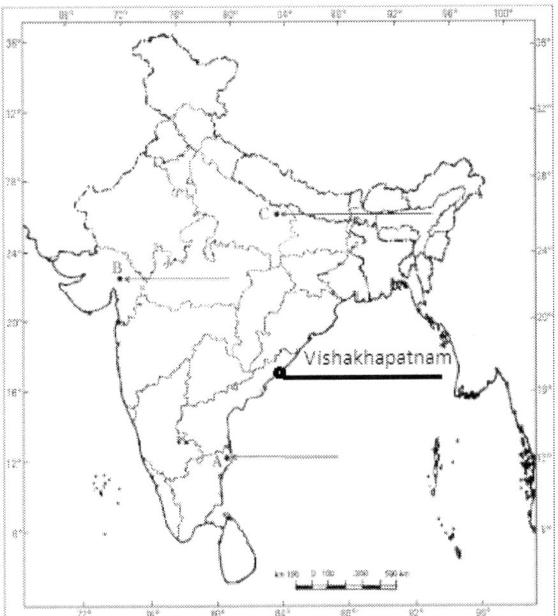

15. (*a*) Chattisgarh [1]

    (*b*) Porbandar [1]

    (*c*) Electronic City [1]

16. In present time, our country is one of the least energy efficient countries in the world. We need to be very careful towards energy consumption and follow the different ways to save energy as much as possible.

Below are a few measures to solve this burning problem:

   (*i*) One should use public transport system instead of individual vehicles more often. [1]

   (*ii*) Switching off the electricity when it is not in use, this should be in practice properly and due to this, we can incorporate a lot in energy conservation. [1]

   (*iii*) Use more power saving devices and non-conventional sources of energy [1]

   (*iv*) By encouraging young brains to innovate in alternative sources of energy.

17.

[1 + 1 + 1]

18. The characteristics of the Durg-Bastar-Chandrapur Iron-ore belt are as follows:

   (*i*) Durg-Bastar-Chandrapur Iron-ore belt lies in Chhattisgarh and Maharashtra. [1]

   (*ii*) Hematite, a high-quality ore of iron is found in Bastar. [1]

   (*iii*) 14 high-quality hematite ore is found in the hills of this region. [1]

19.   [1 + 1 + 1]

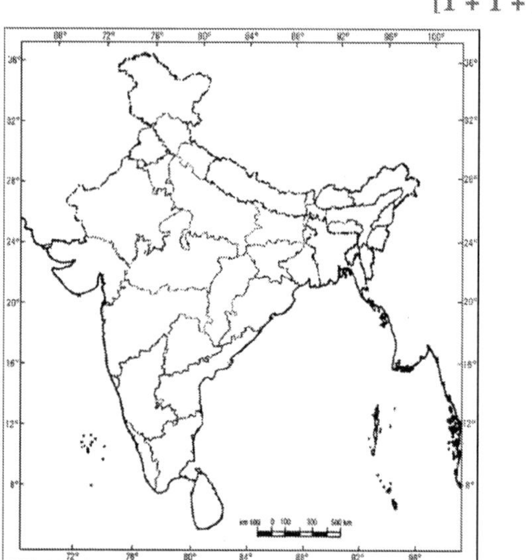

20.

(*a*) Korba   [1]

(*b*) Murshidabad   [1]

(*c*) Chennai   [1]

AND

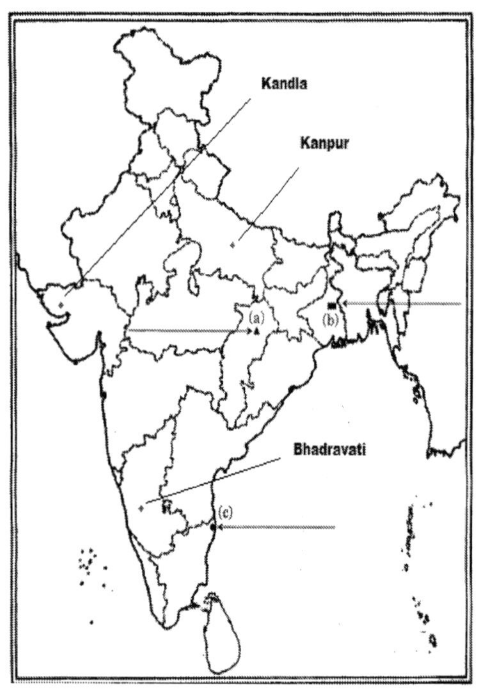

[2]

21.

(*i*) The growing rate of consumption of energy has resulted in the country becoming increasingly dependent on fossils fuels such as coal, oil and gas which are finite. That's why the need for sustainable energy resources like solar, wind and water.   [1]

(*ii*) Renewable energy sources are infinitely cheaper than the conventional ones and are available in the nature in abundance as compared to the non-renewable sources of energy and their ever-rising prices and shortages.   [1]

(*iii*) The uncertainties about the non-renewable sources of energy and their rising prices pose a threat to security of energy supply in future. This in turn leads to uncertainty regarding the future of the national economy and can have serious repercussions.   [1]

(*iv*) There is a phenomenal rise in the prices of oil and gas because of their undisputed demand.   [1]

(*v*) The environment is getting harmed due to increasing use of fossil fuels. It is causing serious environmental problems like pollution and degradation of soil, water and air. On the other hand, renewable energy sources, which are natural sources of energy, are pollution free and eco friendly.   [1]

22. The most abundantly available fossil fuel in India is coal. The different forms of coal are Peat, Lignite, Bituminous and Anthracite. Let's talk about their importance in detail: [1]

(*i*) Peat : Decaying plants in swamps produce peat and it is burnt as fuel or applied to the soil to improve the texture and moisture. [1]

(*ii*) Lignite: It is brown is colour, soft and has high moisture content. Generation of electricity is the main usage of lignite.   [1]

(*iii*) Bituminous: It's usually black in colour and has medium heat per kg. It is used for producing coke.   [1]

(*iv*) Anthracite: The carbon content in per kg is more than 90%. It is used in residential and commercial space heating.   [1]

23. Need to conserve mineral resources are:

(*i*) Mineral resources are limited and non-renewable.   [1]

(*ii*) All minerals are not evenly distributed on the earth surface so it will take time to find all the minerals.   [1]

(*iii*) The geological processes of mineral formation are very slow but the rate of consumption is very high.   [1]

Mineral resources can be conserved by following ways:

(*i*) There should be planned usage of these resources. [0.5]

(*ii*) Bicycle or walk through can be used as a means of transport to travel short distances. Judious and proper uses of minerals should be promoted by government means like as rebate in personal tax for a person who use sustainable means for his transportation or other work . [0.5]

(*iii*) Switch off the vehicles engines at railway crossing or at a red traffic light. [0.5]

(*iv*) The government should implement some strict usage law in order to conserve these resources. [0.5]

MULTIPLE CHOICE QUESTIONS

1. What is a mineral ?
   (*a*) Naturally formed aggregate of minute particles
   (*b*) A naturally occurring substance that has a definite chemical composition.
   (*c*) Heterogeneous naturally occurring substance with a definable internal structure.
   (*d*) None of these

2. Limestone is an example of......
   (*a*) Metallic minerals
   (*b*) Manganese ore
   (*c*) Non-metallic minerals
   (*d*) None of these

3. Copper is used in making....
   (*a*) Utensils
   (*b*) Buildings
   (*c*) Cricket equipment
   (*d*) Both (*b*) and (*c*)

4. What type of energy is obtained from coal, petroleum and natural gas?
   (*a*) Hydro energy
   (*b*) Thermal energy
   (*c*) Renewable energy
   (*d*) Solar energy

5. Shrubs, farm wastes, animal and human wastes are used to produce.......
   (*a*) Rocks
   (*b*) Minerals
   (*c*) Biogas
   (*d*) Cotton

Answer Keys

1. (*b*) 2. (*c*) 3. (*a*) 4. (*b*) 5. (*c*)

FILL IN THE BLANKS

1. A ___________ studies the formation of minerals, their age and physical and chemical properties.

2. a wide range of colours , hardness, crystal forms, lustre and density is found in minerals due to ____________ and ___________ conditions

3. Odisha was the largest ___________ producing state in India in 2009-10.

4. Iron ore is transported as slurry through ____________

5. ___________ is the oldest oil producing State of India.

🔑 Solutions

1. Geologist
2. Physical, chemical
3. Bauxite
4. Pipelines
5. Assam

TRUE OR FALSE

1. Copper is mainly used in electrical cables and electronic industries

2. Nagarcoil and Jaisalmer are well known for effective use of solar energy

3. Minerals occur in beds or layers in sedimentary rocks.

4. Mumbai high is an offshore oil field?

5. Koderma, in Jharkhand is the leading producer of Bauxite

🔑 Solutions

1. True
2. False
3. True
4. True
5. False

CHAPTER 6

Manufacturing Industries

Summary

Manufacturing Industries

Introduction

* Production of goods in large quantities after processing from raw materials to more valuable products.
* The economic strength of a country is measured by the development of manufacturing industries.
* Manufacturing industries helps in modernising agriculture.
* It reduces the heavy dependence of people on agriculture income by providing them jobs.
* Helps in bringing down regional disparities.

Location

* The industrial locations are complex in nature.
* It depends on the availability of raw material.
* Cost of production at site.
* Closeness to market.
* Availability of transport.
* Availability of cheap labours.
* Government policies

Classification

On the basis of raw material sources

Agro Based Industries - Cotton textile, jute textile, sugar and vegetable oil

Mineral Based Industries - iron and steel, petrochemical, aluminium and cement industries.

One the basis of their main role

* Basic or key industries-supply their products to manufacture other goods, ex. Iron and steel and copper smelting .
* Consumer industries–produce goods for direct use of consumers. Ex-sugar, toothpaste, paper, soap etc.

On the basis of capital investment

* Small scale industries-owned and run by individuals having small number of labourers .
* Large Scale Industry-Industries having large number of labourers and employs in each unit.
* Investment is more than one crore Rs, Cotton or jute textile industries are large scale industries

On the basis of ownership

* Private Sector Industries-owned by individuals or firms such as Bajaj Auto or TISCO situated at Jamshedpur are called private sector industries.
* Public Sector Industries-owned by the state and its agencies like Bharat Heavy Electricals Ltd., or Bhilai Steel Plant or Durgapur Steel Plant are public sector industries.
* Joint Sector Industries-owned jointly by the private firms and the state or its agencies such as Gujarat Alkalies Ltd., or Oil India Ltd. fall in the group of joint sector industries.
* Co-operative Sector Industries-owned and run co-operatively by a group of people who are generally producers of raw materials of the given industry such as a sugar mill owned and run by farmers are called co-operative sector industries.

Agro based industries

Textile industry

- It contributes 14 percent in industrial production and provides employment to 35 million peoples directly.
- It contributes 4 percent towards GDP.
- It is self reliant industries, which complete in the value chain.

Cotton industries

- There are nearly 1600 cotton and human made fibre textile mills in the country. 80 percent of mills in private sector and rest in public sector.
- It is concentrated in cotton belt of Maharashtra and Gujarat.
- It supports many other industries like chemical and dyes, mill stores, packaging materials and engineering works.
- The handspun khadi provide large scale employment to weavers in their homes.
- India export yarn to Japan.
- It has second largest installed capacity of spindles in the world next to China.
- There is need to upgrade machinery in the weaving and processing sector.

Jute Textiles

- India is the largest producer of raw jute and jute goods and stand at second place after Bangladesh.
- Due to availability of ideal condition most of the jute mills located in the bank of Hugli river of west Bengal.
- There are about 70 jute mills in India, which supports 2.61 lakh workers directly and another 40 lakh small and marginal farmers are engaged in cultivation for raw material i.e Mesta or Jute.
- To increase in productivity,and to improve quality,the national Jute policy was formulated
- The main market of jute textiles are U.S.A, Canada, Russia, U.K and Australia.

Sugar industries

- India is second largest producer of sugar and stand first in Gur and Khandsari production.
- There are 460 sugar mills in India spread in U.P, Bihar, M.P, Punjab and Harayana.
- Recent year the sugar industries shifted in Maharashtra due to idea condition of growing sugarcane.

Minerals based industries

Iron and steel industries

- It is categorized in heavy industry.
- India stands at ninth rank among world in crude steel production with 32.8 ton steel production in a year.
- In spite of large quantity of production per capita consumption of steel is only 32 kg per annum.
- Steel authority of India, market the steel of all public sector, where TISCO market its produce through Tata Steel.
- The presence of iron and steel industries is mainly found in Chotanagpur plateau region.

Aluminium smelting

- Second most metallurgical industries in India .
- To manufacture aircraft, utensils and wires, it is used.
- India have eight smelting plant.
- Bauxite is the raw materials used in the smelters.

Chemical industries

- It contributes 3 percent of the GDP.
- Third largest in Asia and 12th in world in production.
- It includes small and large manufacturing industries.
- It includes petrochemicals which are used for manufacturing of synthetic fibres, synthetic rubbers plastics, dye stuffs etc.

Fertiliser industry

- It includes the production of nitrogenous fertilizer, mainly Urea, DAP and NPK.
- India is the third largest producer of nitrogenous fertilizers.
- There are fifty seven fertilizers units in India and one cooperative is in Hazira located in Gujarat.

Cement industries

- The first cement plant was setup in Chennai in 1904.

- There are 128 large plants and 332 mini plants in the country.

Information technology

- Due to development of IT in Banglore it is known as Electronic capital of India.
- Eighteen software technology parks provide single window service and high data communication facility to software experts.
- Up to 31 march 2015, it employed over one million person.
- BPOs has emerged as the medium of foreign earning .
- The innovation and development in the hardware and software, the IT industries rising continuously.

Industrial Pollution and Environmental Degradation

Industries contributes in the development and growth of the economy but also caused in the unbalance of nature, caused contamination of resources.

Types of Pollution

- Air - caused by undesirable gases such as sulphur dioxide and carbon monoxide, air borne particles such as dust, sprays, mist & smoke.
- Water Pollution - Caused by organic & inorganic industrial wastes such as release of lead, mercury pesticides, fertilizers, synthetic chemical, plastics, rubber, fly ash, phosphogypsum etc.
- Thermal Pollution - Caused by nuclear power plants nuclear & weapon production cause cancers birth defects & miscarriages.
- Noise Pollution - Causes heaving impairment, increased heart rate & blood pressure by making unwanted noise.

Control of Environment Degradation

- Minimising the use of water by reusing recycling.
- Harvesting rainwater to meet water requirement.
- Treatment of hot water and effluents before releasing in ponds & rivers, involves 3 steps.

  1. Primary treatment by mechanical means.

  2. Secondary treatment by biological process.

  3. Tertiary treatment by biological chemical & physical processes.

Points to know

Agglomeration economy

When a number of companies establish their units at one place to avail maxim benefits nearby the population, both industries and people gets opportunity to develop.

GDP

Gross domestic product.

EMS

Environment management system

PREVIOUS YEARS' EXAMINATION QUESTIONS

▶ 1 Mark Questions

1. Which one of the following has been the major source of foreign exchange for IT industry?

   (a) BHEL

   (b) SAIL

   (c) BPO

   (d) OIL

   [TERM 2, 2011]

2. Which one of the following factors plays the most important role in the location of an industry in a particular region?

   (a) Raw material

   (b) Market

   (c) Least production cost

   (d) Transport

   [TERM 2, 2012]

▶ 3 Mark Questions

3. Explain any three problems faced by Iron and Steel Industry in India.

   [TERM 2, 2011]

4. Describe any three factors that control industrial location.

   [TERM 2, 2011]

5. How do industries pollute air? Explain ill effects of pollution.

   [TERM 2, 2012]

6. Why was cotton textile industry concentrated in the cotton growing belt of Maharashtra and Gujarat in the early years? Explain any three reasons.

[TERM 2, 2012]

7. Locate and label the following items with appropriate symbols and write their correct names on the same map:

   (*i*) Durgapur - Iron and Steel Plant

   (*ii*) Kaiga - Nuclear Power Plant

   (*iii*) Vishakhapatnam - Sea Port

[TERM 2, 2012]

8. Why has the 'Chhota Nagpur Plateau Region' the maximum concentration of iron and steel industries? Analyse the reason.

[TERM 2, 2015]

9. Suggest any three steps to minimize the environmental degradation caused by the industrial development in India.

[TERM 2, 2016]

▶ 5 Mark Questions

10. Explain any five measures to control industrial pollution in India.

[TERM 2, 2013]

11. What is the manufacturing sector? Why is it considered the backbone of development? Interpret the reason.

[TERM 2, 2015]

🗝 Solutions

1. (*c*) BPO [1]

2. (*c*) Least production cost [1]

3. The Iron and Steel Industry is a basic industry since all the other industries are dependent on it for their machinery.

   Problems faced by Iron and Steel Industry in India are:

   (*i*) High costs and capital. [1]

   (*ii*) Limited availability of cooking coal and irregular supply of energy. [1]

   (*iii*) Labour productivity is low. [1]

   (*iv*) Poor Infrastructure for setting up industries.

4. The factors that control industrial location are:

   (*i*) Availability of raw materials and low capital cost. [1]

   (*ii*) Proximity or closeness to the markets. [1]

   (*iii*) Availability of cheap and skilled labour. [1]

   (*iv*) Government policies.

5. Industries pollute air by emitting high proportion of undesirable gases like sulphur dioxide and carbon monoxide.

   The ill effects of pollution are as follows:

   (*i*) It adversely affects human health causing respiratory and water borne diseases. [1]

   (*ii*) It degrades the environment and increases the amount of carbon dioxide causing global warming [1]

   (*iii*) It causes loss of habitat for plants and animals. [1]

6. Cotton textile industry was concentrated in Maharashtra and Gujarat in the early years due to:

   (*i*) The availability of raw cotton. [1]

   (*ii*) The availability of market, labour, transport including accessible port facilities. [1]

   (*iii*) Suitable moist climate for cultivation of cotton. [1]

7.

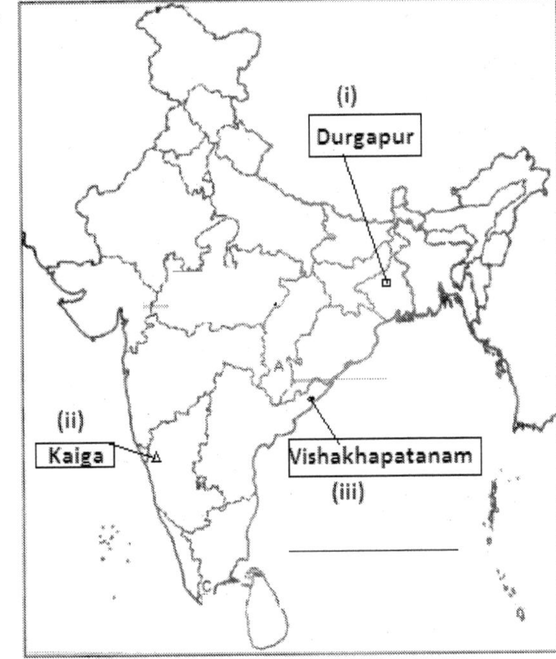

[1 + 1 + 1]

8. Chhotanagpur plateau region has the maximum concentration of iron and steel industries because of the below reasons:

   1. Region is rich in low cost iron ore [1]

   2. High grade raw material in proximity [1]

   3. Cheap labour and vast growth potential in the home market. [1]

9. The industrial development contributes to the economic growth but it also affect the environment. Industries are responsible for degradation in air, water, land etc.

   We can reduce environmental degradation caused by industries by the following ways:-

   (*i*) Minimizing used water for processing by reusing and recycling it in two or more successive stages. [1]

   (*ii*) Water requirement can be met by rain water harvesting [1]

   (*iii*) By dumping, sewage and industries wastage in remote areas from urban population.

   [1]

   (*iv*) Degradration in air can be reduced by using oil or gas instead of coal in factories. Pollution check certificates should be made compulsory for factories to operate and function.

10. Five measures to control industrial pollution in India are as follows:

    (*i*) Particulate matter in the air can be reduced by fitting smoke stacks to factories with electrostatic precipitators, fabric filters, scrubbers and inertial separators. [1]

    (*ii*) Smoke can be reduced by using oil or gas instead of coal in factories. Pollution check certificates should be made compulsory for factories to operate and function. [1]

    (*iii*) Machinery and equipments adopting the latest technology can be used and the existing equipments should be upgraded. Generators should be fitted with silencers.

    (*iv*) Waste generation can be minimized by using ash through ash pond management, ash water recycling system and liquid waste management. [1]

    (*v*) Afforestation should be encouraged and green belts should be set up around factories to maintain ecological balance. [1]

11. In the manufacturing sector, raw products are transferred in to more valuable products, so it is also known as secondary sector. It is considered the backbone of development for the given reasons: [1]

    (*i*) It provides materials like fertilizers, pesticides to the agricultureal sector. [1]

    (*ii*) It creates job opportunities, as a large portion of population is dependent on agriculture which leads to disguised unemployment. [1]

    (*iii*) The export of manufactured goods expands trade and thus adds to foreign exchange. [1]

    (*iv*) It also minimizes the regional differences, when an industry is being set up in the tribal or remote areas. [1]

    (*v*) It plays an major role in eradicating poverty. It also helps in modernizing agriculture, which forms the backbone of our economy.

MULTIPLE CHOICE QUESTIONS

1. What are Public Sector Industries?

   (*a*) Industries which are owned and operated by private agencies

   (*b*) Industries which are owned and operated by government agencies

   (*c*) Industries which are owned and operated by individuals

   (*d*) Industries which are owned and operated by government and private agencies

2. Where was the first cement plant established in India?

   (*a*) Kerala

   (*b*) Assam

   (*c*) Chennai

   (*d*) Maharashtra

3. AMUL is an example of…..

   (*a*) Cooperative Sector Industry

   (*b*) Agro-based industry

   (*c*) Mining industry

   (*d*) Heavy industry

4. To which one of the following countries does India export jute goods?

   (*a*) Japan   (*b*) China

   (*c*) USA   (*d*) France

5. The pollution caused by the discharge of hot water from factories and thermal plants into rivers and ponds before cooling is called as......

   (*a*) Air pollution

   (*b*) Thermal pollution

   (*c*) Water pollution

   (*d*) Soil pollution

Answer Keys

1. (*b*)   2. (*c*)   3. (*a*)   4. (*c*)   5. (*b*)

FILL IN THE BLANKS

1. _______________ is the backbone of any country's economy

2. NMCC stands for ___________________.

3. Sugar is an example of ___________ industry

4. Sulphuric acid, nitric acid, alkalis, soda ash and caustic soda are ___________ types of chemicals.

5. The major drawback of cotton industry is _______________ .

Solutions

1. Steel production

2. National Manufacturing Competitiveness Council

3. Agro-based

4. Inorganic

5. Fragmented nature of cotton processing

TRUE OR FALSE

1. Chhota Nagpur region maximum concentration of iron and steel industries

2. Industries do not cause environmental degradation

3. NTPC markets steel for the public sector plants.

4. Agriculture and industry are complementary to each other.

5. Banglore has emerged as the electronic capital of India..

Solutions

1. True

2. False

3. False

4. True

5. True

Life Lines of National Economy

Summary

Means of Transport

Roadways

- Road networks of India is largely developed in the world.
- The cost of construction of roads is lower.
- Roads can cross relatively more dismembered and undulating geology.
- Roads can arrange higher inclinations of slant and in that capacity can navigate mountains.
- Door to door services can provide easily with the help of roads.
- In state PWD, in districts zila parisad, in rural area maintains the roads.

Golden Quadrilateral Super Highways

- a major road development project launched to connect Delhi, Kolkata-Chennai- Mumbai and Delhi by six-lane super highways by Indian government.
- Srinagar of Jammu & Kashmir and Kanyakumari of Tamilnadu connects with North-South corridors.
- The Silcher of Assam and Porbander of Gujarat connecting by the East-West Corridor .
- To minimize the distance and travelling time is the main goal to link.

Railways

- Railway is the largest public sector undertaking in the country.

- The distribution pattern of the railway network in the country has been largely influence by physiographic, economic and administrative factors.
- The Himalyan mountains regions are unfavourable for the construction of railway lines due to high relief sparse population & each of economic opportunities.
- The northern plains provide most favourable condition having high population density.
- Rivers also create problem for lay down of railway tracts.

Water ways

- Waterways are the cheapest way of transport.
- The Ganga river between Allahabad and Haldia, which cover 1620 km is national waterways.
- The brahmputra river between Sadiya and Dhubri covering 891 km distance is national waterways.
- 95 percent of the country trade is done by sea.

Means of communication

- The personal communication and mass communication including television, radio, press, etc. are the major means of communication.
- India postal network is the largest means of the communication in the world.
- India have one of the largest telecom network in the Asia.
- Doordarshan is the national television of India.
- In India about 100 language newspaper is published.

- India is the largest producer of feature films in the world.

International Trade and Tourism

- The exchange of goods among people; states & countries is referred to as trade.
- Export or import of goods and services between two and more than two countries termed as International Trade.
- Exports and imports are the components of trade. The balance of a trade of a country is the difference between its export and import.
- When the value of exports exceeds the value of imports, it is called favourable balance of trades.

Tourism as a Trade

- Tourism has proved itself as one of the most important aspect of trade.
- Tourism in India has grown substantially. National integration has encouraged it.
- Provide support to local handicrafts.
- Provides support to cultural pursuits.
- Develops of international understanding about our culture and heritage.

Points to know

Pradhan Mantri Gramin Sadak Yojna

The Pradhan Mantri Gram Sadak Yojana is a nationwide plan in India to provide good all-weather road connectivity to unconnected villages.

STD

Subscriber Trunk Dialing

PREVIOUS YEARS'
EXAMINATION QUESTIONS

▶ 1 Mark Questions

1. Which one of the following major ports has been developed to decongest Kolkata port?

    (*a*) Kandla

    (*b*) Haldia

    (*c*) Paradip

    (*d*) Marmagao

    [TERM 2, 2011]

2. Which one of the following is an inland riverine port?

    (*a*) Kandla A   (*b*) Kolkata

    (*c*) Mumbai   (*d*) Tuticorin

    [TERM 2, 2012]

3. Which one of the following ports is the biggest with a spacious, natural and well sheltered harbor?

    (*a*)Kolkata

    (*b*) Chennai

    (*c*) Mumbai

    (*d*) Vishakhapatnam

    [TERM 2, 2013]

4. Name the river related to National Waterways No. 2.

    [TERM 2, 2017]

▶ 3 Mark Questions

5. Explain the importance of railways as the principal mode of transportation for freight and passengers in India.

    [TERM 2, 2015]

6. Examine with example the role of means of transport and communication in making our life prosperous and comfortable.

    [TERM 2, 2017]

▶ 4 Mark Questions

7. Mention any two inland waterways of India. Write three characteristics of each.

    [TERM 2, 2011]

8. "Dense and efficient network of transport and communication is a pre- requisite for national and international trade." Support the statement with four arguments.

    [TERM 2, 2012, DELHI 2018]

▶ 5 Mark Questions

9. Describe any five major problems faced by road transport in India.

    [TERM 2, 2013]

10. "Advancements of international trade of a country is an index to its prosperity." Support the statement with suitable examples.

    [TERM 2, 2014]

11. Classify communication services into two categories? Explain main features of each.

     [TERM 2, 2016]

12. "Roadways still have an edge over railways in India." Support the statement with arguments.

     [TERM 2, 2016]

🔑 Solutions

1. (*b*) Haldia   [1]

2. (*b*) Kolkata   [1]

3. (*c*) Mumbai   [1]

4. Brahmaputra is related to National Waterways No. 2.   [1]

5. For transportation of freight and passengers in India, Indian Railways is the principle mode. People can conduct various activities like sightseeing, business and pilgrimage with the transportation of goods over long distances.   [1]

   It is helping the country to accelerate the development as well as bind the economic life of the industry and agriculture for the country.

   For the current scenario, Railways is the largest public sector undertaking in the country.   [1]

6. Means of transport and communication plays an important role in making our life prosperous and comfortable in following ways:

   (*i*) Now it is easy to export and import good because of means of transport and it helps in the economic development of the country, which helps in raising living standard of peoples   [1]

   (*ii*) People of different regions and different cultures are connected to each other via the internet and mobile phones. People are aware of what is happening in the world.   [1]

   (*iii*) It helps in the fast development of the country which requires advance means of communication and transport. It is easier to travel long distances in very short time, which paced the globalization. For example, in case of a storm, the governments can inform people so that they can ensure their safety.   [1]

7. Two inland waterways of India are:

   (*i*) The Brahmaputra River between Sadiya and Dhubri.   [1]

   (*ii*) The Ganga River between Allahabad and Haldia.   [1]

   Three characteristics of The Brahmaputra River between Sadiya and Dhubri are: [1]

   (*i*) It is also known as National Waterway 2.

   (*ii*) Its length is 891km.

   (*iii*) It facilitates national security and is used as transportation link between states.

   Three characteristics of The Ganga River between Allahabad and Haldia: [1]

   (*i*) It is known as National Waterway 1.

   (*ii*) It is 1,620km long.

   (*iii*) It provides pilgrimage opportunities.

8. Dense and efficient network of transport and communication is a pre-requisite for national and international trade because:

   (*i*) Raw materials can easily reach their respective centres of production by means of good transportation.   [1]

   (*ii*) Good transport infrastructure is very important to enable finished products to reach their respective markets.   [1]

   (*iii*) Communication eases the integration of markets and investments.   [1]

   (*iv*) Communication facilities are of utmost importance in tertiary activities like providing knowledge about events happening in distant places.   [1]

9. Five major problems faced by road transport in India are:

   (*i*) India is a densely populated country and the road network is inadequate and incapable in catering to the needs of such a large population.   [1]

   (*ii*) Volume of traffic is the biggest problem as the number of vehicles is too much in India and it often leads to traffic jams.   [1]

   (*iii*) More than half of the roads in India are unmetalled and this reduces its usage during the rainy season. The roads become slippery and very difficult to drive on. [1]

(*iv*) National highways are made for travelling on long routes but they are less than the situation demands. Also, many highways need upgrading as they are too old and not safe for driving. [1]

(*v*) Casual attitude of the citizens towards the traffic rules is also a major cause of traffic jams and accidents. [1]

10. "Advancements of international trade of a country is an index to its prosperity."

(*i*) India has been earning large foreign exchange through the export of information technology in the recent years and it has thus appeared to become a software giant at the international level. [1]

(*ii*) International trade contributes to India's economic growth, raising income level of people and has helped India to improve its productivity of manufactured goods. [1]

(*iii*) There are many goods or resources possessed by one country and are required by other and vice-versa. These differences create conditions for international trade as the resources are limited and no country can survive without International trade.[1]

(*iv*) Apart from goods and services, in the recent years, exchange of commodities and goods have also been superseded by the exchange of information and knowledge. [1]

Thus, it can be concluded that advancement of international trade of a country is an index of its economic prosperity.

11. The two main categories in which communication can be divided into are Personal communication and mass communication. [1]

Personal communication can be understood as exchange of communication in between two people. [1]

The Indian postal network is the largest in the world. It handles written communication as well as parcels. [1]

Mass communication creates awareness and provides entertainment among people about various national programmes and policies.

It includes radio, television and newspaper, magazines, books and films. [1 + 1]

12. India has a road network of about 2.3 million km which is one of the largest road networks in the world.

"Roadways still have an edge over railways in India." can be supported by the following reasons:

(*i*) Money spent on road construction is much lower in comparison to railway lines. [1]

(*ii*) Roads can be covered and can be comparatively more anatomized. [1]

(*iii*) It can cover traverse mountains and higher gradients of slopes such as the Himalayas. [1]

(*iv*) It is an economical mode of transportation for small amount of goods and for a few people over shorter distances. [1]

(*v*) It can also lower the cost of loading and unloading as it provides door-to-door service. [1]

(*vi*) It is also used as a linkage between railway stations, sea ports and air ports so it acts as a feeder to other modes of transport.

MULTIPLE CHOICE QUESTIONS

1. Which one of the following is the most important modes of transportation in India ?
   (*a*) Pipeline   (*b*) Railways
   (*c*) Roadways   (*d*) Airways

2. In which language is the maximum number of newspapers published in India
   (*a*) Hindi   (*b*) English
   (*c*) Telugu   (*d*) Punjabi

3. Which of these was the first port developed soon after Independence?
   (*a*) Surat
   (*b*) Goa
   (*c*) Kamarajar Port
   (*d*) Kandla

4. Which of these is a super highway?
   (*a*) Sher Shah Suri Marg
   (*b*) Golden Quadrilateral
   (*c*) Jawaharlal Nehru port
   (*d*) National Highway-12

5. Which communication service in India is the largest in the world?

   (a) Railways

   (b) Airways

   (c) Postal

   (d) Waterways

Answer Keys

1. (b)   2. (a)   3. (d)   4. (b)   5. (c)

FILL IN THE BLANKS

1. Jawaharlal Nehru port developed to ______________.

2. The air transport was nationalised in______

3. __________________ airport is situated in Mumbai.

4. __________________ have a length of 14,500 km

5. Indian railways lack __________________.

Solutions

1. Decongest the Mumbai port and serve as a hub port for the region

2. 1953

3. Chhatrapati Shivaji

4. Inland Waterways

5. Repair and maintenance of tracks and bridges

TRUE OR FALSE

1. Border Roads Organisation was established in 1960.

2. National highways are laid and maintained by the CPWD.

3. HVJ pipeline is 1700 Km long

4. Difference between the total value of exports and imports is called balance of payment.

5. Tourism trade brings in much needed foreign exchange.

Solutions

1. True

2. Trie

3. False

4. False

5. True

Unit-III :
POLITICAL SCIENCE

Power Sharing

Summary

Belgium and Sri Lanka and majoritarianism in Sri Lanka

Belgium

- Small country in Europe.
- Have borders with Netherlands, Germany and Luxembourg.
- Ethnic composition of this small country is complex 59 percent live in Flemish and speak Dutch.
- Another 40 percent live in Wallonia and speak French and 1 percent speak German.
- In capital, Brussels, 80 percent speak French and 20 percent Dutch speakers.
- The minority French speaking community was relatively rich and powerful.
- Resented by the Dutch community who got the benefit of economic development and education much later.
- Ethnic difference led tension between two communities.

Sri Lanka

- An inland nation, few km south of Tamilnadu.
- It has a diverse population nearly about 2 crores.
- 74 percent Sinhala speakers, most of them are Buddhist.
- 18 percent Tamil speakers, in which 13 percent are Srilankan Tamils and 5 percent Indian Tamils.
- Srilankan Tamils are concentrated in north and east of country and most of them are Hindu and Muslims.
- 7 percent Christians are Tamil and Sinhalese both.
- Sinhalese community tried to enjoy his will or dominance over minority ,that created a turmoil in Sri Lanka.

Majoritarianism in Srilanka

- Sinhalese community sought to dominance over government by virtue of majority.
- The elected government adopted majoritarion measures to establish Sinhalas supremacy.
- Sinhalas declared official language in 1956, disregarding Tamils.
- Government followed the pre ferential policies for university positions and government jobs.
- Constitution stipulated that the state shall protect and foster Buddhism.
- The government measures increased the feeling of alienation among Srilankan Tamils.
- They felt discrimination in every walk of life due to the Buddhist government policies.
- Srilankan Tamils launched parties and struggles for their autonomy.
- By 1980s they demanded independent state Tamil Elam.
- Distrust turned into civil war between communities, which led the Civil War.

Accommodation in Belgium and Forms of power sharing

Accommodation in Belgium

* A new constitution was formed between 1970-73.
* There were **equal numbers of French and Dutch-speaking ministers** in the central government so that no single community has the privilege of making unilateral decisions.
* The **powers** of central and state government were **shared** so that states are **not subordinate** to the centre.
* There was **a separate government** for Brussels having equal representation of both the communities.
* The Belgian model introduced a third form of government known as the **community government** which is elected by the people belonging **to one language** community.
* This model help to create mutual cooperation between ethnic composition.

Forms of power-sharing

Horizontal distribution of power

Power is shared among **different organs of government** such as the legislature, executive, and judiciary. This type of power sharing is prevalent in India.

* None of the organ can exercise more power, each organ can **check** by others.

Vertical distribution of power - In this, the power can be shared among governments at different levels. This type of power-sharing is prevalent in the USA.

* In India central or union government.
* In India at the provincial or state level, state government is responsible for the development .
* The extended level of the government is called local government or Panchayat.
* The division of the powers involving higher to lower level.

Power sharing among different social groups

* Power can be shared among social gatherings, for example, phonetic and religious gatherings. For example, Community government' in Belgium.

* Constitutional and legitimate game plans whereby socially weaker segment and lady are spoken to in the governing body and organization
* Constituencies are reserved for diverse social group to include them in power.

Other types of power-sharing

Power is also shared in political parties, pressure groups and movements control or influence those in power.

* People have independence to opt have various contenders for power.
* Due to completion in political parties to attract peoples, power does not remain in one hand.
* Interest groups like traders farmers, workers also have a share in governmental powers by bringing influence on decision making process.

Points to know

CIVIL WAR

A violent conflict between opposing groups within the country that become so intense like war.

FEDERAL

Having or relating to a system of government in which several states form a unity but remain independent in internal affairs.

PRESSURE GROUP

A pressure group is an organized group of people who tries to create pressure or persuade government or other authority to change as per their demands.

PREVIOUS YEARS' EXAMINATION QUESTIONS

▷ 1 Mark Questions

1. Who elects the community government in Belgium?

    (*a*) People belonging to one language community only

    (*b*) By the leader of Belgium

    (*c*) The citizens of the whole country

    (*d*) The community leaders of Belgium

    [TERM 1, 2011]

2. Division of powers between higher and lower levels of government is called:

   (*a*) horizontal distribution

   (*b*) parallel distribution

   (*c*) vertical division

   (*d*) diagonal division

   [TERM 1, 2011]

3. What is Majoritarianism?

   [TERM 1, 2013]

4. Which type of powers does the community government of Belgium enjoy?

   [TERM 1, 2014]

5. Name any two countries with which Belgium has borders?

   [CBSE 2015]

6. Which type of powers does the community government of Belgium enjoy?

   [TERM 1, 2013]

▶ 3 Mark Questions

7. Why Sri Lankan Tamils felt alienated?

   [TERM 1, 2011]

8. What were the special elements of the Belgian model?

   [TERM 1, 2012]

9. Explain the vertical division of power giving example from India.

   [TERM 1, 2011]

▶ 5 Mark Questions

10. Describe the tension that existed between the Dutch and the French speaking people in Belgium.

    [TERM 1, 2013]

11. Explain moral reasons to explain that Power sharing is desirable.

    [TERM 1, 2013]

12. State the main elements of the power sharing model evolved in Belgium.

    [TERM 1, 2014]

13. "Both Belgium and Sri Lanka are democracies with a difference". Support the statement by giving three points of difference

    [TERM 1, 2016]

14. Examine any five features of federalism practiced in India.

    [TERM 1, 2017]

🔑 Solutions

1. (*a*) People belonging to one language community only. [1]

2. (*c*) Vertical division [1]

3. It's a form of democracy based on the philosophy that the majority of the people has the right to take decision or form a policy according to their needs by dominating minority. e.g., **Sri Lanka** opted for majoritarianism in which majority **Sinhalas** ruled the country. [1]

4. The community government of Belgium enjoy the power related with **cultural, educational** and **language issues** of the community. [1]

5. **Netherlands and Germany** are the two countries with which Belgium has borders. [1]

6. To safeguard the communities, the community government of Belgium enjoys the constitutional **powers that are not dependent on the Central and state government.** [1]

7. Sri Lankan Tamils felt alienated from the majority group Sinhalese because of the following reasons:

   (*i*) They felt that the Buddhist Sinhalese, who led one of the major political parties, were insensitive towards the Tamil culture and language. All they cared about was Sinhalese culture and language. [1]

   (*ii*) The constitution and government policies of Sri Lanka denied Sri Lankan Tamils equal political right . [1]

   (*iii*) Also, the Tamils felt that that government had ignored their interests and discriminated against them in getting equal jobs and other opportunities [1]

8. The special elements of the Belgian model are distinguished as following:

   (*i*) There were **equal numbers of French and Dutch speaking ministers** in the central government so that no single community has the privilege of making unilateral decisions. [1]

   (*ii*) The **powers** of central and state government were **shared** so that states were **not subordinate** to the centre. [1]

(*iii*) There was **a separate government** for Brussels having equal representation of both the communities. [1]

(*iv*) The Belgian model introduced a third form of government known as the **community government** which is elected by the people belonging **to one language** community.

9.

(*i*) Sharing of power among different levels of the government that **involve higher and lower levels of government,** is called the **vertical division of power.** [1]

(*ii*) In India, the general level power is given to the **central or union government (higher level of government)** and regional level power is given to **the state government (lower level of government).** [1]

(*iii*) In India, the power is further divided to government lower than state governments in the form of **municipality and panchayats.** [1]

10. There was **economic inequality** between the Dutch- and the French-speaking community. The **French-speaking** population who was in **minority** was comparatively **rich** and **powerful** whereas, the **Dutch**-speaking population was **poor** but in the majority. The social differences between Dutch-speaking and French-speaking communities during the 1950s and 1960s led to **tensions** between them. The stress between the two communities **was acuter in Brussels.** The constitution was amended **four times** between **1970 and 1993** so as to work out a settlement that would help everyone to live together within the same country. [1 + 1 + 1 + 1 + 1]

11. The moral reasons to explain that Power sharing is desirable are:-

(*i*) To make an **accountable, responsible and lawful government.** [1]

(*ii*) It ensure the spirit of democracy by involving popular participation through **de-centralization of powers.** [1]

(*iii*) To promote **national integrity.** [1]

(*iv*) To notational any citizen

(*v*) To not concentrate power in one place.

12. Belgium has a very **innovative arrangement** which is different from other countries. The elements of its power-sharing model are as follows:

(*i*) The first feature of the model is an **equal number of seats for Dutch and French-speaking** ministers. Equal reputation is given to them in the central government. It **does not allow any single majority to take decisions unilaterally.** [1]

(*ii*) The many power of central government is given to the state governments for the two regions and **does not treat** state governments as **subsidiary to the central government.** [1]

(*iii*) The capital city of Belgium, Brussels also **has equal representation of Dutch** as well as French people. [1]

(*iv*) It also has a third type of government called **Community Government** in which the people of one language community elect the government. [1]

(*v*) The preferment and preservation **of verbal and cultural variation** are also assured by this power model. [1]

13. Difference in power - sharing of Belgium and Sri Lanka:

(*i*) In Belgium the government **does not follow special policies in matters of jobs and education.** In Sri Lanka the government **follows special policies in matters of government jobs and education.** [1.5]

(*ii*) In Belgium there is a singular government called **'community government'** to look after the cultural, educational and language related issues. In Sri Lanka the major political parties are **not dedicated to the language and culture of the Tamils.** [1.5]

(*iii*) In Belgium there is **no differentiation between different religions.** In **Sri Lanka Buddhism** is the formal religion. [2]

14. (*i*) **Written Constitution**: The Indian constitution fulfils the basic requirement of government since it is a written document which has **448 articles and 12 schedules.** [1]

(*ii*) **Two or more levels of government**: Indian federal system is a system of government in which there are two or more levels of government and the power is **divided between a central authority** and its **various constituent** units which is called **federalism.** [1]

(*iii*) **Rigid constitution**: No one can change the constitution unilaterally. If the fundamental provisions are to be changed, they require the consent of the **both the levels of the government**. [1]

(*iv*) **Supremacy of Constitution**: Existence and authority of **each tier** of the government are constitutionally safeguarded since jurisdictions of the respective levels of the government are specific in the constitution.[1]

(*v*) **Supreme authority of the courts**: In Indian federal system courts have the power **to interpret the constitution.** In case of dispute arising between different levels of the government the highest court acts as referee. [1]

MULTIPLE CHOICE QUESTIONS

1. Power sharing is desirable because:
   (*a*) It helps to reduce the possibility of conflict between social groups
   (*b*) It allows everyone to do whatever they wish to
   (*c*) It gives equal importance to all farmers
   (*d*) It makes politicians extremely powerful

2. Organisations that attempt to influence the policies of the government to safeguard their own interests are called as:-
   (*a*) Coalition Government
   (*b*) Legitimate government
   (*c*) Pressure groups
   (*d*) Democratic groups

3. What measure was adopted by the democratically elected government of Sri Lanka to establish Sinhala supremacy?
   (*a*) Constitutional Reforms
   (*b*) Monarchy Rule
   (*c*) Community Government
   (*d*) Majoritarian measure

4. The body that is concerned with the interpretation of the laws and has the power to punish those who commit crimes or break the laws is called as:
   (*a*) Judiciary
   (*b*) Executive
   (*c*) Legislature
   (*d*) Coalition government

5. The ethnic composition of Belgium is very.....................

   (*a*) Simple
   (*b*) Complex
   (*c*) Of a single type
   (*d*) Dominated by Persian community

Answer Keys

1. (*a*)   2. (*c*)   3. (*d*)   4. (*a*)   5. (*b*)

FILL IN THE BLANKS

1. ___________ was made the official language of Sri Lanka in 1956

2. A war which is fought between different groups of people who live in the same country is called as ____________.

3. ______________ implies that all citizens should have the same political rights and should have equal access to all offices of authority

4. Horizontal division of power is an arrangement in which power is shared among different _________ of the government.

5. In Belgium, the government does not follow _____________ policies in matters of jobs and education.

🔑 Solutions

1. Sinhala
2. Civil War
3. Political equality
4. Organs
5. Preferential

TRUE OR FALSE

1. Brussels is the capital of Belgium.
2. Marathas is the major ethnic group of Sri Lanka.
3. In a democracy, people rule themselves through institution of self-governance.
4. Horizontal distribution of power results in a balance of power among various institutions.
5. The system of 'checks and balances', ensures that none of the organs of government can exercise only limited power.

🔑 Solutions

1. True
2. False
3. True
4. True
5. False

Federalism

Summary

Federalism and India as a Federal country

Federalism

* Is an arrangement of government in which control is separated amongst focal and different constituent units.
* Both of these levels of government make the most of their capacity autonomous of other.
* Different levels of government benefits the power, which is pre characterized by the constitution.
* The basic arrangement of the constitution can't be transformed one level of the administration.
* The power is given to courts to decipher the constitution and intensity of various levels of the administration.
* The most elevated court go about as an Umpire.
* Wellsprings of the revenue of the two levels are clearly determined.
* For fruitful Federation have the soul of common trust and consent to live respectively in the two levels.
* When autonomous states meeting up individually to shape a greater unit ,by pooling power and holding character is named as meeting up alliance. Ex USA, Switzerland and Australia
* When a huge nation partition its capacity between the constituent states and national government is named as Holding together Federation. Ex India, Spain, Belgium.

India as a Federal country

* In India the two tier system of government is provided by the constitution, the union government and the state government.
* A third tier of federalism was added in the form of Panchayat and Municipalities.
* The constitution clearly provided a three fold distribution of legislative powers between

Union and state government by creating three list

* **Union list** - includes 97 subjects of the national importance e.g. Defence, foreign affairs, banking currency etc.
* Union government alone can take decision and make laws on it.
* **State list** - it includes 66 subjects of the state and local importance such as polices, trade, commerce.

State government alone can make law on these subjects.

Concurrent list - includes 45 subjects of common interest of both the union government and state government such as education, forests, trade unions, marriage, adoption and succession

* Both union and state government can make laws, in case of any issue the law made by union government will prevail.

Residuary subjects - includes the subjects, which came up after making constitution like computer software, IT.

* Union government have the power to legislate on these subjects.

Federalism in Practice and Decentralisation in India

Federalism in Practise

Linguistic state

- New states were created to by changing old states.
- Boundaries of old states changed to ensure people speaking same language.
- Based on culture, ethnicity or geographical some states like Jharkhand, Nagaland, Uttarakhand created to identify the differences.
- Development of the states on the premise dialect ,made the nation more joined together and organization more less demanding.

Language policy

- None of the language is given the status of national language.
- Hindi is the mother tongue of 40 percent Indians.
- 21 other language categorised as a scheduled language.
- States are independent to work in their own official language.
- Use of English to stop in 1965 as language of official purpose.
- Government of India encourages the promotion of Hindi.
- Flexibility shown by India to avoid any kind of strife or intense like Sri Lanka.

Check from here

Centre state relations - constitutional arrangements for sharing power works in reality depends to a large extent on how ruling parties and leaders follow these arrangements.

- State government not worked independently if the union ad state both have government of same party.
- The centre government always overlook the development of state when state have different party government.
- Regional parties came into existence after 1990.
- Regional parties affect the vote bank of major parties therefore no any party got a clear majority in Legislative body, to form a government major parties have to enter in alliance.
- Now states are enjoying autonomy due to culture of alliance government.

Decentralisation in India

- Municipalities are set up in towns. They are controlled by elected bodies consisting of people's representatives.
- Municipal Chairperson is the political head of the municipality.

Points to know

JURISDICTION

A specified area where the authorities can take decision, and right of taking decision is given by law.

COALITION GOVERNMENT

A government which is formed with the support of other parties as no one have full majority.

PANCHAYAT SAMITI

Mandals, taluka panchayats, block panchayats, or panchayat samiti are rural local governments at the intermediate level in panchayat raj institutions (PRI).

PREVIOUS YEARS' EXAMINATION QUESTIONS

▶ 1 Mark Questions

1. Rural local government is popularly known as:
   (a) Panchayati Raj
   (b) Zila Parishad
   (c) State government
   (d) Gram Panchayat
   [TERM 1, 2011]

2. What was the main objective of the Constitutional Amendment made in 1992 in India?
   [TERM 1, 2013]

3. Write one merit of coalition government?
   [TERM 1, 2013]

4. Name the country which follows coming together style of federalism.
   [TERM 1, 2014]

5. What is the official post for the chairperson of a Municipal Corporation?
   [TERM 1, 2015]

6. Which country is an example of coming together type of federation?
   [TERM 1, 2017]

▶ 3 Mark Questions

7. What do you mean by 'coming together federation' and 'holding together federation'? Give one example each.

[TERM 1, 2012]

8. Mention any three main features which make India a federal country.

[TERM 1, 2015]

9. Describe any three provisions of amendment made in 'Indian Constitution' in 1992 for making 'Three-Tier' government more effective and powerful.

[DELHI 2018]

▶ 5 Mark Questions

10. Define decentralization? Explain briefly the structure of Local government.

[TERM 1, 2012]

11. Examine the role of new system of local governments in the Indian democratic set-up. Highlight any two difficulties which it still faces.

[TERM 1, 2014]

12. What provisions have been made in the constitution of India to make it a secular state? Describe.

[TERM 1, 2016]

🔑 Solutions

1. (a) Panchayati Raj   [1]

2. The main objective of the Constitutional Amendment made in 1992 in India was the effective **de-centralization** of India. It made the **third-tier of democracy** more powerful and effective by reservation of seats in local government to SC, ST and women.   [1]

3. One of the merits of the coalition government is that the majority based decisions are taken considering **views of every party**.   [1]

4. **USA, Switzerland and Australia** follow the coming together style of federalism   [1]

5. The official post for the chairperson of a Municipal Corporation is of **Mayor**.   [1]

6. **Switzerland** is a country, which is an example of coming together type of federation.   [1]

7. When **independent states combine themselves** together to form a bigger unit, that scenario is called coming together **federation**. All the states usually **share equal power** to increase the security among its units.   [1]

Eg- USA, Switzerland and Australia.   [0.5]

When a geographically large country divides its power between the states and national government to ensure the spirit of **democracy**, it is termed as holding together federations.[1]

Eg.; India, Spain, Belgium.   [0.5]

8. (i) India is governed by two tiers or levels of governments- central and state government.   [1]

(ii) **In India the central** government **cannot interfere** instate government issues or subjects. It ensures the spirit of Federalism.   [1]

(iii) India has a **three tier** government, where powers are divided between the **Legislature, Executive and the Judiciary.**   [1]

(iv) **Elections** for each government are held **separately**, this proves India is Federal nation, as **separate jurisdiction** is meant for them.

(v) **Division of power:-** Power has been divided between the **Union and the state** governments in our written constitution.

9. Amendment in Indian Constitution in 1992-

(i) It is **constitutionally mandatory to hold regular elections** to local government bodies.   [1]

(ii) **Seats reserved** for the Scheduled Caste, Scheduled Tribes and Other Backward Classes.   [1]

(iii) **At least one third of all positions are reserved** for **women**.   [1]

(iv) **Creation of State Election Commission.**

(vi) The state governments are directed to **share some powers** and **revenue** with local government bodies.

10. Decentralization is a process in which the **activities, responsibility and financial resources** are shared or distributed among different levels, to ensure the development. [1]

There are two local government. One is for **rural** areas and on is for **urban** areas. Rural local government is called **Panchayat Raj** in which either each village or a group of villages have a **gram panchayat**. Gram panchayat is a council that has many ward members who are known as panch and it also includes a president known as **sarpanch**. They are directly elected by the adult population of each village.   [1 + 1]

Urban local government is called **Municipality**. Municipality operates in towns and Municipal cooperation in big cities. Head of municipalities is known as **chairman** and head of municipal cooperation is called **mayor**. [1 + 1]

11. The role of new system of local government in the Indian democratic set-up can be understood in the following ways:

   (*i*) The three steps system in the democratic decentralization has been reflected from village local self-government to the district level. It contains the **power transfer, responsibilities and resources**. This idea focuses on the **participation of the whole community** and has been countersigned by the political leaders. [0.5]

   (*ii*) The constitutional status has been bestowed to the local self-government in the **73rd and 74th constitutional amendments acts of 1992**. Well organized elections, financial autonomy and the power **transfer between centre, state and local bodies** is bestowed by it. [0.5]

   (*iii*) Efficacious **participation of the people** has been provided by it. [0.5]

   (*iv*) It makes **democracy comprehensive and symbolic in nature** by taking it to the grass root level. That is why the notion of democracy has been extended by it. [0.5]

   (*v*) It has encouraged active participation of all the groups of the society by reserving the seats **for women, SC and ST classes**. [0.5]

   (*vi*) The democracy has become more **comprehensive** by the existence of **panchayats** as a view of **planning and better management** of the resources has been introduced in the people. [0.5]

   (*vii*) The different groups can **participate in the governance** of the country by which the diversity of the country has been identified.

   This system still faces these two difficulties:

   (A) Our society still faces **the caste and illiteracy issues** that affect the functioning of the local government bodies. [1]

   (B) The activities of these local bodies **are often interfered in by the MLAs** as they field their own candidates for elections. [1]

12. The provisions made in the constitution of India to make it a secular state are as follows:-

   (*i*) There is **no official religion** of the Indian state. Unlike the status of Buddhism in Sri Lanka or Islam in Pakistan, **our constitution does not give a special status to any religion**. [1 + 1]

   (*ii*) The constitution **allows the state to intervene in the matters of religion** in order to ensure equality within religious communities. [1]

   (*iii*) Under the Right to Freedom of Religion, our constitution provides to all citizens freedom to **profess, practice and propagate any religion**, or not to follow any. [1]

   (*iv*) The constitution of India puts **ban on the discrimination** on grounds of religion. [1]

MULTIPLE CHOICE QUESTIONS

1. Which of these is a feature of Federalism?
   (*a*) All revenue related matters are handled by the legislature.
   (*b*) It encourages dynastic politics
   (*c*) The country is ruled by a monarch
   (*d*) There are two or more levels (or tiers) of government

2. Which of these subjects falls under concurrent list?
   (*a*) Trade & commerce
   (*b*) Agriculture
   (*c*) Marriage
   (*d*) Foreign affairs

3. Under which type of federation India comes?
   (*a*) Holding together federations
   (*b*) Coming Together Federation
   (*c*) Bringing Together Federation
   (*d*) All of the above

4. What is the decision making body of a village?
   (a) Gram Panchayat
   (b) Municipal Corporation
   (c) Sarpanch
   (d) Ward Councilor

5. In which year was a major step towards decentralization taken?
   (*a*) 2004   (*b*) 1992
   (*c*) 1897   (*d*) 1991

Answer Keys

1. (*d*)   2. (*c*)   3. (*a*)   4. (*a*)   5. (*b*)

FILL IN THE BLANKS

1. India is a ______________ country where people speak different languages.
2. Indian Federation has ________ states and ______ union territories
3. ________________ are formed when independent states come together to form a bigger state.
4. ________________ local body has a 'Mayor' as its head.
5. ________________ is the only Indian state that has its own Constitution.

 **Solutions**

1. multilingual
2. 29, 7
3. Coming Together Federations
4. Municipal Corporation
5. Jammu & Kashmir

TRUE OR FALSE

1. The report of the States Reorganisation Commission was implemented on 2nd November, 1956.
2. Federalism has succeeded in India due to the nature of democratic policies in our country.
3. Unitary government has only one level of government.
4. 32 languages which are listed in the Eighth Schedule of the Indian Constitution
5. Argentina is a communist country.

Solutions

1. False
2. True
3. True
4. False
5. False

CHAPTER 3

Democracy and Diversity

Summary

Origin of social difference and it types

Origin of social difference

- Social differences is mainly caused due to birth.
- They might be male or female, tall or short, have various types of appearances, or on the other hand have distinctive physical capacities or handicaps.
- Choice also creates difference.
- What one wants to study, may be different from others in the same community.
- Some do not believe God and are atheists.
- People have difference to one another due to social division.
- There is caste difference in people having same religion.
- We have more than one identity and can belong to more than one social group.

Types

Over lapping

- Social differences of one type become more important than other.
- People started to feel separation based on communities.
- Difference between the black and white became social division in the US is overlapping division.
- In India, Dalits tend to be poor and landless and face discrimination.

- A social division and tensions may be possible due to overlapping .

Cross cutting

- It is not always that a group having common interest on a subject is same on other subject.
- People of northern Ireland and the Netherlands divided between catholic and protestant, me but both were followers of same religion.
- If you are catholic of northern Ireland you have a tendency to be poor.
- The result is catholic and protestant have had conflict in Northern Ireland.
- In Northern Ireland class and religion overlap with each other.

Politics of social division-ranges of outcomes

- Democracy involves political competition among various political parties.
- The competition tend to divide society, it makes social division into political division and lead to conflict, violence and sometime disintegration.

Outcomes

- In northern Ireland 53 percent are protestants and 44 percent Roman Catholics.
- Catholics represented by Nationalist parties demanded that Northern Ireland be unified with the republic of Ireland.
- Protestants represented by Unionist ,who wanted to remain with UK.

* Hundreds of civilians, militants and security forces lost their lives in the fight between Unionist and Nationalist.

* In 1998 UK government and Nationalist reached a peace treaty and suspended their armed struggle.

* In Yugoslavia political competition along religious and ethnic lines led the disintegration of Yugoslavia in six independent countries.

Three determinants

* Three elements are significant in choosing the result of legislative issues of social division.

* The result relies upon how individuals see their characters.

* If people think in singular terms then it becomes difficult to accommodate.

* Having been different in caste, language, group and citizen of different state, we see our identity as Indian.

* It is substantially less demanding if the general population see that their characters are numerous and are reciprocal with the national personality

* A larger part of Belgians presently feel that they are as much Belgian as they are Dutch or German speaker.

* The second aspect depends on how the demands of any community raised by political leaders.

* It is easier to accommodate demands which is in the constitutional framework and not to undermine the interest of other community.

* The demand for only Sinhals was at the cost of the interest and identity of Tamil community which led the civil strife.

   The third aspect depends on how the demands of different groups are raised before the government

* When government have will to fulfil the demands of demands of minority community by sharing power, the threat of the social divisions is minimize in country. Eg - Belgium and Srilanka

* When the government try to suppress the demands the result will be opposite.

* In democracy political expression of social division is very normal and can be healthy it depends how the government, citizens, various group take it.

Points to know

CIVIL RIGHT MOVEMENT

The civil rights movement was a struggle by African Americans in the mid-1950s to late 1960s to achieve civil rights equal to those of whites, including equal opportunity in employment, housing, and education etc.

HOMOGENEOUS

A society that has similar kind of people, especially where there are no significant ethnic difference.

PREVIOUS YEARS' EXAMINATION QUESTIONS

▶ 1 Mark Questions

1. List out the reasons for the growth of Civil Right Movement in America.

    [TERM 1, 2015]

2. How can you say that democracies are based on political equality?

    [TERM 1, 2015]

3. What does Overlapping difference signify?

    [TERM 1, 2016]

4. Explain the meaning of democracy.

    [TERM 1, 2017]

▶ 3 Mark Questions

5. Explain any two reasons why differences occur in society. Give an example to show that social differences do not lead to social division.   [TERM 1, 2011]

6. "Every social difference does not lead to social division". Explain giving an example.

    [TERM 1, 2012]

7. How are social differences not always an 'accident of birth'? Why are most of the countries of the world emerging as multi-cultured countries?

    [TERM 1, 2015]

8. Taking the example of Carlos, Smith and Norman, explain how social differences divide similar people from one another but also unite very different people.

    [TERM 1, 2016]

9. Why do some people think that it is not correct to politicize social division? Give three reasons.

[TERM 1, 2016]

10. "We have different identities in different contexts." Support the statement with three facts.

[TERM 1, 2016]

11. "Social divisions exist in most of the countries". Explain.

[TERM 1, 2016]

12. Explain the process of decision making in your family. Is it democratic? Explain.

[TERM 1, 2016]

13. "Overlapping social differences create possibilities of deep social divisions and tensions". Justify the statement with an example.

[TERM 1, 2016]

14. Explain any three reasons for the conflicts between the Catholics and the Protestants in Northern Ireland. [TERM 1, 2016]

15. Suggest any two measures to check the social divisions.

[TERM 1, 2016]

16. Explain with examples the two bases for the origin of social differences.

[TERM 1, 2016]

17. Compare overlapping and cross cutting of social differences with one example each.

[TERM 1, 2016]

▶ 5 Mark Questions

18. Explain the three factors that determine the outcome of politics of social divisions. What role do the political leaders play in this area? [TERM 1, 2013]

19. What lessons have been learnt from the Civil Rights Movement of Martin Luther King in the USA? [TERM 1, 2016]

20. Describe any five characteristics of democracy. [TERM 1, 2017]

🔑 Solutions

1. Factors for the growth of Civil Right Movement in America are:

(i) When African Americans served their country during World War II they discovered that racial discrimination was not nearly as cruel in European countries like Great Britain and France.

(ii) Unequal distribution of rights and injustice in America on the basis of ccolour, skin and race with Afro Americans. [1]

2. In the democracy every person has a **right to vote** which establishes political equality. [1]

3. When one type of social **difference overlaps another difference** it leads to overlapping difference. [1]

4. Democracy means, **for the people, by the people.** It is a type of government **in which people elect the ruler of the country.** [1]

5. The following factors are responsible for differences in a society:

(i) **By accident of birth**: No one can choose to be born into a particular community.

Some people are short, some are tall, some have disabilities but some don't have disabilities. [1]

(ii) **By our choices**: Some people do not believe in any religion, such people are called **atheists**. Some people want to follow a **different religion** leaving their own religion in which they are born. [1]

But these **social differences do not lead to social division** like people share **similar thoughts** but they belong to different groups. For example, some people belonging to the same community may feel the difference because their caste is different but in another way some people belonging to different communities may feel close to each other because their caste is same. [1]

6. Every social difference may not lead to social division. It **depends upon the cultural, social and political circumstances and how the people perceive their identities.** Social differences divide similar people, but unite a very different people. The people from different social groups share **differences and**

similarities beyond the limitation of their groups. [1 + 1]

For example- There were two black people Carlos and Smith, both were African-American and thus they differ **from Norman who was white**. But they all were same in other ways i.e. they were athletes who together raised a voice against racial discrimination. [1]

7. The differences are **based on the accident of Birth**. Normally we don't choose to belong to our community. We belong to it simply because we are born into it. For example people around us are **male or female**, they are tall or short, and have different physical abilities or disabilities. All are grouped accordingly in different communities. It is possible to say that most countries are **multicultural** because of the increased rate of migration, the flow of trade and commerce as compared to centuries before. [1 + 1 + 1]

8. (*i*) Both Tommie Smith and John Carlos were **African-Americans** and were facing **racial discrimination** in the United States. [1]

   (*ii*) They both belonged to different nations but in the end, **they both were athletes**. [1]

   (*iii*) All of the three athletes Tommie Smith, John Carlos and Norman, were **united** on the issue of **racial discrimination** even though one of them (Norman) was white. [1]

9. (*i*) It can lead to **conflict, violence** and even affect the **integration** of the country. [1]

   (*ii*) If the political parties start competing on the basis of social divisions, it can **create differences among** different groups in the country. [1]

   (*iii*) People **use caste, religion** to gain more number of seats in an election, but in the long run it can be **harmful for the country**. [1]

10. We all belong to different social groups so we have different identities in different contexts like:-

    (*i*) People who belong to the **same religion** feel that they do not belong to the same community just because **their caste is different**. [1]

    (*ii*) Sometimes people from **different religions** can have same caste which gives them a sense of **belongingness**. [1]

    (*iii*) At the same time, rich and poor persons from the same family often **do not keep close relations** with each other as their perception is very different about each other. [1]

11. 'Social divisions' refers to regular **patterns of division in society** that are associated with membership of particular social groupings, generally in terms of advantages and disadvantages, **inequalities and differences**. Social divisions do not exist only in India. To state other examples we can tell about economic **backwardness of Blacks in US, discrimination** against **Dalits** in India and discrimination faced by Muslim women, discrimination based on religious beliefs in Muslim countries and division of labour in several European countries. [1 + 1 + 1]

12. Decision making is a term used to describe the process by **which families make choices, determine judgments**, and come to conclusions that guide behaviors. When all members have **an equal opportunity to join in the decision-making process**, it tends to make the democratic family relationships develop most effectively. It's always good to plan a family meeting to plan family fun and to share good experiences and positive feelings toward each other. [1 + 1 + 1]

13. When **one social difference overlaps another difference**, it is known as overlapping social differences.

    (*i*) Overlapping **social differences between Blacks and Whites** became a social division in the United States. The main factor for the Black Power Militant Movement was overlapping **social difference**. [1]

    (*ii*) Even in India, **the Dalits faced discrimination** and injustice and these sort of incidences produce social divisions which **harm** and **weaken the basic foundation of democracy.**   [1]

14. The main reason of conflict was the constitutional status of Northern Ireland. **Unionists** wanted it to **remain the part of UK** as they were mostly Protestants and **considered themselves British.**   [1]

The **nationalists were mainly Irish** and thus wanted to be a part of **Ireland.**   [1]

Religious difference also became one of the reason for conflict as **they were Catholic** and wanted to be a part of catholic nation.

The employment opportunities were **very low for the Catholics** as compared to the Protestants, as most of **the business owners were Protestants**   [1]

15. Two measures to check the social division:

(i) Ban the use of the name of caste, creed, religion in political campaigns for election.   [1.5]

(ii) **Reservations of seats in educational** institutions and government jobs for the weaker sections of society.   [1.5]

16. Most social differences are based on the **accident of birth.** For example, people may be tall, strong, and weak, girl or boy. Some social differences emerge because **people choose to follow certain practices or principles.** For example, a person may be an atheist or may be a feminist. Some people may convert to another religion. All **social differences do not result in social divisions.** Sometimes, even people belonging to different religions may have common interests   [1 + 1 + 1]

17. Overlapping differences happen when some **social differences overlap other differences.** And then it becomes a social division when some social differences are joined by another set of social differences. For example, the difference in the Blacks and the **Whites in America** is due to their different race which is a social difference. Cross-cutting differences happen when one type of social difference is weakened by another set of **social differences.** Then, it becomes difficult to group people into a single category because they

are going to have different opinions and views on different matters. For example, people in the Netherlands are predominantly Christian, but divided between Catholics and Protestants.

[1 + 1 + 1]

18. The factors that determine the outcome of politics of social divisions are-

(i) **Raising demands of political leaders-** The outcome of politics also depends on how political leaders raise the demands of any community. It is easier to **accommodate demands** that are within the Constitutional framework.   [1.5]

(ii) **How people perceive-** This is the most important factor that decides the outcome of politics of social division because if the **people see their identities in singular** and **exclusive terms** then it will lead to social division and violence.   [1]

(iii)**Reaction of the government-** The outcome of politics of social division also depend on reaction of government, that is how the government reacts to the demand of different groups.   [1.5]

19. The lessons learned from the Civil Rights Movement of Martin Luther King in the USA are:

(i) Nonviolence can fight **"the triple evils"** of **racism, materialism, and militarism.** [1]

(ii) King also turned his passion to oppose **the Vietnam War,** thus entering the **international realm** and the struggle **for human rights** for all oppressed peoples, which shows how human issues are similar across the world.   [1 + 1]

(iii)He was sure that a non-violent movement can succeed in securing **victory** against the evils of **discrimination** between **Blacks and Whites** which is a lesson for all communities.   [1]

(iv) Society cannot be organized on the basis of **discriminatory rules forever.**   [1]

20. Following are the characteristics of democracy:

(i) In a democracy, people of the country have the power **to elect their representatives.** These representatives hold the supreme power and frame policies for citizens. [1]

(*ii*) Democracy works on the basic value of equality and inclusiveness. [1]

(*iii*) There should be a free and fair election. All the adult citizens must have the right to vote in the election. [1]

(*iv*) People abide by the law and they are required to respect minority option. They can raise their voice for their rights. [1]

(*v*) Policies and working of the ruling party are observed by the opposition party. [1]

MULTIPLE CHOICE QUESTIONS

1. What is a homogenous society?
   (*a*) A society that has different kinds of people
   (*b*) A society that has similar kinds of people, especially where there are no significant ethnic differences
   (*c*) A country that has similar kinds of vegetation
   (*d*) Both (*b*) and (*c*)

2. Which university installed a 20 - foot high sculpture representing the protest by Tommie Smith and John Carlos in 2005?
   (*a*) Yale University
   (*b*) Russian University
   (*c*) San Jose University
   (*d*) University of Delhi

3. In which year did the Civil Rights Movement start?
   (*a*) 1890   (*b*) 2001
   (*c*) 1947   (*d*) 1954

4. Who was the leader of the Civil Rights Movement?
   (*a*) Martin Luther King Junior
   (*b*) Mahatma Gandhi

    (*c*) Abraham Lincoln
    (*d*) None of these

5. What penalty was imposed on Carlos and Smith for their action at the 1968 Mexico Olympics?
   (*a*) The International Olympics Committee took back the medals of Carlos and Smith
   (*b*) The International Olympics Committee pushed them out of the stadium.
   (*c*) The International Olympics Committee took back the money prize given to Carlos and Smith
   (*d*) Both (*a*) and (*c*)

Answer Keys

  1. (*b*)   2. (*c*)   3. (*d*)   4. (*a*)   5. (*a*)

FILL IN THE BLANKS

1. The descendants of Africa who were brought into America as slaves between the 17th century and early 19th century were termed as ____________________.

2. ____________________ is a system of government in which the citizens exercise power directly or elect representatives from among themselves to form a governing body, such as a Parliament.

3. Social division takes place when some ____________ overlap with other differences.

4. The Civil Rights Movement aimed to abolish __ ____________________________.

5.) Northern Ireland population was divided into ______________ and ____________.

Solutions

1. African American
2. Democracy
3. social differences
4. racial discrimination against African-Americans
5. Protestants, Roman Catholics

Gender, Religion and Caste

Summary

Gender and Politics.

Public /private division.

- A form of hireachical social division seen everywhere but is rarely recognised in the study of politics.
- Division of labour in our society is based on gender ,women is only for work in house and man is for work outside to earn.
- When these jobs are paid for, men are ready to take up these jobs.
- Earlier,only men were allowed to participated in public affairs in many countries of world.
- Women in different parts of the world organized and agitated for equal rights.
- World wide agitation for gender division mobilisation improved women's role to in public life.
- Many Scandinavian countries such as Sweden, Norway and Finland have a high ratio of working women in public life.

Women in India

- In India still have Patrachial
- The literacy rate among women is only 54 percent compared with 76 percent among men.
- Girls drop out rate is higher than boys in school as well as higher education.
- The proportion of women among highly paid jobs is very small.
- The specific sector like films ,sports ,factories don't follow the equal pay equal work act, even in same work.
- The urban areas have become particularly unsafe for women, even they are not safe in their home also.
- Women percentage is low in the participation of public affairs and legislature but woman representation is ensured in local government after after 73rd amendment.

Religion, Communalism and Politics.

Religion

Religious difference are regularly communicated in the field of politics

- Gandhiji used to state that religion can never be isolated from governmental issues. According to him, politics must be guided by ethics drawn from all religions.
- According to Human right minorities are always targeted in communal riots. They have demanded that the government should take special steps to protect religious minorities

- Women's movements have argued that family laws of all religions discriminate against women,they demanded to ensure their equality by improving the existing law.
- People should be able to express their needs ,interests and demands as a member of a religious community.
- Sometimes government respond positively regarding demands to prevent discrimination and oppression.

Communalism

- Religion is the principal basis of social community is main idea on which Communal politics is based
- Communalism involves thinking that the followers of particular religion must belong to one community.
- Extreme forms of communalism leads to the belief that people belonging to different religions cannot live as a equal citizen within one nation.
- Religious prejudices, stereotypes of religious communities and beliefs in the superiority of ones religion over the other.
- Political predominance of one's own religious network, generally expressed by communal mind.
- Political mobilisation on religious mind is done by using sacred symbols, religious leader ,emotional appeals. etc
- some times communalism expressed as a form of ethnic violence, riots and massacre.
- Partition of India is worst example of it.

Caste and Politics

- Caste system is an extreme form of this.
- The hereditary occupational division was sanctioned by rituals. Members of the same caste group practised the same occupation, married within the caste group
- Caste system was based on discrimination against the 'outcaste' groups. They were subjected to the inhuman.
- Practice of untouchability political leaders and social reformers like Jotiba Phule, Gandhiji, B.R. Ambedkar and advocated and worked to establish a society in which caste inequalities are absent

- Caste system in modern India have undergone great changes due to Growth of literacy,education, occupational mobility and urbanisation
- The Constitution of India prohibited any caste-based discrimination and laid the foundation of policies to reverse the injustices of the caste system

Caste in politics

- People belonging to the same caste belong to a natural social community and have the same interests which they do not share with anyone from another caste
- **Caste can take various forms in politics** When parties choose candidates in election, they keep in mind the caste composition of the electorate and nominate candidates from different castes so as to get necessary support to win elections.
- Political parties used the notion of caste to muster supports. Some political parties favour some castes.
- Universal adult franchise brought new consciousness among the people of caste that were earlier treated as inferior and low
- No parliamentary constituency in the country has a clear majority of one single caste. So, every candidate and party needs to win the confidence of more than one caste and community to win elections.
- No party wins the votes of all the voters of caste or community. When people say that a caste is 'vote bank' of one part, it usually means that a large proportion of the voters from that caste vote for that party.
- Many political gatherings set up applicants from a similar position. A few voters have in excess of one competitor from their rank.
- The decision party and the sitting MP or MLA every now and again lose races in our nation. That couldn't have happened if all positions and networks were solidified in their political inclinations.
- Voters host solid connection to political gatherings which is frequently more grounded than their connection to their stations or network.

- Rich and poor or people from a similar rank regularly vote in an unexpected way.
- People's evaluation of the execution of the administration and the ubiquity rating of the pioneers likewise matter.

Politics in caste

- Each position bunch endeavours to wind up greater by joining inside it neighboring ranks or subcastes which were prior barred from it.
- Various rank gatherings are required to go into a coalition with different positions or networks and in this way go into a discourse and arrangement
- New sorts of rank gatherings have come up in the political field like 'in reverse' and 'forward' standing gatherings.
- In a few circumstances, articulation of position contrasts in legislative issues gives many detrimental networks the space to request their offer of intensity. e.g. Dalits and OBC have increased better access to basic leadership.
- Several political and non-political associations have been requesting for a conclusion to victimization.
- Specific rank, for greater respect and more access to arrive assets and openings.
- Religion, legislative issues in view of station personality are not exceptionally solid in a majority rule government. It can occupy consideration from other problems that are begging to be addressed like neediness, improvement and debasement.

Points to know

FEMINIST

A supporter of the equality of rights and opportunities of men and women

CASTE HIREACHY

A ladder like formation in which all the caste groups are placed from the highest to lowest caste.

PREVIOUS YEARS' EXAMINATION QUESTIONS

▶ 1 Mark Questions

1. According to 2001 census the sex ratio in India was__________.
   - (a) 1000 males 950 females
   - (b) 1000 males 850 females
   - (c) 1000 males 927 females
   - (d) 1000 males 933 females

   [TERM 1, 2011]

2. What term is used for the number of girl children per 1000 boys?

   [TERM 1, 2014]

3. Which term is used for a country which allows its people to follow any religion?

   [TERM 1, 2015]

4. In which country the participation of women in public life is very high?

   [TERM 1, 2015]

5. On which factor communalism is based on?

   [TERM 1, 2016]

6. What is the literacy rate among Indian women?

   [TERM 1, 2016]

▶ 3 Mark Questions

7. Describe the adverse effects of caste in politics in India.

   [TERM 1, 2017]

8. "Secularism is not an ideology of some political parties or persons, but it is one of the foundations of our country." Examine the statement.

   [DELHI 2018]

9. The outcome of politics of social division depends on how the political leaders raise the demands of any community. Explain the statement.

   [TERM 1, 2014, DELHI 2018]

10. Why is combination of politics and social divisions considered very dangerous and explosive? Explain with suitable examples.

    [TERM 1, 2015]

▶ 5 Mark Questions

11. What was the fear of printed books on religion?

[TERM 1, 2012]

12. (*a*) Define Caste Hierarchy.

(*b*) "Caste system has not disappeared from contemporary India." Support your answer with suitable examples.

[TERM 1, 2012]

13. Describe any five features of the caste system prevailing in India.

[TERM 1, 2013]

14. What is secular state? How does the constitution of India ensure that India remains a secular state? Explain.

[TERM 1, 2014]

15. What have been the consequences of the political expression of gender division in free India? What is the status of women's representation in India's legislative bodies?

[TERM 1, 2016]

16. Elections are all about caste and nothing else. Explain the statement.

[TERM 1, 2016]

🔑 Solutions

1. (*d*) It is 1000 males 933 females. [1]

2. Sex ratio is the term used for the number of girl children per 1000 boys. [1]

3. Secular State is the term which is used for a country which allows its people to follow any religion. [1]

4. Sweden, Norway and Finland are the countries where the participation of women in public life is very high. [1]

5. It refers to the differences of social communities based on religious beliefs. [1]

6. The female literacy rate is 65.46% according to census of 2011. [1]

7. There can be several adverse effects of caste in politics in India:

(*i*) People prefer to vote the candidate of their caste in elections rather than voting a right person who would hold the responsibilities properly. [1]

(*ii*) Inclusion of caste in politics leads to disparities and social violence. [1]

(*iii*) It leads to disintegration of people and societies of a country on the basis of caste and religion. [1]

(*iv*) Many times the rightful heir of a post does not get a chance because of reservations.

8. Secularism is the foundation of our country

(*i*) There is no official religion of India. [1]

(*ii*) Our constitution does not give a special status to any religion. [1]

(*iii*) The constitution prohibits discrimination on grounds of religion. [1]

(*iv*) The constitution provides all individuals and communities freedom to profess, practice and propagate any religion or not to follow any religion.

(*v*) The constitution allows the state to intervene in the matters of religion in order to ensure equality.

9. In order to win the elections and take the power, political parties and leaders often talk about the **social divisions**. They also make **various promises** with the various communities. In the name of **injustice** done with the disadvantaged communities, they often do **politics**. The aim of political parties is to **convince the voters of any particular community** so that they can have **maximum votes and win the elections**. As a result of it, a **specific party is supported by a specific community**. And that's how, the **social division is dependent on the political leaders whether** they are raising the demands of any community within constitutional framework or for self interest [1 + 1 + 1]

10. The factors that determine the outcomes of politics of social divisions are written as follows:

(*i*) If the political parties start stimulating in terms of present social divisions in society, it can make **social divisions into political divisions and lead to struggle**, **violence** or even **breakdown** of a country. [1]

(*ii*) Politics and social divisions **must not be allowed to mix** for self interest as in case of Srilanka preference were given to Sinhalese, undermining the Tamils in society and politics too, which led to a civil war in Srilanka. [1]

(*iii*) Social divisions affect **polling in most** of the countries. People from one country tend to prefer some party more than others due to social divisions, which creates political competitions. **In case of Yugoslavia the political competitions based on social division led to disintegration into six countries.** [1]

11. Many people feared the spread of print. This can be easily explained with the help of an example. [1]

In India, the Muslim Ulamas were deeply anxious about the spread of print because of which the colonial rulers could change the personal laws of Muslims. They also countered this with the help of print. [1 + 1]

In Europe: Many people read books and came with ideas that supported reason and rationality. They stood up against the churches. One such movement gave rise to the Protestants. [1 + 1]

12. (a) Caste Hierarchy is a system of social stratification in our society. It is a social structure in which people are placed in highest to lowest brackets based on their caste. Caste system is a process of putting people in occupational groups. It tells which sort of occupation a person can pursue and the social interaction one can have with the society. [1 + 1]

(b) There are many aspects in Indian society which show that Caste system has not disappeared from contemporary India. One such aspect is marriage. In Indian society people still do not want to marry their children with someone of other caste. In India there is caste based reservation as well, which shows that caste system has not disappeared from contemporary India. [1 + 1 + 1]

13. The caste system features prevailing in India are:-

(i) In India the occupational structure is sanctioned by rituals, which is unique to the world. [1]

(ii) People have to marry within their caste group. [1]

(iii) They practice their hereditary occupation. [1]

(iv) They cannot eat with other caste people. [1]

(v) In some parts of India people of low caste face injustice like un-touchability. They are not allowed to enter temples etc. [1]

14. A state is called secular if it does not have any legal religion. In a secular state, all the religions have equal values and respect. For example India is a secular state as it has granted equal rights to all the religions in it. Indian constitution ensures secularism in the following ways: [1]

(i) India has no official language. Each and every person in India has freedom to use any language and they all have equal rights. [1]

(ii) There is no special reputation granted to any particular religion in India. Indian constitution gives equal rights to every religion in India. This is dissimilar to the countries like Pakistan, Sri Lanka and England etc. [1]

(iii) The Indian constitution mentions the Right of Freedom of Religion in which it gives freedom to every native to follow or accept any religion and also not to accept any religion. [1]

(iv) It also forbids any type of inequality on the basis of religion. [1]

(v) It has given right to the states to interfere in any incident related to religion so that equality can be maintained inside the religious communities.

15. The gender issue as a result of the feminist movement was raised in politics. [1]

The political expression and political parties helped to improve the women's role in public life. As a result now we can find women working as scientist, doctors, engineers, managers and University teachers jobs which were earlier supposed to be not suitable for women. Also in India Equal wage for equal work act, reservation of one third seats for women in panchayati raj, reservation in jobs for women etc. are the outcomes of political expression of gender division in India. [1 + 1]

But in spite of all these women are still lagging behind in comparison to their male counterparts [1]

When it comes to representation of women in Legislative bodies, India is among the bottom group of nations in the world. Women's representation has always been less than 10% in Loksabha and 5% state assemblies. On the other hand, the situation is different in the case of local government bodies as one-third of the seat in local government bodies i.e. panchayats and municipalities are reserved for women. There are more than 1 million elected women representative in rural and urban local bodies. [1]

16. (i) The politicians of our country have found an easier way of collecting votes, through their vote banks. People from different castes are now called vote banks and they play an important role at the time of elections. [1]

(ii) The caste based policy is more popular than development based politics because the political system has divided the people with respect to their castes. [1]

(iii) Most of the political parties put up the candidate from the majority caste, which helps them in winning the election. As there will be a number of people in majority caste and eventually, they will vote for the person of their caste only. [1]

(iv) To win elections, it becomes really important that the party wins the confidence of more than one caste. [1]

(v) It's unfortunate that in a country like India, people still prefer this caste system rather than the development policies. We need to look forward and work together so that we can have more transparent and development-oriented government, which will lead India towards prosperity and growth. [1]

MULTIPLE CHOICE QUESTIONS

1. Which of these is an indicator of social division?
   (a) Discrimination on the basis of figure
   (b) Discrimination on the basis of caste
   (c) Discrimination on the basis of qualification & skills
   (d) All of the above.

2. How many seats are reserved for women in Panchayati- Raj?
   (a) 1/10th   (b) 2/3rd
   (c) ½   (d) 1/3rd

3. Under which system is father the head of the family
   (a) Patriarchy
   (b) Feminism
   (c) Casteism
   (d) Matriarchy

4. Which of these factors influence the political set up in our country?
   (a) Sex ratio   (b) Religion
   (c) Both (a) & (b)   (d) None of these

5. Who said 'Religion can never be separated from politics?
   (a) Mahatma Gandhi   (b) Jawaharlal Nehru
   (c) Jyotiba Phule   (d) B.R. Ambedkar

Answer Keys

   1. (b)   2. (d)   3. (a)   4. (b)   5. (a)

FILL IN THE BLANKS

1. ______________ gives all Indian citizens whose age is 18 years the right to vote.

2. A man or a woman who believes in equal rights and opportunities for women is called a ________.

3. Political mobilisation on religious lines is a frequent form of ____________.

4. The gender division is not based on biology but on social expectation and ....

5. A ladder like formation in which all caste groups are placed from the highest to the lowest is called as ____________.

Solutions

1. Universal Adult Franchise
2. Feminist
3. Communalism
4. Stereotypes
5. Caste hierarchy

TRUE OR FALSE

1. A secular state has two official religions.
2. Shift of population from rural areas to urban areas is called as Occupational Mobility
3. Social and economic development is a factor for breaking down the caste system.
4. A person who demands equal rights for women is called as a secularist.
5. Despite constitutional prohibition, evil of casteism has not ended completely

Solutions

1. False   4. False
2. False   5. True
3. True

CHAPTER 5

Popular Struggles and Movements

Summary

Movement for Democracy in Nepal

- Nepal was under the rule of monarch. However, with changing times, Nepal adopted a constitutional monarch. King Birendra, who has accepted this transition from absolute monarchy to constitutional monarchy, was killed in a mysterious massacre of the royal family in 2001.

- King Gyanendra, the new king of Nepal, was not prepared to accept democratic rule. He took advantage of the weakness and unpopularity of the democratically elected government.

- The movement of April 2006 was aimed at regaining popular control over the government from the king. All the major political parties in the parliament formed a Seven Party Alliance (SPA) and called for a four-day strike in Kathmandu, the country's capital. This protest soon turned into an indefinite strike in which MAOIST insurgents and various other organisations joined hands.

Bolivia's Water War

- Bolivia is a poor country in Latin America. The World Bank pressurised the government to give up its control of municipal water supply. The government sold these rights for the city of Cochabamba to a multi-national company that immediately increased the price of water by four times.

- In January 2000, a new alliance of labour, human rights and community leaders organised a successful four-day general strike in the city. The government agreed to negotiate and the strike was called off. Yet nothing happened. The police resorted to brutal repression when the agitation was started again in February

- But the power of the people forced the officials of the MNC to flee the city and made the government concede to all the demands of the protesters. The contract with the MNC was cancelled and water supply was restored to the municipality at old rates. This came to be known as Bolivia's water war.

- The protest against water privatisation in Bolivia was not led by any political party. It was led by an organisation called FEDECOR. This organisation comprised local professionals, including engineers and environmentalists who were supported by a federation of farmers who relied on irrigation, the confederation of factory workers' unions, middle class students etc.

Pressure Groups and Movements:

- Pressure groups are organisations that attempt to influence government policies. But unlike political parties, pressure groups do not aim to directly control or share political power.

- Usually interest groups seek to promote the interests of a particular section or group of society. Trade unions, business associations and professional (lawyers, doctors, teachers, etc.) bodies are some examples of this type

- Pressure groups and movements exert influence on politics in a variety of ways:

  a) They try to gain public support and sympathy.

  b) They often organise protest activity like strikes or disrupting government.

  c) Business groups often employ professional lobbyists or sponsor expensive advertisements.

How do we Assess Democracy's Outcomes?

PREVIOUS YEARS'
EXAMINATION QUESTIONS

▷ Very Short Answer Type Questions

1. Which organization led the project against water privatization in Bolivia?

   [Board Term-II, 2016, Delhi Set I, II, III]

2. What was the main role of 'FEDECOR' organization in Bolivia?

   [Board Term-II, 2015 Set I, II, III]

3. What was the main aim to start movement in April 2006, in Nepal?

[Board Term II, 2015, Set I, Outside Delhi 2013]

4. The "Third Wave' country that had won democracy in 1990.   [Board Term-II, 2012]

5. Who dissolved the popularly elected Parliament in February 2005, in Nepal

   [Board Term-II 2012, Delhi]

▷ Short Answer Type Questions

6. What was the Green Belt Movement? What was the attitude of the government towards this movement?

   [Board Term-II, 2016, Set TYCJQ6VD]

7. Who led the Project against water privatization in Bolivia? Describe the ways of protest adopted by that organization.

   [Board Term-II, 2016, Foreign Set-I, II, III]

8. State the issue of struggle in Bolivia. Which groups participated in it?

   [Board Term-II, 2015, Set-RKZQI05]

9. "The struggle of the Nepali people in a source of inspiration to democrats all over the world." Support the statement.

   [Board Term-II, 2015 Delhi Set-II]

10. How are popular struggles integral to the working democracy? Explain with an example of Bolivia's struggle against privatization of water.

   [Board Term-II, 2014]

11. Explain any three common feature of the popular mass struggle in Nepal and Bolivia.

   [Board Term-II, 2014]

12. Mention any three indirect ways in which people can force government to listen to their demands.

   [Board Term-II, 2011, Set-68008]

13. In what two ways do organizations influence the decisions in a democracy ?

   [Board Term-II, 2011, Set- 68010]

🔑 Solutions

1. FEDECOR.   [1]

2. The protest against water privatization in Bolivia was led by FEDECOR and it made the government concede to all the demands of the protesters.   [1]

3. To restore democracy in Nepal.   [1]

4. Nepal   [1]

5. King Gyanendra dissolved the popularly elected Parliament in February 2005, in Nepal.   [1]

6. (i) The Green Belt Movement was the tree plantation movement in Kenya.

   (ii) 30 million trees had been planted across Kenya.

   (iii) The leader of this movement was Wangari Maathai.

   (iv) The government officials and politicians did not show any response towards this movement.   [3]

7. **Protest against water privatization in Bolivia:**

   FEDECOR (comprised local professionals, including engineers and environmentalists), human right and community leaders.

   Ways of their Protest :

   Organized a successful four-day general strike in the city.

   Influenced the decision through direct participation in competitive politics.

   Created parties and formed governments.

   Formed pressure groups for the protest.

   (Any two)   [1 + 2 = 3]

   [CBSE Marking Scheme, 2016]

8. The World Bank pressurized Bolivian government to privatize municipal water supply (Privatisation of Water.

   The government sold the right to an MNC which increased the price of water by four times. Groups- FEDECOR consisting of professionals like engineers and environmentalists, federation of farmers, confederation of factory workers' union, students of university of Cochabamba and city's homeless street children.

   [CBSE Marking Scheme, 2015)

9. The struggle of the Nepali people is a source of inspiration to democrats all over the world :

   The autocratic decision of King Gyanendra in February 2005 resulted in protest by the political parties and people of Nepal. Political parties having diverse ideology joined together and defied the curfew. The leaders rejected the half hearted concessions by the king, ultimately the king was compelled to concede all the three demands made by the protesters. Hence, this struggle of Nepalis known as the Second Movement for Democracy became a source of inspiration to democrats all over the world.

(CBSE Marking Scheme, 2015) [3]

10. The popular struggles are integral to the development of democracy :

(a) Popular struggles are a part of working democracy.

(b) Struggle are essential to save democracy. For example, Nepal's struggle for restoration of democracy and Bolivia's Water War.

(c) It is only in democracy that different individual groups can express their feelings.

(d) The people do not agree with policies of the government, they can oppose it with all their might and constant popular struggle to achieve their goal.

(e) Democracy evolves through popular struggle.

(Any three)

[CBSE Marking Scheme, 2015] [1 × 3 = 3]

Pressure Groups

PREVIOUS YEARS'
EXAMINATION QUESTIONS

▶ Very Short Answer Type Questions

1. How are issue specific movements different from generic movements ?

Board Term-II, 2016, Delhi Set-I, II, III]

2. Distinguish between pressure groups and political parties by stating any one point of distinction.

[Board Term-II, 2016, Outside Delhi Set-I, II, III]

3. Name any two sectional interest groups.

[Board Term-II, 2016, Outside Delhi Set-I, II, III]

4. Differentiate between 'Sectional Interest Groups' and 'Public Interest Groups'.

[Board Term-II, 2016, Foreign Set-I, II, III]

5. State the main aim of Backward and Minority Communities Employees Federation.

[Board Term-II, 2016, Foreign Set-I, II, III]

11. (a) Both these are instances of political conflict that led to popular struggles.

(b) In both cases, the struggle involves mass mobilizations and public demonstration of mass support clinched the dispute.

(c) Both instances involved the critical role of political organization.

[CBSE Marking Scheme, 2014]

12. Indirect ways to forces the government:

(a) By forming organization.

(b) By undertaking activities.

(c) By deciding to act together without forming organization. [1 × 3 = 3]

[CBSE Marking Scheme, 2011]

13. The different organizations influence the decisions in a democracy in two ways :

(a) **Direct ways:** Participation in competitive politics. This is done by creating parties, contesting election and forming government.

(b) **Indirect ways:** They could do so by forming an organization and undertaking activities to promote citizens interest or view point through interest groups or pressure groups.

[CBSE Marking Scheme, 2011] [1½ × 1½ = 3]

▶ Short Answer Type Questions

6. What are sectional interest groups ? Describe their functioning.

[Board Term-II, 2016, Delhi Set-I, II, III]

7. What are public interest pressure groups ? Describe their functioning.

[Board Term-II, 2016, Outside Delhi Set-I, II, III]

8. Explain any three types of pressure groups.

[Board Term-II 2015, Set-WVIVSA5]

9. Describe any three features of sectional interest groups.

[Board Term-II, 2015, Foreign Set-III]

10. What are pressure groups ? How are they formed? Explain. (R) [Board Term-II, 2014]

11. What are interest groups ? Give two features of promotional pressure groups in India.

[Board Term-II, 2011, Set-2080]

12. What do you understand by sectional interest groups ? Explain With examples.

[Board Term-II, 2011, 2016]

13. How would you differentiate between sectional interest groups and public interest groups ?

[Board Term-II, 2011, Set-2027]

 Solutions

1. Issue specific movements seek to achieve a single objective within a limited time frame, while generic movements seek to achieve a broad goal in the long term.   [1]

2. Pressure groups do not aim to directly control or share political power but political parties directly control and share political power.   [1]

3. The two sectional interest groups are:
   (a) Trade Unions
   (b) Business associations
   (c) Professional bodies-lawyers, doctors, teachers etc.
   (Any two)   [1½ + 1½ = 3]

4. Sectional interest groups seek to promote the interest of a particular section while public interest groups promotes collective rather than selective good.   [1]

5. Its main aim is with social justice and social equality for the entire society.   [1]

6. **Section interest groups :**
   The groups that seek to promote the interests of a particular section or a group of society is called sectional interest groups.
   Functioning :
   They perform a meaningful role in countering the undue influence of other groups.
   They create awareness about the needs and concerns of their own society.
   Their principal concern in the betterment and well-being of their members not society in general.
   (Any two)   [1 + 2 = 3]
   [CBSE Marking Scheme, 2016]

7. Public interest groups are those that promote collective rather than selective interests.
   Their functioning is as follows :
   It aims to help groups other than their own members.
   They represent some common interest that need to be defended.
   The members of the organization may not benefit from the cause that the organization represents. e.g., a group fighting against bonded labour fights not for itself but for those who are suffering under such bondage.
   (Any two)   [1 + 2 = 3]
   [CBSE Marking Scheme, 2016]

8. (1) Social/Identify Group-have a special identity.
   (a) Community based-Ram Krishna Mission.
   (b) Sectional-Vishva Hindu Parishad.
   (2) Associational/Identify based group-promote vocational or professional interest.
   (a) Business group-FICCI
   (b) Trade Union-INTUC, CITU
   (c) Farmers and peasants.
   (3) Institutional Group-
   Groups within the government e.g.,-IAS Officers' Association, IPS Officers' Ad hoc group formed for temporary cause, e.g., to open a college or hospital.
                                          [1 × 3 = 3]
   [CBSE Marking Scheme, 2015]

9. Features of sectional interest groups :
   (a) Interest groups seek to promote the interests of a particular section or group of society.
   (b) Trade unions, business associations, professional etc. are the examples.
   (c) They are sectional because they represent a section of society.
   (d) Their principal concern is the betterment and well-being of their members, not society in general.
   (Any three)   [1 × 3 = 3]
   [CBSE Marking Scheme, 2015]

10. Pressure groups are organizations that attempt to influence government policies. These organizations are formed when people with common occupation, interest, aspirations or opinions come together in order to achieve a common objective.   [3]
    [CBSE Marking Scheme, 2014]

11. (a) Interest groups or pressure groups are organizations that attempt to influence government politics. They do not aim to directly share political power. These are formed when people with common occupation, interest, aspirations or opinions come together for common objective.
    (b) Two features of promotional groups are :
    (i) They promote collective rather than selective good.
    (ii) They aim to help groups other than their own members.
                                          [1 + 2 = 3]
    [CBSE Marking Scheme, 2011]

12.*(i)* Usually interest groups seek to promote the interests of a particular section or group of society.

(ii) They are sectional interest groups as they represent a section of society-workers, employees, business persons etc.

(iii) BAMCEF-Backward and Minority Community Employees Federation-It is an organization largely made of government employees and it addresses the problems of its members who suffer discrimination in trade unions and business organizations.

[1 + 2 = 3]

[CBSE Marking Scheme, 2011]

13.

	Sectional Interest Group	Public Interest Group
(a)	Promotes interest of a particular section or group of society.	Promotes the general interest of society as a whole.
(b)	Aim of section interest group is the selective good.	Aim of public interest group is collective good.
(c)	Example : FEDECORE, associations, etc.	Represents the common people of the society. Example : Women's group; group fighting against child labour.

MULTIPLE CHOICE QUESTIONS

1. What does SPA stands for?
   (a) Six Party Alliance
   (b) Seven Party Alliance
   (c) Secular Party Alliance
   (d) None of these

2. Which agency in Bolivia pressurised the government to give its control of municipal water supply?
   (a) World Bank
   (b) UNICEF
   (c) NAM
   (d) UNESCO

3. Who dissolved the popularly elected Parliament in February 2005, in Nepal ?
   (a) King Gajenendra
   (b) Dalai Lama
   (c) Both *(a)* and *(b)*
   (d) King Gyanendra

4. What was the Green Belt Movement that started in Kenya?
   (a) Resource Management movement
   (b) Movement against corruption
   (c) Tree plantation movement
   (d) None of these

5. Which of these demands was put forward by the Seven Party Alliance in Nepal?
   (a) Restoration of Parliament
   (b) Restoration of Monarchy
   (c) Restoration of Dictatorship
   (d) None of these

Answer Keys

1. *(b)*   2. *(a)*   3. *(d)*   4. *(c)*   5. *(a)*

FILL IN THE BLANKS

1. The popular struggles are integral to the development of____________.

2. FEDECOR is an example of _______________.

3. The World Bank pressurised ____________ government to privatise municipal water supply.

4. The aim of Backward and Minority Communities Employees Federation is ____________________.

5. Usually interest groups seek to promote the interests of a _________ section or group of society

Solutions

1. Democracy

2. Public interest group

3. Bolivian

4. Social justice and social equality for the entire society.

5. Particular

CHAPTER 6

Political Parties

Summary

Political parties-An introduction and role

- A group of people who agree with some dogma or tenets and contest elections with the goal of formation of government.
- Their dogma and tenets for the development and welfare of society .
- All parties try to impress people for their support by comparing their policies from with other political parties
- They seek to implement these policies by wining popular support through elections.
- A basic political division of a society is reflected by the parties. Being a part of a society ,parties involves in Partisanship.
- Party is known by his dogma, policies which they support and by whom they associated.
- A political party has three components (*i*) the leaders (*ii*) the active members, and (*iii*) the followers.
- Parties contest elections.
- The candidates for contesting in elections are opted by the top most leaders of parties .
- A party reduces a vast multitude of opinions into a few basic positions which it supports.
- The major decisions are taken by political executive that formed by political parties after winning election and forming government .
- Parties recruit leaders train them and then make them ministers to run the government in the

- Those parties that lose in the elections play the role of opposition to the parties in power, by voicing different views and criticizing government for its failures or wrong policies.
- public opinion is shaped by parties. Issue is raised and highlighted by parties .
- Many of the pressure groups are the augmentation of political gatherings among various areas of society.
- Parties here and there likewise dispatch developments for the determination of issues looked by individuals.

Types of Party System.

One-Party System

- In some countries only one party is allowed to control and run government. These are called one-party system.
- In China only the Communist party is allowed to rule. Although, legally speaking, people are free to form political parties.
- We cannot consider one party system as a good option.
- Any democratic system must allow at least two parties to compete in elections and provide a fair change for the competing parties to come to power.

Two-Party System

- In some countries power usually changes between two main parties. Several other parties may exist, contest elections and win a few seats in the national legislatures.

- If only the two main parties have a serious chance of winning majority of seats to form government, such a party system is called two-party system.

- In United Kingdom and USA the two-party system.

Multi-Party system

- When the two parties have a reasonable chance of coming to power either on their own strength or in alliance with others, is termed as a multiparty system.

- In India, we have multi-party system, the governments is formed by various parties coming together in a coalition.

- When several parties in a multiparty system join hands the purpose of contesting elections and winning power it is termed as **alliance or a front**

- The multi-party system often appears very messy and leads to political instability.

- At the same time, this system allows a variety of interests and opinions to enjoy political representation.

National and regional parties.

National Political Parties

- The national political parties have their units in various states. But by and large all these units follows the same policies, programmes and strategy that is decided at the national level.

- Election Commission provide recognition to every political parties by registering them. The Commission treats all parties equally, some special facilities is provided to large and established parties.

- The criteria to be registered National Party is to get at least 6 percent total votes in Lok Sabha elections or Assembly elections in four states and wins at least four seats in the Lok Sabha.

- six national recognised parties in the country in 2006.

- **Indian national congress** founded in 1885,build moder secular democratic republic under the leadership of Jawahar Lal Nehru.

- it emerged as the largest party with 145 member in Loksabha election held in 2004.

  BJP founded in 1980 want to bulid a strong and modern India by following ancient culture and

value. Hindutatva is an important element in its conception.

- It came in power in 1998 as NDA but lost in 2004. currently it is in power.

  BSP Kanshi Ram founded in 1984,it upholds the dalits, adivasis, OBC's and religious minorities.

- It believes in the ideas of Oyotiba Phule and Naiker and follows their tenets.

- It has its main base in U.P and substantial presence in Delhi, Punjab.

  Communist Party of India (Marxist), is founded in 1964.

- It based on Marxism-Leninism,enjoy,it is in strong majority in West Bengal, Kerala and Tripura have impact among the factories worker,farmers, and labourers.

- In Bengal, it is in power more than 30 years without break.

  Communist Party of India (CPI) formed in 1925 based on the ideology of Marxism –Leninism.

- it accepts democracy as the means of the promoting the interest of working class.it is split in 1964.

  National congress party due to split in congress party in 1999 NCP is formed.Peoples Maharashtra ,Meghalaya and Assam have strong feeling with it.

Regional parties

- The Election commission registered a party as a National party which gets at least 6 per cent of the total votes in an election of the State and wins at least two seats.. Eg Samajwadi party,Janta dal, Samta Dal

- State parties generally reffered as Regional Political Party. It exists, operates and functions at the regional level.

- It gives importance to state related issues, specific problems of the region and it has great influence only on the people of that region.

Challenges faced by Political parties and reforms.

Challenges faced by Political parties

Lack of internal democracy within parties. It is found in parties of all over the world.

- The concentration of power in one or few leaders at the top Parties do not have open list of its members.
- Parties do not hold its routine organisational meetings, fail to conduct its internal elections regularly and refuse to share information.
- Ordinary members of the party do not get sufficient information on what happens inside the party.
- Since one a few leaders exercise paramount power in the party, those who disagree with leadership find it difficult to continue in the party.
- More than loyalty to party principles and policies, personal loyalty to the leader becomes more important.

  Challenge of Dynastic succession relates to the first one. Since most political parties do not practice open and transparent procedures for their functioning.

- There are very few ways for an ordinary worker to rise to the top in a party. Those who happen to be the leaders are in a position of unfair advantage to favour people close to them or even their family members.
- In many parties, the top positions are always controlled by members of the one family.
- They do not have adequate experience or popular support come to occupy positions of power. It is oftenly seen in India.
- **The growing role of money and muscle** power in parties especially during elections. Since parties are focussed only on winning elections, they tend to use short-cuts to win elections.
- They tend to nominate those candidates who have or can raise lots of money. Rich people and companies who given funds to the parties tend to have influence on the policies and decisions of the party
- In some cases parties support criminals who can win elections.
- voters are not provided a meaningful choice by parties.

Reforms

The constitution was amended to prevent elected MLAs and MPs from changing parties.

- This was done to stop indulging in defection.
- This new law has helped bring defection down. At the same time this has made any dissent even more difficult.

The Supreme Court passed an order to reduce the influence of money and criminals.

- Now it is mandatory for every candidate who contests elections to fill an affidavit giving details of his property and criminal cases pending against him.
- The new system has made a lot of information available to the public. But there is no system of check if the information given by the candidates is true.

  Hold organisational election and file their income tax return.

- The election commission passed an order making it necessary for political parties to hold their organisation elections and file their income tax returns.
- The parties have started doing so, sometimes only in formality. It is not clear if this step has led to greater internal democracy in political parties.
- Beside these **many suggestions** are often made to reform political parties especially reservation of women in parties.
- Strong law should be to regulate internal affairs of party.

Points to know

PARTISAN

A person strongly committed to a party group or faction .

LEFTIST PARTIES

Having radical, ideological conservative nature

OPPOSITION

The political party or group of parties who failed to make their own government and working as a criticiser of a government.

DEFECTION

Changing party allegiance from the party on which a person get elected to a different party

PREVIOUS YEARS'
EXAMINATION QUESTIONS

▶ 1 Mark Questions

1. The political party which believes in Marxism-Leninism is
   (a) Nationalist Congress Party
   (b) Communist Party of India
   (c) Dravida Munnetra Kazhagam(DMK)
   (d) Bahujan Samaj Party
   [TERM 2, 2011]

2. Which one of the following countries has one party system?
   (a) China   (b) Indo-China
   (c) Japan   (d) Germany
   [TERM 2, 2013]

3. Why do political parties involve partisanship?
   [TERM 2, 2015]

4. Distinguish between pressure groups and political parties by stating any one point of distinction.
   [TERM 2, 2016]

5. Why did India adopt multi-party system?
   [TERM 2, 2016]

▶ 3 Mark Questions

6. Explain how the relationship between political parties and pressure groups can take different forms.
   [TERM 2, 2011]

7. Why can't modern democracies exist without political parties? Explain any three reasons.
   [TERM 2, 2012]

8. Explain the three steps taken by the different authorities to reform political parties and their leaders in India.
   [TERM 2, 2012]

9. Name the national political party which gets inspiration from India's ancient culture and values. Mention four features of that party.
   [TERM 2, 2013]

10. What is meant by regional political party? State the condition required to be recognized as a 'regional political party'.
   [TERM 2, 2016]

▶ 4 Mark Questions

11. Explain how dynastic succession is a major challenge for political parties in India.
   [TERM 2, 2011, 2015]

▶ 5 Mark Questions

12. "About hundred years ago there were few countries that had hardly any political party. Now there are few countries that do not have political parties." Examine this statement.
   [TERM 2, 2014]

13. What is meant by a political party? Describe the three components of a political party.
   [TERM 2, 2015, 2016]

14. Suggest any five effective measures to reform political parties.
   [TERM 2, 2015]

15. "Political parties are a necessary condition for a democracy". Analyze the statement with examples.
   [TERM 2, 2016]

🔑 Solutions

1. (b) Communist Party Of India   [1]
2. (a) China   [1]
3. Political parties represent basic political divisions in a society. A party is known by which part it stands for, which policies it supports and whose interest it upholds by which they try to convince people for their supports. This reflects fundamental political divisions.   [1]
4. Political party.
   A Political party is a group of people who come together to contest elections and hold power in government.
   Pressure group.
   A pressure group is a group of people, working together to change the policy or to influence the decision of the government by democractic means. Sometimes it is extention of a political party among different sections of society.
   Political party sometimes launches movements for the revolution of problems faced by people. These groups actively participate to create pressure.   [1]
5. India adopted multi-party system because India is a democratic country where all individual are free to make their own party. Any democratic system must allow at least two parties to compete in election and provide a fair chance for the competing parties to come to power. To

ensure the sharing of the power among different section of society based on ideology, tenets, religions etc india adopted the multi party system. [1]

6. The relationship between political parties and pressure groups can take different forms in the following ways. [1]

Pressure groups are often formed by the politicians and political parties. Most of the Employee trade unions and students organizations in our country are either established by or affiliated to one or the other major political party of the country. Most of the leaders of the pressure groups are also the leaders or activist of any political party. [1]

Sometimes, political parties grow out of such movements. Due to reform movements of 1930s and 1940s parties like DMK and AIADMK were formed.

Political parties take up the issues raised by pressure groups, resulting in a change in the policies of the political parties at times. [1]

7. Modern democracies cannot exist without political parties because of the following reasons:

(i) The political parties provide a platform and representation to various sections of the society. [1]

(ii) These parties provide a forum for public debates and articulation of different opinions. [1]

(iii) They also give shape to policies and legislations on the basis of their election manifestos that direct the developmental path of a country. [1]

8. Some steps taken by the different authorities to reform political parties are as follows:

(i) The Constitution was amended to prevent elected MLAs and MPs from changing their parties. If an MLA or an MP changes parties, he or she will lose the seat in the legislature. [1]

(ii) The Supreme Court made it important for every candidate who contests elections to file an affidavit by providing details of his/ her property and criminal cases pending against him/ her. [1]

(iii) Election Commission has made it necessary for political parties to hold organizational elections to maintain inner party democracy and file their income tax returns. [1]

9. The national political party which gets inspiration from India's ancient culture and values is Bharatiya Janata Party. Four features of BJP are as follows:

(i) A uniform civil code was promoted for people living in the country, irrespective of different castes and religion and have put ban on religious conversions. [1]

(ii) The party wants the complete state of Jammu and Kashmir to be integrated with India (both politically and territorially). [1]

(iii) Cultural nationalism is an important element of its conception of Indian nationhood and politics, BJP wants to build a modern and strong India. [1]

(iv) The party was founded in 1980 by reviving the previous Bharatiya Jana Sangh.

10. A regional political party is a political party that is recognized and has its influence in a particular state of the nation. [1]

The condition required to be recognized as a 'regional political party' are:

(i) The party must have secured at least 6 percent of the total votes polled in all the constituencies of the parliament. [1]

(ii) The party must win at least one seat from the state in Lok Sabha general elections. [1]

11. Dynastic succession is a major challenge for political parties in India:

Most political parties do not practice open and transparent functioning procedures. [1]

In a party, an ordinary worker mostly cannot rise to the top. It has confined the spirit of political parties. Leaders favour the people close to them or their family members and chase the unfair advantage of being in position, which leads the favourism and flatterism in the party. [1 + 1]

In Dynastic Succession the top most position is always occupied by the members of a family, which is unfair to the other party members. it leds the unexperience leading which always diverts the principles of party . [1]

12. There was a shift from anarchy or imperialism to people's government or democracy about a hundred years ago in various counties. after the French revolution and American independence, colonial countries paced their freedom struggles and formed their own demcractic government,rooting out the imperialism.The starting age of democracy was deepened with improvements especially in sharing of powers in different sections of society, giving rights to express their views. The freedom rights leds the

creation of different section of ideology, in society. People with different ideologies organized themselves for their interest with a firm doctrine to come in power, accepted as party in a country. The deepening of democracy led to the formation of different political parties. [1 + 1 + 1]

The change in the map of world democracy led the formation of political parties based on their views. Today we have few country without democracy. [1 + 1]

13. A group of people who come together to contest elections and hold position in the government is called a political party. [1]

They agree on the same policies, beliefs and programs for the society with a view to promote the collective good. [1]

The three components of a political party are as follows:

(i) Leader is the person who has been chosen by all the party members and will have all the responsibility to take decision. [1]

(ii) Active members. are the members of the party, who actively participate in all type of activities i.e. meeting, rally, organizing, promotions etc. [1]

(iii) Followers. are the people who believe in the particular political party and try to make others believe in their agendas and favorable work for the country. Actually the number of followers of any party gives a clear picture of the future of the party. [1]

14. Five effective measures to reform political parties are as follows:

(i) Any candidate that has any pending conviction should be barred from contesting election. [1]

(ii) All political parties should file income tax and the financial accounts must be audited, with that their accounts must be made public. [1]

(iii) Introduction of party hopping law preventing an individual from defecting to another party without seeking fresh mandate from the electorates. [1]

(iv) All parties must create positions for women and people with disabilities. there should be a transparent and democratic selection of successors of leaders . [1]

(v) Parties must encourage inner party democracy, and thus should have regular elections. [1]

15. "Political parties are a necessary condition for a democracy".

The importance of political party is directly linked to the emergence of representative democracies. [0.5]

As societies became large and complex, they also needed some agency to gather different views on various issues and to present these to the government. [0.5]

They needed some ways, to bring various representatives together so that a responsible government could be formed. [0.5]

They needed a mechanism to support or restrain the government, make policies, justify or oppose them. [0.5]

Political parties fulfill these needs that every representative government has.

(i) The existence of political parties in a representative democracy allows the democratic machinery to function smoothly and ensures that the country runs as per its policies and ideologies and has a responsive and accountable government. They serve as both policy makers and opposition. [0.5]

(ii) Without political parties there would be chaos and turmoil in the society. As societies are becoming larger and more complex, there is a general will for dialogue that has to be facilitated by bringing together of representatives from different parts of a country. Only then can there be a responsible government. [0.5]

(iii) If there no political parties, every candidate is going to be an independent candidate and will be accountable to their constituency for what they do in the locality, but no one can then be held accountable for larger issues. [0.5]

(iv) Modern form of democracies also need representatives from various political parties to form the government and to keep a check on the ruling party by being in the opposition. [0.5]

(v) Political parties are required so that a country is governed as per set ideologies and will be responsible for how the country will be run. They put forward various policies and programmes for the electorate's consideration, they participate in parliamentary legislation process, they form and run governments, they provide people access to government machinery and welfare schemes and shape and articulate public opinion. [1]

MULTIPLE CHOICE QUESTIONS

1. What are the three components of a political party?

    (a) The leaders, the passive members and general public

    (b) The leaders, the active members, and the followers

    (c) Party symbol, Party manifesto, and the followers

    (d) None of these

2. Which of these is the most common party system?

    (a) One-Party   (b) Monarchy

    (c) Two-Party   (d) Multi-Party

3. Which of these is a major political party in India?

    (a) Bahujan Samaj Party

    (b) Akhil Bharatiya Ashok Sena

    (c) Akhil Bharatiya Dal

    (d) Akhil Bharatiya Desh Bhakt Morcha

4. Which autonomous constitutional authority responsible for administering election processes in a country?

    (a) Municipal Corporation

    (b) UPSC

    (c) Election Commission

    (d) CAG

5. When was the Communist party of India – Marxist (CPI-M) formed?

    (a) 2005   (b) 1964

    (c) 1857   (d) 2000

Answer Keys

    1. (b)   2. (d)   3. (a)   4. (c)   5. (b)

FILL IN THE BLANKS

1. ____________________is not recognised as a national political party.

2. One party political system not considered a good democratic system because________________.

3. The guiding philosophy of Bharatiya Janata Party is________________

4. Nationalist Congress party was formed in ______________

5. Concentration of power in one or few leaders leads to lack of .... within political party.

Solutions

1. Samajwadi Party

2. It does not support the idea of democracy

3. Cultural nationalism

4. 1999

5. Internal democracy

TRUE OR FALSE

1. Telugu Desam Party is a state party.

2. Political parties do not face the challenge of dynastic succession

3. An important function of political party in India is to contest elections.

4. Political parties play the role of both party in power as well as opposition.

5. Political defection is not a very serious problem faced by political parties in India.

Solutions

1. True

2. False

3. True

4. True

5. False

Outcomes of Democracy

Summary

How do we Assess Democracy's Outcomes.

Points to know

Topic -1. How do we assess democracy's outcomes.

- Democracy is a better form of government.
- Democracy was better it Promotes equality among citizens
- It Enhances the dignity of the individual.
- It Improves the quality of decision-making, and Provides a method to resolve conflicts
- It Allows a room to correct mistakes.
- Democracy is the form of the government it can create conditions for achieving something, the citizens have to take advantage with condition and achieve goals.

Political outcomes.

- In a democracy, we are most concerned with ensuring that people will have the right to choose their rules and people will have control over the rulers.
- Whenever possible and necessary, citizens should be able to participate in **decision making** that affects them all.
- Democracy should be **accountable to** the citizen, and responsive to the needs and expectations of the citizens.

- The idea of deliberation and negotiation is a important base of democracy.
- The democratic government will take more time to follow procedures before **arriving at a decision**
- But because it has followed procedures, its decisions may be both **more acceptable to the people and more effective.**
- Democracy ensures that decision making will be based on norms and procedures. So a citizen, who wants to know if a decision was taken through the correct procedures, can find this out.
- Anyone has the right and the means to examine the process of decision making. This is known as **transparency.** Transparency is a best outcome of democracy
- Regular free and fair election; open public debate on major policies and legislations and citizens' right to information about the government and its functioning is the actual performance of democracies.
- Democratic government is people owns government ,it may be slow not always very responsive but it is legitimate government overwhelmed by all over the world.

Economic outcome and Reduction of in equality and poverty

- For the fifty years between 1950 and 2000, dictatorship have slightly higher rate of **economic growth.**
- Evidence shows that in practice many democracies did not fulfil this expectation.

- The difference between less developed countries with dictatorships and democracies is negligible.
- We can expect democracy not to lag behind dictatorship *in the respect of economic development.*
- Within democracies there can be very high degrees of inequalities.
- In democratic countries like South Africa and Brazil the top 20 per cent people corned more than 60 per cent of the national income, leaving less than 3 per cent for the bottom 20 per cent population
- Countries like Denmark and Hungary are much better in this respect.

Reduction of in equality and poverty

- democracies are based on political equality ,but due to economic inequality it seems difficult .
- A small number of ultra rich enjoy a highly disproportionate share of wealth and incomes .
- The peoples who are at the bottom of the society loosing their income level and compel to sustain low standard of life.
- Democratic countries do not appear to be successful to reduce poverty but their efforts to reduce inequality can't criticise as the economic disparities depends on many things.

Accomodation of social diversity

- Democracies usually develop a procedure to conduct their competition. This reduces the possibility of these tensions becoming explosive or violent.
- The conflicts among different groups can't be fully solved by any society .
- democracy can successfully handle the social difference, divisions and conflicts.

Majority rule government must satisfy two conditions to accomplish this result

(*i*) It is important to comprehend that vote based system isn't just run by dominant part supposition.

  - The greater part in every case needs to work with the minority.
  - With the goal that administration capacity to speak to the general view.

(*ii*) It is likewise important that govern by major part does not progress toward becoming guideline by greater part network as far as religion or race or phonetic gathering, and so forth.

  - If someone is barred from being in majority on the basis of birth, then the democratic rule ceases to be accommodative for that person or group.

Points to know

MONARCHY

The governing of country is in the hand of the of king, who avails despotic power.

DIGNITY

The word denotes privileged position, honourable rank or importance given to any particular post or personating.

TRANSPARENCY

Right or means to examine the process of decision making.

Points to know

JURISDICTION

The area it may be the geographical boundaries or certain kinds of subject over which someone has legal authority.

COALITION GOVERNMENT

A government in which many or multiple political parties cooperate, reducing the dominance of any one party within that "coalition". The usual reason for this arrangement is that no party on its own can achieve a majority in the legislative body.

PANCHAYAT SAMITI

Mandals, taluka panchayats, block panchayats, or panchayat samiti are rural local governments at the intermediate level in panchayat raj institutions (PRI).

PREVIOUS YEARS'
EXAMINATION QUESTIONS

▶ 1 Mark Questions

1. Which one of the following is not the quality of democracy?

   [TERM 2, 2012]

   (a) It promotes equality among citizens

   (b) It takes quick decisions

   (c) It improves the quality of decision making

   (d) It enhances the dignity of the individual

2. Which one of the following features is common to most of the democracies?

   (a) They have formal constitution

   (b) They hold regular elections

   (c) They have political parties

   (d) All the above

   [TERM 2, 2013]

▶ 3 Mark Questions

3. Explain the role of democratic governments in reducing economic disparities.

   [TERM 2, 2011]

4. How do democracies accommodate social diversity? Explain.

   [TERM 2, 2011]

5. "An ideal government would not only keep itself away from corruption but also make fighting corruption and black money a top priority". Justify the statement by highlighting the values attached to it.

   [TERM 2, 2014]

6. How is democracy accountable and responsive to the needs and expectations of the citizens? Analyse.

   [TERM 2, 2015]

7. On the basis of which values will it be a fair expectation that democracy should produce a harmonious social life? Explain.

   [TERM 2, 2017]

▶ 5 Mark Questions

8. "Democracy is seen to be good in principle but felt to be not so good in practice". Justify the statement.

   [TERM 2, 2013]

9. "Democracy stands much superior in promoting dignity and freedom of the citizen". Justify the statement.

   [TERM 2, 2016]

10. "Democracies lead to peaceful and harmonious life among citizens." Justify this statement.

   [DELHI 2018]

🔑 Solutions

1. It takes quick decisions [1]

2. (d) All the above [1]

3. The government plays an important role in reducing economic disparities by adopting the following measures:

   (i) Government provides public facilities to uplift the economically weak class therefore economic gulf between poor and reach can be breached. [1]

   (ii) Government undertakes extensive social welfare schemes and strives to achieve universal literacy rate. [1]

   (iii) Government takes care to provide equal opportunities to all and answer that the income is eventually distributed among the people [1]

4. Democracy accommodates social diversity in following ways:

   (i) It allows methods to resolve conflicts. It takes into account views from both Majority and Minority, so as to provide a general view of the situation. [1]

   (ii) It allows equality, fair representation to all irrespective of caste, creed, colour, region, religion or language. [1]

   (iii) The weaker sections of the society are given the economic benefits to help them improve their living standards and live a dignified life. [1]

5. "An ideal government would not only keep itself away from corruption but also make fighting corruption and black money a top priority". This can be justified by highlighting values such as legitimacy, responsiveness and accountability:

   (i) Legitimacy – Social evils like Inflation, Poverty and poor political ethics arise from big sources of corruption and black money. A government elected by people is expected to work for their well being and prosperity, and when a government fails to control corruption it loses all its legitimacy to rule. [1]

(*ii*) Accountability – A government is responsible for management of polity and its resources, whereas corruption and black money always impede the prime allocation of resources. [1]

(*iii*) Responsiveness – People's representatives who have the mandates of people of their constituencies are the ones who run the government. [1]

6. Democracy is all about using the right to choose or vote. A democratic government is dependent on people's viewpoint. A leader is only able to win the democratic country, if he or she has given the valued people's opinion and make them top priority. However doing this is not enough. Once the leader has been chosen by the people, right from the next day citizens start evaluating their deeds and the process becomes very transparent. So transparency is the main factor of a democratic government by which a leader needs to be very responsive to the needs and expectation of the citizens. [1 + 1 + 1]

7. In a democratic country, majority and minority should work together. It should be the duty of government that both the groups respect each other's cultures. Needs and aspirations of every section of society should be looked by a democratic country. There should be equal participation of the citizen in government policies. The government should be able to solve conflicts between two communities without any discrimination. For example, in Belgium, the government negotiated the differences between two linguistic communities. [1 + 1 + 1]

8. "Democracy is seen to be good in principle but felt to be not so good in practice". The reasons for this are:

(*i*) In a democracy, people expect to have their needs fulfilled but it is not possible to look after everyone's needs as every country has diverse culture and regions. This often frustrates the common people. [1]

(*ii*) Ideally in a democracy everyone should be treated equally but there are instances where the minority opinion is not taken into account for a general view. [1]

(*iii*) Democracy is a people's government and it is imperative that people cast their vote to choose a government. But, many people skip the voting which does not serve the purpose of democracy. [1]

(*iv*) Regular elections may lead to change in ruling party and every party works in a different way. This may cause instability. [1]

(*v*) The people as well as the country will suffer if people are not wise enough in choosing a decent representative. [1]

9. In today's society, every individual expects to get proper respect. Democracy stands for every individual's freedom and respect. Democracy gives the power to each individual, so s/he can fight back for their dignity. [1 + 1]

Still, there are societies which have been built for long on the basis of subordination and domination. it is not a simple thing to accept that all individual are equal. [1]

If we talk about the respect of women, it's been ages that most of the societies are male dominated. Women struggled for long to get their respect and dignity. They also need to be treated equally and for such a situation Democracy comes forward and stands to promote dignity. [1 + 1]

10. Democracy leads to peaceful and harmonious life among citizens –

(*i*) Democracy accommodates various social divisions. [1]

(*ii*) Democracy reduces the possibility of tensions becoming explosive and violent. [1]

(*iii*) Ability to handle social differences and conflicts among different groups is a plus point of democracy. [1]

(*iv*) Democracy develops procedure to conduct healthy competitions among different groups in a society. [1]

(*v*) Democracy respects differences and provides mechanism to resolve them. [1]

(*vi*) Democracy always accommodates minority view.

MULTIPLE CHOICE QUESTIONS

1. Democracies have not helped in removing:
   - (*a*) Economic inequalities
   - (*b*) Infrastructural problems
   - (*c*) Political conflicts
   - (*d*) All of the above

2. Democracies are based on political equality as:
   - (*a*) It assures employment for all
   - (*b*) It establishes constitutional monarchy
   - (*c*) It grants every individual the right to vote
   - (*d*) None of these

3. What is meant by an accountable government?
   - (*a*) In an accountable government, people have the right to elect the leaders to form government and if possible they participate in decision-making process
   - (*b*) In an accountable government, people do not have the right to elect the leaders.
   - (*c*) In an accountable government, people are not a part of decision-making process.
   - (*d*) In an accountable government, only under privileged section of the society are allowed to vote

4. A legally chosen government is called as......
   - (*a*) Dictatorship
   - (*b*) Legitimate government
   - (*c*) Monarchy
   - (*d*) None of these

5. Non – democratic regimes suppress ......
   - (*a*) External social differences
   - (*b*) Internal economic differences
   - (*c*) External gender differences
   - (*d*) Internal social differences

Answer Keys

1. (*a*)
2. (*c*)
3. (*a*)
4. (*b*)
5. (*d*)

FILL IN THE BLANKS

1. A democratic government provides .... for arriving at a decision.
2. Increase in domestic production and services leading to an all – round growth in people's standard of living are known as________________.
3. Democracy is based on the idea of ___________ and negotiation.
4. In Bangladesh, more than half of its population lives in _____________.
5. Accommodating the demands of ___________ communities reduces the possibility of problems

Solutions

1. Rules and procedures
2. Economic growth
3. Deliberation
4. Poverty
5. Minority

TRUE OR FALSE

1. Democratic form of government is considered as the best.
2. Unequal distribution of income and opportunity between different groups in society is called as gender inequality.
3. Democracy provides an opportunity for rectifying errors.
4. Dictatorships have higher rate of economic growth..
5. Every society can fully and permanently resolve conflicts among different groups..

Solutions

1. True
2. False
3. True
4. True
5. False

CHAPTER 8

Challenges to Democracy

Summary

Define challenges and its types.

- A challenge is not just any problem. We usually call only those difficulties a 'challenge' which are significant and which can be overcome.

- A challenge is a difficulty that carries within it an opportunity for progress.

- Once we overcome a challenge we go up to a higher level than before.

- Different type of country face different type of challenges,it can be categorized in three.

Foundational challenge is making the transition to democracy and then instituting democratic government.

- It involves bringing down the existing non-democratic regime, keeping military away from controlling government and establishing a sovereign and functional state

The challenge of expansion is face by most of the established democracies.

- It involves applying the basic principle of democratic government across all the regions, different social groups and various institutions.

- Ensuring greater power to local governments, extension of federal principle to all the units of the federation, inclusion of women and minority groups, etc., falls under this challenge.

- Means that less and fewer decisions should remain outside the arena of democratic control.

- India and other democracies like the US face this challenge.

- Third **challenge of deepening of democracy** is looked by each majority rules system in some frame.

- It includes reinforcing of the foundations and practices of popular government.

- It ought to occur such that individuals can understand their desires for vote based system.

- It takes distinctive implications and ways in various parts of the world.

- when all is said in done terms, difficulties of extending implies fortifying those foundations that assistance individuals' investment and control.

- It requires an endeavour to cut down the control and impact of the rich and ground-breaking individuals in settling on administrative choice.

Reforms and Redefining Democracy

Reforms

- Law has an imperative part to play in political change.

- Carefully formulated changes in law can debilitate wrong political practices and support great ones.

- A legitimate established changes without anyone else can't conquer difficulties to majority rules system, just changes are to be completed primarily by political activists, gatherings, developments and politically cognizant natives.

- Any lawful change should precisely take a gander at what results it will have on legislative issues. Once in a while the outcomes might be counter-profitable.

- Best laws are those which enable individuals to complete vote based changes.
- Right to Information Act is a decent case of a law that enables the general population to discover what is going on in government and go about as guard dogs of majority rule government.
- Democratic changes are to be realized primarily through political practice.
- Main focus of political reforms should be on ways to strengthen democratic practice and the most important concern should be to increase and improve the quality of political participation by common people.

Redefinig Democracy

- The rulers chosen by the general population must take all the real choices.
- Elections must offer a decision and reasonable opportunity,to the general population to change the present rulers
- This decision and opportunity ought to be accessible to every one of the general population on an equivalent premise.
- The activity of decision must prompt an administration constrained by essential tenets of the constitution and natives' rights.

Points to know

CHALLANGE

Difficulties which are significant and which can be overcome are known as challenges.

POLITICAL REFORM

Improvements in setbacks on such issues which is related with governing system and politics.

RIGHT TO INFORMATION ACT

The act which ensure the public questioning regarding the decision making and other issue related with government.

BUREAUCRACY

Type of governing system controlled by officials

BY ELECTIONS

Election is held in the mid of period or after normal election due to vacation of seat .

PREVIOUS YEARS'
EXAMINATION QUESTIONS

▶ 1 Mark Questions

1. The Seven Party Alliance (SPA) in Nepal has succeeded in removing monarchy, holding elections and forming a government. This comes under which one of the following challenges

   (a) Foundational challenge.

   (b) Challenge of expansion of democracy.

   (c) Challenge of deepening of democracy.

   (d) All the above

   [TERM 2, 2011]

2. 'A challenge is not just any problem but an opportunity for progress.' Analyse the statement.

   [DELHI 2018]

▶ 3 Mark Questions

3. Explain 'the challenge of expansion of democracy' by stating three points.

   [TERM 2, 2011]

4. "A challenge is an opportunity for progress." Support the statement with your arguments.

   [TERM 2, 2015]

5. How are some countries of the world facing the 'challenge of expansion of democracy'? Explain with examples.

   [TERM 2, 2012]

6. "Legal-constitutional changes by themselves cannot overcome challenges to democracy". Justify the statement with an example.

   [TERM 2, 2013]

▶ 5 Mark Questions

7. Explain any five major challenges being faced by the Indian democracy.

   [TERM 2, 2014]

8. Describe "It is very difficult to reform politics through legal ways". Evaluate the statement.

   [TERM 2, 2017]

🔑 Solutions

1. (a) Foundational Challenge   [1]

2. A challenge is an opportunity. Overcoming a challenge gives an opportunity to go up to a higher level than before and it provides

motivation as a positive experience to fight tge challenges. [1]

3. The challenges of expansion of democracy can be the following:

(*i*) Extension of democratic ideas, approaches and government to various regions and social groups. [1]

(*ii*) Distribution of power between the federation and the local bodies. This means that more social groups, regions and institutions are following democracy. [1]

(*iii*) Including women and minority groups in the democracy. [1]

4. At different points in this age of democracy, we have noted the serious challenges that democracy faces all over the world. [1]

A challenge is form of a difficulty which has an opportunity for progress. One goes up to a lever higher than before once he overcomes the challenges. [1]

A challenge can't be stated as any problem. The difficulties that could be overcome and are important can be said to be a challenge. Immense learning happens when one overcomes a challenge through the period of struggle and once one succeeds, it raises confidence for future. [1]

5. Some of the democratic countries of the world are facing the challenge of expansion of democracy in the following ways:

(*i*) By applying the principles of democratic government across all regions, social groups and different institutions [1]

(*ii*) By giving greater power to local government. [1]

(*iii*) By extending federal principles to different units of federation, including women and minorities. [1]

(*iv*) By ensuring that least number of decisions stay outside the democratic control.

Ex. In India still there is not a 100% participation of peoples in election. In Loksabha election of 2014, 66% peoples participated.

6. In political reform Law has an important role to play. Planned changes in law promotes good political practices and discards the wrong ones. By legal constitutional changes the challenges faced to democracy can never overcome. Any legal change should be carefully looked into that what changes it will bring on politics. [1.5]

For example.

If law says a convicted person cannot stand for elections, unsuspicious politician make their relatives the face but handle the power themselves. So carry out democratic reforms we need political parties, activists, movements and politically conscious citizens. [1.5]

7. The five major challenges faced by the Indian democracy are-

(*i*) Political and Economic Instability. Political and economic instability in a democratic country affects its economic growth because it has negative effects on productive economic decisions such as investment and savings. The instability of the government implies uncertain future policies. A very important concern is commitment towards national interest, reduction of interference of unlawful elements in politics, public accountability and growth oriented policies of the government. [1]

(*ii*) Illiteracy. Education is a fundamental right which is ensured to the citizens. According to a report, India possesses the largest illiterate population. Illiteracy in India is mainly due to gender, income and caste imbalances. So there is not an activate participation of people in decision making. [1]

(*iii*) Agricultural Changes. The new techniques of farming are posing a problem for the farmers who are used to old techniques of farming. There is lack of sufficient irrigation facilities. Also, there is no law for security of fragmented land holdings for farmers.[1]

(*v*) Corruption. One of the major challenges to any democracy is Corruption. Corruption in India is at a very alarming rate.It creates obstacles in the welfare work of the government, which leads serious gulf between principles and reality of democracy. [1]

(*iv*) Poverty. Over population is one of the major reasons of poverty in India. This is a vicious cycle that leads to high level of illiteracy, poor health care facilities and lack of access to financial resources. It's a serious issue before Indian democracy to uplift the socially and economically backward peoples

(v) Casteism, Communalism, Regionalism: Divison of a society based on caste, specific belief for one religion and particular geographical area is a serious threat for democracy which create a social division, where people are always working for their own interest by undermining others. [1]

8. Wrong political practices can be discouraged by carefully implying new laws but the challenge to democracy is that these changes are not enough to reform the politics. Thinking of legal ways of reforming politics is very tempting because new laws can ban undesirable things. Law plays an important role in political reform. For example, in cricket, changes in rules of the game are not enough to improve the quality of the game but mainly it depends on administration, coaches and players. In the similar way, political reformation depends on political parties, activists, movements. Sometimes the result of these changes is counter-productive. For example, people with more than two children have been banned from contesting panchayat elections that restricted many poor women and men to take part in the election. It is the denial of the democratic opportunity but it was not intended. So we can say "It is very difficult to reform politics through legal ways". [1 + 1 + 1 + 1 + 1]

MULTIPLE CHOICE QUESTIONS

1. Which of these is a feature of a good democracy?
   (a) Economic inequalities
   (b) Elections give an opportunity and choice to the people to change the current ruler
   (c) Unaccountable government
   (d) None of the above

2. Which of these challenges is faced by countries that do not have a democratic form of government?
   (a) The challenge of bringing down the existing non-democratic regime and keeping the military away from controlling the government.
   (b) The challenge of gender equality
   (c) The challenge of cleanliness
   (d) All of the above.

3. The challenges to democracy linked to the possibility of.......
   (a) Economic reforms
   (b) Infrastructural reforms
   (c) Change in the mindset of people
   (d) Political reforms

4. A Challenge is an opportunity for ....
   (a) Regretting about our mistakes
   (b) Cursing people around us
   (c) Progress
   (d) None of these

5. A challenge that democracy faces in contemporary India is......
   (a) Extreme availability of monetary resources
   (b) Caste discrimination
   (c) Weak Infrastructure
   (d) Threat of an external attack

Answer Keys

1. (b)   2. (a)   3. (d)   4. (c)   5. (b)

Unit-IV : ECONOMICS

Development

Summary

Different people, different goals

- The stage which satisfy the demand or need of ones is termed as Development.

- Different person have different development goals.

  Some person have different goals in income and others in terms of more income, equal wages, freedom, job security, health and environment, respect of others etc.

- Development of ones may be destructive to or conflicting with others.

National development

- The development of a country is determined by the Average income.

- Total income of a particular country divided by its total population is average income which categorizes a country in developed, developing or under developing.

- According to the world Bank report in 2004, the countries with **per capita income** of Rs 45,300 p..a are considered as rich

  Countries below Rs 37,000 p.aa are poor countries

- India's per capita income is Rs 28,000 p.a.

- UNDP is an organ of UNO. It works to achieve the eradication of poverty, and the reduction of inequalities and exclusion.

- It measures the development of countries based on various indicators and publishes HDR.

- In HDR the HUMAN DEVELOPMENT INDEX shows the level of the development of countries among its members.

- HDR is based on indicators like per capita income, life expectancy at birth, literacy rate etc.

- India was ranked 131 in the 2016 Human Development Index (HDI) among 188 countries.

Public facilities

- Money in your pocket cannot buy all the goods and services that we may need to survive in our life.

- Income is not an adequate indicator of material goods and services that citizens are able to use.

- Normally, money cannot buy a pollution-free environment or ensure that you get unadulterated medicines unless you can afford to shift to a community that already has all these things.

- Money may also not be able to protect us from infectious diseases.

- The government provides some basic facilities collectively at affordable price like school, health facilities, food grains to ensure the development of the country. These facilities are termed as Public Facilities

Sustainable development

- Development without damaging the environment is sustainable development.

- The scarcity of resources is due to the overuse of natural resources. Resources are not conserved by us for our future generations.

- We can take the example of groundwater. The excess use of water in agriculture sector and domestic uses have led to the decrease of ground water level.

- We should discover the alternatives of resources and should encourage how to use these alternatives.

- Overuse of the resources led to the environmental degradation, which created the global threat, for all countries.

Points to know

Goal – receive or achieve something; idea, object, success

Per capita income – average income is known as Per capita income

Infant mortality rate – the number of children that die before the age of one year as a proportion of 1000 live children born in a year.

Literacy rate – measure of the proportion of literate population in the seven and above age group.

Net attendance ratio – the total number of the children of the age group of six to ten attending school as a percentage of total number of children in the same age group.

BMI - BMI is a person's weight in kilograms (kg) divided by his or her height in metres squared. An adult who has a BMI of 25-29.9 is overweight, and an adult who has a BMI over 30 is obese. A person with a BMI of 18.5-24.9 has a normal weight.

PREVIOUS YEARS'
EXAMINATION QUESTIONS

▶ 1 Mark Questions

1. Which one of the following is also called average income?
   (a) National Income
   (b) Per Capita Income
   (c) Gross Income
   (d) None of the above
   [TERM 1, 2011]

2. Which of the following is true of the people's goals in addition to higher income?
   (a) Equal treatment
   (b) Freedom

   (c) Respect and security
   (d) All the above
   [TERM 1, 2011]

3. How can development goals of different sections of our society be achieved?
   [TERM 1, 2015]

4. According to the World Development Report 2006, what is the Capita income of the low income countries in 2004?
   [TERM 1, 2017]

5. Define average income?
   [TERM 1, 2017]

6. Which is the most correct way of measuring a country's development?
   [TERM 1, 2017]

7. State any two goals of development other than income.
   [DELHI 2018]

▶ 3 Marks Questions

8. What is the main criterion used by the World Bank in classifying different countries? What are the limitations of this criterion, if any?
   [TERM 1, 2012]

9. What is Per Capita Income? Mention any two limitations of Per Capita Income as an indicator of development.
   [TERM 1, 2017]

10. Explain the three components of Human Development Index.
    [TERM 1, 2017]

11. Explain inferences which have been drawn by comparing the development levels of Punjab, Kerala and Bihar.
    [TERM 1, 2017]

12. Sustainability of development is most desirable'. Explain?
    [TERM 1, 2017]

13. How is the issue of sustainability important for development? Explain with examples.
    [DELHI 2018]

▶ 5 Marks Questions

14. (a) Define per capita income.
    (b) What is the criterion used by the UNDP for classifying countries?
    (c) Compare the literacy rate and life expectancy of India and Sri Lanka.
    [TERM 1, 2012]

15. What historical changes have been bought about in Primary, secondary and tertiary sectors?
    [TERM 1, 2012]

16. Describe any five public facilities needed for the development of a country.
[TERM 1, 2013, 2016, 2017]

17. What is development? What are the indicators used by UNDP for measuring development? Compare it with the World Bank report.
[TERM 1, 2016]

Solutions

1. (b) Per Capita Income   [1]

2. (d) All the above   [1]

3. Economic Growth is the way to achieve the development goals of different sections of our society. It could be done by more investment in the economy and by providing equal job opportunity, which can be ensured by providing proper education system.   [1]

4. According to the World Development Report 2006, the Capita income of the low income countries in 2004 was Rs 37,000 or less than Rs 37,000.   [1]

5. The average income is total income earned by each person in a given area in a specific year divided by total population.   [1]

6. Measuring the HDI (Human Development Index) is the most correct way of measuring development of any country.   [1]

7. Goals of development other than income include:
   (i) Equal treatment
   (ii) Freedom
   (iii) Security   [1]

8. The main criterion used by the World Bank in classifying different countries is Per Capita Income. It measures the average income earned per person in a given area in a year. This is used for measuring development of any country. [1]
   Per Capita Income has limitations which include:
   (i) Covering only the economic aspect and ignoring factors like education, health, environment etc.   [1]
   (ii) There is no transparency regarding distribution of income.   [1]

9. The total income of the country divided by its total population is called the average income or the per capita income.

   There are following limitations of Per Capita Income:
   (i) The equitable distribution of income is not visible. It does not give any idea about how many people are rich and how many people in a country are poor, which could decide the development.   [1]
   (ii) Average income is useful for comparison, but it does not tell us how this income is distributed among people.   [1]

10. The three components of Human Development Index (HDI) are:
    (i) Life expectancy: It denotes the average expected length of life of a person at the time of birth.   [1]
    (ii) Gross Enrolment Ratio: It means enrolment ratio for primary school, secondary school and higher education beyond secondary school.   [1]
    (iii) Per capita Income: It is calculated in dollars for all countries so that it can be compared. It is also done in a way so that every dollar would buy the same amount of goods and services in any country.   [1]

11. Inferences which have been drawn by comparing the development levels of Punjab, Kerala and Bihar are:-
    (i) Average income or per capita income is not the best criteria to compare the economic growth precisely.   [1]
    (ii) Despite having a lower per capita income, Kerala is more developed than Punjab for several other factors.   [1]
    (iii) Therefore, per capita income is not the ideal index to measure development because it does not include non-monetary aspects of development.   [1]

12. Sustainable development is most desirable development as we work on the things that can meet the need of present generation without compromising the needs of the future generation. Development without damaging environment is termed as sustainable development. In sustainable development we work toward the common future of present and future generations by not misusing and overusing the natural resources that we have.   [1 + 1 + 1]

13. Importance of Sustainable Development -
    (i) Sustainable development aims at managing the needs of today in such a way that the future generation does not have to compromise their needs.   [1]
    (ii) Sustainability is the capability to use the resources judiciously and maintain the ecological balance.   [1]
    (iii) It lays emphasis on environmental protection and check environmental degradation. [1]
    (iv) To stop over exploitation and over use of resources.

Example: Resources like petroleum, coal and groundwater need to be used judicially so that it's available for our future generation as well.

14. (*i*)   Per capita income or average income measures the average income earned per person in a given region in a specified year. We calculate it by dividing the area's total income by its total population.   [1]

   (*ii*)   Human Development Index (HDI) is the criteria used by UNDP (United Nations Development Programme) for classifying countries regarding development   [2]

   (*ii*)   Literacy rates of Sri Lanka and India are 90.6 and 62.8 respectively and life expectancy of Sri Lanka and India are 75.1 and 65.8 respectively.   [2]

15. Following are the historical changes that have been brought about in Primary sector:

   (*i*)   People in primary sector can take up other jobs because now farmers produce much more food than before because of change of methods in farming.   [1]

   (*ii*)   Buying and selling activities increased multiple times than before because of increment in numbers of craft persons and traders.   [1]

Following are the historical changes that have been bought about in secondary sector:

   (*i*)   Over a long time factories were introduced and started expanding especially because new methods of manufacturing were introduced.   [1]

   (*ii*)   People started working in factories who were earlier working on farms in large numbers. People are beginning to use many more goods that were produced in factories at cheap rates.   [1]

Following are the historical changes that have been brought about in tertiary sector:

   (*i*)   In developed countries there have been further shifts from secondary sector to tertiary sector in past 100 years.   [1]

   (*ii*)   In developed countries most people are now working in services sector, and also services sector have become the most important in terms of total production.

16. Five Public facilities needed development of a country are described below:

   (*i*)   The Public Distribution System (PDS), which provides average quality of food grains and other items at subsidized prices to the weaker sections.   [1]

   (*ii*)   Government schools which provide elementary education up to class 8 free of cost for all children up to the age of 14 years.   [1]

   (*iii*)   Healthcare in government hospitals provided to the weaker sections at subsidized rates. This includes outpatient as well as hospitalization facilities.   [1]

   (*iv*)   Sanitation is very important to keep a city and country clean which improves personality as well.   [1]

   (*v*)   Water is an essential resource that everyone needs to fulfill their day to day activity and their personal demands like washing clothes, bathing and maintaining hygiene.   [1]

   (*vi*)   Improvement of road and transport facilities: There should be good quality roads to reach any destination and proper public transport so that people can afford better and cheaper transport facilities to commute.   [1]

17. Development can be defined as a process of economic and social advancement in terms of quality of human life. The indicators used by UNDP for measuring development are: [1]

   1. Literacy/education,   [0.5]

   2. .Life Expectancy .   [0.5]

   3. Net Enrollment Ratio   [0.5]

   4. Net Attendance Ratio   [0.5]

World Bank only considers Per Capita Income as the measure to compare countries. UNDP also includs Health and Education to compare countries.   [2]

MULTIPLE CHOICE QUESTIONS

1. Which of these is a feature of a developed nation?

   (*a*)   Corruption

   (*b*)   Political inequality

   (*c*)   Gender inequality

   (*d*)   High per capita income

2. UNDP stands for........

   (*a*)   United Nations Developmental Programme

   (*b*)   United Nations Development Programme

   (*c*)   United Nations Developed Programme

   (*d*)   Unidentified Nations Development Programme

3. Who is responsible for providing public facilities?

   (*a*)   The government

   (*b*)   Private firms

    (c) The defense ministry

    (d) None of these

4. According to per capita income prepared by the world Bank in 2004, in which category is India included in

    (a) Rich countries

    (b) Middle income countries

    (c) Low income countries

    (d) None of the above

5. National development means:

    (a) Economic development

    (b) Social development

    (c) Political development

    (d) All round development

Answer Keys

1. (d)   2. (b)   3. (a)   4. (c)   5. (d)

FILL IN THE BLANKS

1. A composite statistic of life expectancy, education and per capita income indicators, which is used to rank countries into four tiers of human development is called as ____________.

2. Sustainable development is important for __________.

3. the most common indicator for measuring economic development of a country is ____________.

4. Sunlight is an example of ____________ resource.

5. Per Capita Income is calculated in________________.

Solutions

1. Human Development Index

2. Economic growth

3. Per capita Income

4. Renewable

5. Dollars

TRUE OR FALSE

1. India stands 131 in the HDI rank in the world.

2. Developmental goals are different for different people"

3. Kerala has the highest Infant Mortality Rate

4. Illiteracy rate measures the proportion of literate population in 7 and above age group

5. Human development is the ultimate goal of all economic activities.

Solutions

1. True

2. True

3. False

4. False

5. True

CHAPTER 2

Sectors of the Indian Economy

Summary

Sectors of economic activities

Primary sector

- The sector in which the production of goods is done by exploiting natural resources. It form the base for the production of all other products. It is also known as agricultural sector.

Secondary sector

The sector in which the products of primary sector are changed into other form with the help of technology and human skills. It is also known as industrial sector.

Tertiary sector

The sector which helps in the development of primary and secondary sector.

How to create more employment

- To create more employment government should invest money in transportation and storage of crops, which will support agriculture production.

- Government can promote and locate industries and services in semi rural areas, where a large number of people may be employed.

- Government should establish industries related with vegetables and agricultural products in villages near forest areas.

- By ensuring the net attendance ratio of students, governments can create more employment in the education sector. As per planning commission, 20 lakh jobs can be created in the education sector.

- Government should encourage tourism sector as it can give jobs to thirty five lakh people, every year.

NREGA ACT

- It is a quick measure taken by Central Government of India to create more employment in **rural areas**.

- In the first year (2006-2007), Right to work scheme was implemented in 200 districts.

- 100 day work guaranteed work.

- There is provision of unemployment allowance.

- Types of work is given in National rural employment guarantee act 2005, are mainly related with increase in the production of land in future.

Division of sectors as organized and unorganized

Organized sector

Registered by the government

Terms of employment are regular

Follow various acts like Minimum wages act, Payment of Gratuity act etc.

Workers enjoy security of employment.

Workers are supposed to get medical and other benefits.

Unorganized sector

- Small and scattered units, which are largely outside the control of the government.
- Employment is not secure.
- Rules and regulations are not followed.
- Terms of employment are not regular.

Points to know

GDP – the value of the sum of the production of the final goods and services in the three sectors during a particular year is known as Gross domestic product.

Disguised unemployment – It is type of unemployment in which the final output remains unchanged when a person leaves working. It is usually seen in agricultural sector.

Public sector

- The government owns most of the assets and is responsible for providing services. It is for the development of society. e.g. Railway, Post office

Private sector

Ownership of assets and delivery of services is in private hand. Tata iron, TISCO, RIL etc.

PREVIOUS YEARS'
EXAMINATION QUESTIONS

▶ 1 Mark Questions

1. Workers enjoy job security in:
   (a) Agriculture Sector
   (b) Private sector
   (c) Unorganized sector
   (d) Organized sector

   [TERM 1, 2011]

2. Which of the following was the objective of NREGA 2005?
   (a) To control the unorganized sector in rural areas
   (b) To provide 100 days employment in a year by the government.
   (c) To control the flow of money from private sector to public sector.
   (d) None of the above.

   [TERM 1, 2011]

3. Where has the government of India Implemented the right to work?

   [TERM 1, 2016]

4. Which economic sector has the highest share in GDP In 2003?

   [TERM 1, 2016]

5. Where is the disguised unemployment found mostly?

   [TERM 1, 2017]

6. How do big private companies contribute in the development of a nation?

   [TERM 1, 2017]

7. When we produce goods by exploiting natural resources, in which category of economic sector such activities come?

   [DELHI 2018]

▶ 3 Marks Questions

8. Explain the NREGA Act 2005.

   [TERM 1, 2012]

9. What is GDP? Who undertakes the task of measuring GDP in India? How is this task done?

   [TERM 1, 2012]

10. "Agriculture and industry move hand in hand." Analyze the statement with three examples.

    [TERM 1, 2013]

11. Why is it said that money cannot buy all the goods and services that one needs to live well?

    [TERM 1, 2015]

12. Analyze the role of the manufacturing sector in the economic development of India.

    [TERM 1, 2017]

13. How can the workers in the unorganized sector be protected? Explain.

    [TERM 1, 2017]

14. What are final goods and intermediate goods? How do they help in calculating Gross Domestic Product (G.D.P)?

    [TERM 1, 2017]

15. Why is agriculture an activity of unorganized sector in India? Explain.

    [TERM 1, 2017]

16. Explain the concept of underemployment in the urban areas with the help of examples.

    [TERM 1, 2017]

17. What has been the role of NREGA in creating employment for the people in India? Explain.

    [TERM 1, 2017]

18. Distinguish the service conditions of organized sector with that of unorganized sector.

[DELHI 2018]

▶ 5 Marks Questions

19. Analyze the role of chemical industries in the Indian economy.

[TERM 1, 2017]

20. Explain measures that can be adopted to remove disguised unemployment in the agriculture sector.

[TERM 1, 2017]

21. "Workers are not exploited in organized sector". Do you agree with the statement? Explain reasons in support of your answer.

[TERM 1, 2017]

22. Explain the tertiary sector? Why is this sector becoming important in India? Give four reasons.

[TERM 1, 2017]

23. "There has been a big change in the three sectors of economic activities, but a similar shift has not taken place in the share of employment". Explain the above statement on the basis of facts.

[TERM 1, 2017]

24. Compare the employment conditions prevailing in the organized and the unorganized sectors.

[TERM 1, 2017]

🔑 Solutions

1. (d) Organized sector [1]

2. (b) To provide 100 days employment in a year by the government. [1]

3. At least 100 days of guaranteed wage employment in a financial year to every household to do unskilled manual work is implemented in rural areas [1]

4. Service Sector. [1]

5. Disguised unemployment is found mostly in agricultural sector. [1]

6. Big private companies contribute in the development of a nation by the following ways:
   (i) They provide huge employment opportunities. [0.5]
   (ii) They help in economic development by creating and expanding the infrastructure. [0.5]

(iii) They produce good quality products and create an environment of competition among local companies

7. Primary Sector [1]

8. National Rural Employment Guarantee Act 2005 or NREGA is a social security measure implemented by the government of India in 200 districts of the country starting from 1st april 2008, it is implemented in all districts of india. It ensures 100 days of employment in a year by the government to all those who can work and increases livelihood securities in local areas. There is also a provision of unemployment allowance given to people. The gram panchayat is responsible for official verification of people under this act. 33% seats are reserved for women. [1 + 1 + 1]

9. Gross Domestic Product or GDP, is the value of all final goods and services produced in each sector during a specific year. [1]

The task of measuring GDP is done by CSO, undertaken by the ministry of central government. [1]

The task is done with the help of various government departments of all states and Union Territories. The central ministry collects information relating to total volume of goods and services and their prices and then estimates the GDP. [1]

10. Below are the ways which justify that agriculture and industry move hand in hand:
    (i) Transportation provided by different industries to import raw materials from fields to different places helps bring finished goods to the market. [1]
    (ii) Excess Labour in agriculture sectors are employed by industrial sector. [1]
    (iii) Agriculturally produced raw materials are processed in the industries. For example, cotton used to produce textile. [1]

11. There are many things which money alone cannot buy. It includes security, friendship, happiness, freedom and many more. Money cannot buy pollution free environment, unadulterated medicines and peace. Money possessed by an individual even cannot provide us with a type of government which takes decision for the Welfare of the common people. We can buy only

the things that have a price on it but we cannot buy health with money. [1 + 1 + 1]

12. The role of the manufacturing sector in the economic development of India is following:
    (*i*) The agriculture sector has been modernized because of manufacturing industries. So, people are not heavily dependent on agriculture income. [1]
    (*ii*) Manufactured goods are being exported to foreign countries that bring in foreign exchange which creates the flow of money in market. [1]
    (*iii*) Transformation of raw material into a variety of furnished goods of a great value helps in the economic development of the country. [1]

13. The unorganized sector in rural areas mostly consists of landless agricultural farmers, sharecroppers, laborers and artisans, etc. These farmers need to be supported through adequate facility for timely delivery of seeds, agricultural inputs, credit, storage facilities and marketing outlets. [1 + 1]

   In urban areas, workers in the unorganized sector can be protected by providing better wages on time and providing them basic facilities like proper sanitation, hospital aids and cheap and clean living houses. [1]

14. Final goods are completely processed goods that are meant for final consumption. For example: biscuits, breads, etc. [1]

   Intermediate goods are unfinished goods. They need more processing to get ready for the final consumption. Intermediate goods are used up in producing final goods and services. For example: flour. [1]

   Only the final goods are counted for calculating the G.D.P. This is because the value of final goods already includes the value of all the intermediate goods that are used in making the final good.[1]

15. The unorganized sector consists of small and scattered units, mainly which are not under the control of the govt. Jobs in this sector are low-paid and often not regular. Also the employment in this sector is not secure. [1]

   Agriculture is an activity of unorganized sector in India because in India, agriculture is mostly season dependent. There are laborers who work on large fields on daily basis and the methods of farming are mostly traditional. The laborers can be anytime asked to leave the job if the produce

is not good. Moreover, they are paid very less and there are no basic rules and leaves provided to the workers. [1 + 1]

16. Unemployment is a condition in which the labour force is apparently working but all of them are made to work less than their potential. example- in Urban areas highly qualified people like managers, engineers are working in call centers, BPO's due to lack of jobs or unemployment. [2 + 1]

17. The role of NREGA in creating employment for the people in India is as follows:-
    (*i*) It provides 100 days employment per year for every person. [1]
    (*ii*) It was present in 200 districts and extended to all the districts of India. [1]
    (*iii*) 33% of total vacancies is reserved for women. [1]

18. Service conditions of Organized and Unorganized Sectors-
    (*i*) Organized sector is registered by the government whereas the unorganized sector is largely outside the control of the government. [1]
    (*ii*) In organized sector the workers enjoy security of employment whereas, in unorganized sector jobs are insecure, low paid and irregular. [1]
    (*iii*) In organized sector the numbers of working hours are fixed whereas in unorganized sector the numbers of working hours are not fixed. [1]
    (*iv*) In organized sector workers get several benefits such as paid leaves, payment during holidays, provident fund etc, whereas in unorganized sector such facilities are not available.

19. Chemical industries play an important role in Indian economy which are following:
    (*i*) The contribution of chemical industries is approximately 3% of the GDP. [1]
    (*ii*) Both large and small-scale manufacturing units present here. [1]
    (*iii*) It is responsible for the rapid growth of both inorganic and organic sector. [1]
    (*iv*) Most of the industries use its chemical products like fertilizer industries, synthetic fiber industries, medicines etc. [1]
    (*v*) It is growing with a rapid rate leading to the development of Indian economy. [1]
    (*vi*) The largest consumer of the chemical industry is the chemical industry itself.

20. Disguised unemployment is that type of employment in which there are many workers working in a field, but there is a very limited work for them. If we remove some of the workers from the field, there will be no effect on production. To remove disguised unemployment, we need to improve the agricultural practices so that we can increase the marginal productivity of these employees. There should be arrangement for their skill building so they can work in other sectors. Disguised unemployment is hidden unemployment. [1 + 1 + 1 + 1 + 1]

21. Below are the points, which shows that workers are not exploited in organized sector:-

    (*i*) In organized sector people have assured job, because organized sector covers those enterprises where terms of employment are regular. [1]

    (*ii*) In organized sector there is security of job. [1]

    (*iii*) Organized sectors are registered by the government. [1]

    (*iv*) In organized sector employees cannot be terminated in a casual manner without notice as they work under fixed terms of employment. [1]

    (*v*) In organized sector there are other benefits like leaves, social security in the form of provident funds and gratuity. [1]

22. Tertiary sector includes all the activities that support the development of both primary and secondary sectors. Tertiary sector does not produce any goods but aids or supports the production process. Since this sector generates services in spite of goods, the tertiary sector is also called the service sector. [1]

    Now-a-days, tertiary sector is becoming quite important in India because of the following reasons:

    (*i*) With the development of several government programs like Make in India, there is a growing need for the facilities like good communication and transport facilities, which come under the tertiary sector. [1]

    (*ii*) With the development of different businesses, there is a growing need and importance of loan facilities and other banking services. [1]

    (*iii*) Trade is the most important factor for the transfer of manufactured materials to the place where there is a demand so as to maintain the equilibrium between demand and production service sector is needed.[1]

    (*iv*) With the growth of manufacturing and production, the proper place for storage of processed goods is mandatory, which comes under the tertiary sector. [1]

23. Consider the graph. By having a close look at the graph, it can be inferred that from year 1973 to year 2000:

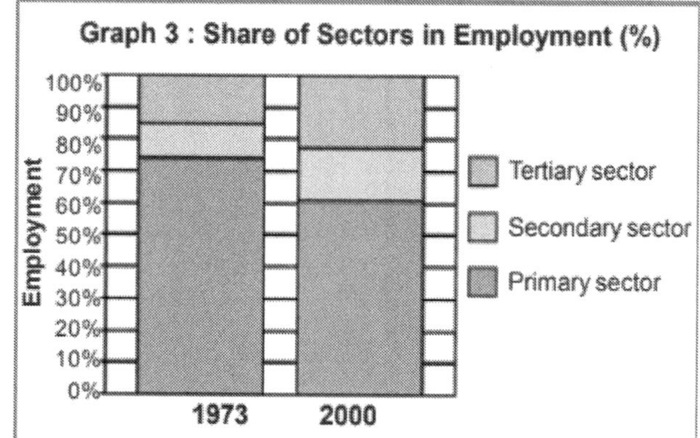

    (*i*) The industrial output or the production of goods has gone up by eight times during the period. However, employment in the industry has risen only by 2.5 times. [1]

    (*ii*) While production in the tertiary sector (or service sector) has risen by 11 times, employment in the same sector has risen less than three times. [1]

    (*iii*) It can be noted that more than half of the workers in the country are working in the primary sector, mainly in agriculture, producing only a quarter of the GDP(Gross Domestic Production). [1]

    (*iv*) On the other hand, the secondary and tertiary sectors produce three-fourth of the produce whereas they employ less than half the people. [1]

    (*v*) The graph shows that there are more people in agriculture than is necessary. It means that primary sector has disguised employment whereas workers in secondary and tertiary sectors work overtime. [1]

24. Employment conditions in the organized and the unorganized sectors can be compared as follows:

	Organized sectors	Unorganized sectors
1.	There are specified rules and regulations which are followed properly.	There are rules and regulations, but are not always followed.
2.	Jobs are appropriately paid.	Jobs are low paid.
3.	There is job security and the jobs are regular.	There is no job security and mostly the jobs are not regular.
4.	There is provision for overtime, paid leave, holidays, leave due to sickness etc for the welfare of employees.	There is no provision for overtime, paid leave, holidays, leave due to sickness etc for the welfare of employees.
5.	People cannot be asked to leave without a concrete reason.	If there is no or less work, people can be asked to leave anytime without a reason.

MULTIPLE CHOICE QUESTIONS

1. What is Gross Domestic Product?
   (a) Sum of taxes collected in a month
   (b) The value of only final goods and services produced within the domestic territory of a country.
   (c) The value of raw materials produced within the domestic territory of a country.
   (d) All of the above

2. In which sector, workers do not fear exploitation?
   (a) Unorganised   (b) Technology
   (c) Organised   (d) Production

3. The activities in primary, secondary and tertiary sectors are........
   (a) Dependent   (b) Inter dependent
   (c) Critical   (d) All of the above

4. Which of the following is an example of private sector enterprise?
   (a) Reliance Industries (b) DDA
   (c) NDMC   (d) Railways

5. Economic Survey is published by the
   (a) National Sample Survey Organisation
   (b) Ministry of Statistics and Planning
   (c) Ministry of Finance
   (d) Ministry of Commerce and Trade

Answer Keys
   1. (b)   2. (c)   3. (b)   4. (a)   5. (c)

FILL IN THE BLANKS

1. ________________ includes all those economic activities which are connected with the extraction and production of natural resources
2. The unemployment which takes place due to the variation in the season is called__________.
3. NREGA guarantees ______ days of assured work to the people who are able and in need of work.
4. The sectors are classified into public and private sector on the basis of__________.
5. All activities that give an income in return are called____________.

Solutions

1. Primary sector
2. Seasonal unemployment
3. 100
4. ownership of enterprises
5. Economic activities

TRUE OR FALSE

1. The tertiary sector has very less importance in the Indian economy.
2. Disguised unemployment is generally found in agriculture sector.
3. The purpose of the public sector is just to earn profits.
4. Construction of multi-purpose projects cannot create more employment.
5. NREGA was introduced in 2005.

Solutions

1. False
2. True
3. False
4. False
5. True

CHAPTER 3

Money and Credit

Summary

Money and Credit

- Money is a medium of exchange.
- Money includes currency paper notes and coin.
- Money is in the form of currency authorized by the government as medium of exchange.
- In India the Reserve bank of India issues currency on behalf of the Central Government.

Banks

- People deposit their extra cash in banks by opening accounts in their names.
- Banks accept the deposits and also pay an amount as interest on deposits.
- As cash Banks keeps only a small share of their deposits as per RBI guidelines.
- Bank charges money on providing facilities.
- Bank mediates between depositors and borrowers.

Credit terms and types

Term of credit

- Collateral
- Interest rate
- Documentation
- Mode of repayment

Type

Formal sector

- Formal sector loan is given by commercial banks.
- Collateral is required in this sector.
- It has a low rate of interest on loan.
- It is controlled or supervised by Reserve Bank of India.

Informal sector

- The loan taken from friends, moneylenders, and relatives is termed as informal sector loan.
- Interest is not fixed, it is usually higher than formal.
- There is no supervisory body for this sector.
- Collateral is not required in most cases
- It often creates a situation of debt trap.

Points to know

Double coincidence of wants

What a person desires to sell is exactly what the other wishes to buy

Cheque

A cheque is a paper instructing the bank to pay a specific amount to the person, in whose name the cheque has been issued.

Collateral

An asset of borrower that is used as a guarantee to obtain a loan from lender.

SHG

A **self-help group (SHG)** is a village-based financial intermediary committee usually composed of 10–200 local women or men. They are exclusive groups started primarily to empower women in rural and suburban areas, make them economically independent and help them contribute to the socio-economic development of the nation.

PREVIOUS YEARS'
EXAMINATION QUESTIONS

▶ 1 Mark Questions

1. Which one of the following is not a feature of money?
   (a) Medium of exchange
   (b) Lack of divisibility
   (c) A store of value
   (d) A unit of account

   [TERM 2, 2011]

2. Professor Muhammad Yunus is the founder of which one of the following banks?
   (a) Co-operative Bank
   (b) Commercial Bank
   (c) Grameen Bank
   (d) Land Development Bank

   [TERM 2, 2011]

3. Which one of the following statements is most appropriate regarding transactions made in money?
   (a) It is the easiest way
   (b) It is the safest way
   (c) It is the cheapest way
   (d) It promotes trade

   [TERM 2, 2012]

4. Which of the following is the main informal source of credit for rural household in India?
   (a) Friends   (b) Relatives
   (c) Landlords   (d) Money Lenders

   [TERM 2, 2013]

5. What is meant by double coincidence of wants?

   [TERM 2, 2015]

6. How does money act as a medium of exchange?

   [TERM 2, 2015]

7. Why are most of the poor households deprived from the formal sector of loans?

   [TERM 2, 2016]

8. Give any two examples of informal sector of credit.

   [DELHI, 2018]

▶ 3 Marks Questions

9. What is money? Why is modern money currency accepted as a medium of exchange?

   [TERM 2, 2012, 2013]

10. Why is cheap and affordable credit important for the country's development? Explain three reasons.

    [TERM 2, 2012]

11. Why is modern currency accepted as a medium of exchange without any use of its own? Find out the reason.

    [TERM 2, 2015]

12. Explain any three loan activities of banks in India.

    [TERM 2, 2017]

▶ 4 Marks Questions

13. Explain any four terms of credit with examples.

    [TERM 2, 2011]

▶ 5 Marks Questions

14. How do banks play an important role in the economy of India? Explain.

    [TERM 2, 2015]

15. How can the formal sector loans be made beneficial for poor farmers and workers? Suggest any five measures.

    [TERM 2, 2017]

🔑 Solutions

1. Lack of divisibility   [1]
2. Grameen Bank   [1]
3. It promotes trade   [1]
4. (d) Money Lenders   [1]
5. Double coincidence of wants mean, if a person desires to sell what exactly other person wishes to buy. Goods are directly exchanged without the use of the money in this coincidence.   [1]
6. For all the sellers, money acts as a medium of exchange for the goods they sell. A seller has to find a buyer for his goods, who can pay a good amount in the reversal of goods seller sells. When money acts as a medium of exchange, the need for double coincidence of want eliminates as the person only find the buyer for their goods.   [1]
7. Most of the poor households are deprived from the formal sector of loans because:

(*i*)   In rural India formal banks are not present everywhere. **[0.5]**

(*ii*) Absence of collateral and proper document. **[0.5]**

(*iii*) Moneylenders charge very high rates of interest keeping no records of the transactions and then they harass the poor borrowers but they preferred to take loan from moneylenders as no paper work or other formalities are needed in it

8. (*i*) Moneylenders **[0.5]**

(*ii*) Traders **[0.5]**

(*iii*) Employers

(*iv*) Relatives or friends

9. Something that acts as a medium of exchange in transactions of goods and services can be taken as Money. It also serves as a standard unit to determine their value. **[1]**

The government of the country has authorized the currency therefore modern money currency is accepted as a medium of exchange for easier transactions and promotion of trade. **[1]**

Example:

Indian rupee is widely accepted as a medium of exchange in India. The rupee currency notes issued on behalf of Indian government by the Reserve Bank of India, cannot be refused by anybody. They have to accept rupees in exchange of goods and services in India. **[1]**

10. Cheap and affordable credit is important for the country's development because:

(*i*)   The more lending, the higher the incomes and that encourages people to invest in agriculture, engage in business and set up small scale industries. **[1]**

(*ii*) Affordable can end the cycle of debt trap and lead to sustainable economic activity that allows borrowers to invest in better technology to make their business more competitive. **[1]**

(*iii*) Cheap credit would also allow weaker sections of society to enter formal sector of lending and rid them of exploitation at the hands of informal moneylenders. **[1]**

11. Modern currency is accepted as a medium of exchange despite having no use of its own because the currency is authorized by the government of the country. The currency is issued by Reserve bank of India on the behalf of central government. This bank has all rights reserved to issue the currency and no other organisation is allowed to issue the currency. The law has permitted the use of rupee as a medium of payment that cannot be refused in making any transaction in India. **[1 + 1 + 1]**

12. Following are the loan activities of banks in India:

(*i*)   For economic activities, loans are provided by the bank. **[1]**

(*ii*) Bank offers less interest on deposit but charges more interest on loans. **[1]**

(*iii*) A small proportion of deposit is kept by the bank as cash to provide a loan. It acts as an intermediate between those who have a fund (deposit) and those who need that fund. **[1]**

13. The terms of credit basically comprises of Interest rate, Collateral and documentation requirement, and the mode of repayment.

(*i*)   Interest rate: The amount due for a particular period of time on the amount lent, deposited or borrowed is known as Interest rate. This is paid by the borrower to the lender along with the principal amount. **[1]**

(*ii*) Collateral: Collateral is an asset that the borrower owns and uses this as a guarantee to a lender until the loan is repaid. **[1]**

(*iii*) Documentation: Documentation required by the lender before lending money includes identification of the borrower such as the employment records or salary slips. **[1]**

(*iv*) Mode of Repayment: This defines the way or the duration on the basis of which the borrower will return back the money to the lender. **[1]**

14. (*i*)   Banks provide credit at cheap and affordable rates to the poor. **[1]**

(*ii*) Banks accept the deposits and also pay an amount as interest on the deposits. **[1]**

(*iii*) Banks use a major portion of the deposits to give loans. **[1]**

(*iv*) Banks helps in establishment of large scale industries which brings foreign exchange, and thus adds to the national income of the country. **[1]**

(*v*)   Provides employment and growth opportunities to the low income groups. **[1]**

Above all, banks ensure the flow of liquidity in market and help to generate capital by various means.

15. Below are the five measures to make the formal sector loans beneficial for poor farmers and workers.

    (*i*) Unlike the informal lenders, formal sector loans should charge less interest on loans.[1]

    (*ii*) Number of banks should increase in rural areas, so services can reach most of the poor people. [1]

    (*iii*) There should be an availability of information and help counter in each bank, so a person can get information regarding the loan properly. [1]

    (*iv*) More and more people should be encouraged to take loan from formal sectors instead of going to other sectors. [1]

    (*v*) It should be checked that each person is getting right amount as a loan and their transaction should be checked properly.[1]

MULTIPLE CHOICE QUESTIONS

1. Which of these is an advantage of money?

    (*a*) It is available to everyone

    (*b*) It can be used as for direct exchange of goods

    (*c*) It eliminates the need for double coincidence of wants

    (*d*) Both (*b*) and (*c*)

2. Who has the authority to issue currency in India?

    (*a*) RBI- Reserve Bank of India

    (*b*) SBI- State Bank of India

    (*c*) TATA

    (*d*) BHEL

3. Which of these is a modern form of money?

    (*a*) Silver coins

    (*b*) Exchange of food

    (*c*) Renting property

    (*d*) Paper currency

4. Which of these is a source of credit?

    (*a*) Banks

    (*b*) Parents

    (*c*) Teachers

    (*d*) Neighbors

5. What is Collateral?

    (*a*) It is a gift provided by a borrower (such as land, building, vehicle, livestock, deposits with banks) against a loan, and it can be sold in case of non-payment of loan.

    (*b*) It is the security provided by a borrower (such as land, building, vehicle, livestock, deposits with banks) against a loan, and it can be sold in case of non-payment of loan.

    (*c*) It is a promise provided by a borrower

    (*d*) Both (*a*) and (*c*)

Answer Keys

  1. (*c*)   2. (*a*)   3. (*d*)   4. (*a*)   5. (*b*)

FILL IN THE BLANKS

1. A _____________ is a written instruction to a bank by an account holder to pay a specific sum to a specific person from his deposit.

2. Farmers require credit to purchase_____________.

3. Banks use only a small portion of the _____________ to extend loans.

4. _____________ and _____________ are sources of formal sector loans.

5.) Payments which are to be made in the future are known as_____________.

✎ Solutions

1. Cheque
2. The raw materials and inputs for agriculture
3. Deposits
4. Banks, Cooperatives
5. Deferred Payments

TRUE OR FALSE

1. Banks play an important role in developing the economy of India.

2. A loan is usually given for a specific duration of time and needs to be completely repaid by a specified date.

3. Informal lenders charge low rate of interest.

4. Before the introduction of coins, a variety of objects were used as money.

5. Deposits with the banks are not beneficial to the depositors or to the nation.

✎ Solutions

1. True
2. True
3. False
4. True
5. False

Globalisation and The Indian Economy

Summary

Globalisation

- **Globalisation** is the process of sharing ideas, goods and services, culture between countries by the help of various means.

- Globalisation paced due to development in transportation and communication technology.

- The economic interactions enabled Globalisation, which also help in the intermingle of social and cultural aspects.

- Globalisation enables the production of goods and services, globally.

- MNCs divide the production of goods and services in small parts and spread out across the globe.

- MNCs setup production jointly with local companies.

- Joint production provides money for additional investment and latest technology for production.

- MNC's generally, work with local companies as a partner, sometimes they buys local companies. In both condition, MNC's use the market setup by the local companies.

Foreign trade and integration of the market

- Foreign trade was the main channel of connecting countries.

- Exchange of goods, across the geographical boundaries of countries.

- Creates an opportunity for the producers to reach beyond the domestic markets or their countries' market.

- Goods travel from one market to another.

- In the market, choice of goods go up.

- Price of similar goods in two markets tend to be equal.

- Producers of two companies closely compete against each other even if they are distant. In this way foreign trade connects markets.

Challenges and Factors that enabled Globalisation

- Rapid improvement in technology is a major factor which paced the Globalisation process.

- Technological change, especially in communications technology. Internet enables us to send instant electronic mail and talk across the world at negligible costs.

- Free Trade. Many barriers to trade have been removed. Some of this has been done by regional groupings of countries such as the EU. Most of it has been done by the WTO. This makes trade cheaper and therefore more attractive to business.

Challenges

- To make globalization beneficial for developing countries.

- To ensure the sharing of benefits among all countries.

- To ensure the proper and strict functioning of the organization involving in trade rules .

- To ensure the minimization of growing disparities between rich and poor.

- To ensure the development of small scale industries.
- To ensure the safeguarding of workers

Globalisation and its impact

- Greater competition among producers both local and foreign producers has been of advantage to producers.
- Greater choice for consumers of improved quality and lower price of products.
- Living standard of people is changing to higher standards.
- Foreign investments have increased.
- New jobs have been created.
- Increased competition has encouraged top Indian companies to invest in newer technology and production methods and raise their production quality.
- Globalisation has enabled some large companies to emerge as multinational companies.
- Creates new opportunities for companies providing services particularly those involving Information Technology

Points to know

MNCs

Multinational companies like Nestle, Cargil foods, Reebook etc

Trade Barrier

Tax on import or export to control foreign trade.

Liberalisation

Removal of barriers from trade set by the government.

SEZs

Special economic zone is set up by the government to attract foreign companies to invest in India by providing infrastructure and giving five year tax waive off in the initial period.

PREVIOUS YEARS'
EXAMINATION QUESTIONS

▶ 1 Mark Questions

1. Which of the following is not a feature of a Multi-National Company?
   (a) It owns/controls production in more than one nation.
   (b) Its sets up factories where it is close to the markets.
   (c) It organizes production in complex ways.
   (d) It employs labour only from its own country.

   [TERM 2, 2011]

2. 'Cargill Foods' is the largest producer of which of the following in India?
   (a) Medicines
   (b) Asian Paints
   (c) Edible oil
   (d) Garments

   [TERM 2, 2012]

3. Which of the following is a 'barrier' on foreign trade?
   (a) Tax on import
   (b) Quality Control
   (c) Sales Tax
   (d) Tax on local trade

   [TERM 2, 2013]

4. Why do MNCs set up their offices and factories in those regions where they get cheap labour and other resources?

   [TERM 2, 2014]

▶ 3 Marks Questions

5. Explain any three advantages of globalization.

   [TERM 2, 2011]

6. What is a trade barrier? Why did the Indian Government put up trade barriers after Independence? Explain.

   [TERM 2, 2011]

7. How are M.N.Cs. spreading their production across countries? Explain with an example.

   [TERM 2, 2012]

8. What would happen if Government of India puts heavy tax on import of Chinese toys? Explain any three points.

   [TERM 2, 2012]

9. How do Multi-National Companies manage to keep the cost of production of their goods low? Explain with examples.

   [TERM 2, 2013]

10. "Foreign trade integrated the markets in different countries." Support the statement with arguments.

    [TERM 2, 2015]

11. How do Multi-National Corporations (MNCs) interlink production across countries? Explain with examples.

    [TERM 2, 2017]

▶ 5 Marks Questions

12. How have our markets been transformed in recent years? Explain with examples.

    [TERM 2, 2013]

13. "Globalization has been advantageous to consumers as well as to producers." Support the statement with suitable examples.

    [TERM 2, 2014]

14: "Globalization and greater competition among producers has been advantageous to consumers." Support the statement with examples.

    [TERM 2, 2015]

15. Describe the impact of globalization on Indian economy with examples.

    [TERM 2, 2016]

16. Analyze any five positive effects of Globalization on the Indian economy.

    [TERM 2, 2017]

17. What is liberalization? Describe any four effects of liberalisation on the Indian economy.

    [TERM 2, 2017]

18. How do we feel the impact of globalization on our daily life? Explain with examples.

    [DELHI 2018]

🔑 Solutions

1. (d) It employs labour only from its own country. [1]

2. (c) Edible oil [1]

3. (a) Tax on import [1]

4. MNCs set up their offices and factories in those regions where they get cheap labour and other resources to save costs and increase profit. [1]

5. Globalization is the process or trend of increasing interaction between people or companies on a world wide scale with the help of various means

    (i) It helped many large companies in India to turn into MNCs which are spreading their operations worldwide. Globalization has also created new opportunities for various sectors like IT. [1]

    (ii) There is a greater choice before the consumers who now enjoy products with improved quality at lower prices. [1]

    (iii) Globalization also broadened minds. It has led to the flow of ideas across national boundaries. [1]

6. Trade Barrier is a kind of restriction that has been set up on the foreign trade and foreign investment by the Indian government. Quotas and taxes on imports are used to regulate trade. Tax on imports is an example of trade barrier. It can be used to regulate foreign trade and decide what and how much should come into the country. [1 + 1]

After Independence, the Indian Government had to put the trade barriers on the foreign trade and investment. This was emphasized at that time so as to get rid of the foreign competition. During 1950s and 1960s, Inian industries were coming it up and foreign competition at that stage won't allow them to settle. Thus, India allowed imports of only essential items such as machinery, fertilizers, petroleum, etc. [1]

7. MNCs spread their production across countries through the following ways:

    (i) MNCs set up offices and factories for production in regions where they can get cheap labour and other resources. [1]

    (ii) MNCs set up production jointly with some of the local companies of these countries. [1]

    (iii) MNCs make capital and technology investments and buy up local companies and then expand production.

    For example: Cargill Foods, a very large American MNC, has bought over smaller Indian companies such as Parakh Foods. Parakh Foods had built a large marketing network in various parts of India, where its brand was well-reputed. Also, Parakh Foods had four oil refineries, whose control has now shifted to Cargill. Cargill is now the largest producer of edible oil in India. [1]

8. If the Government of India puts heavy tax on import of Chinese toys the following situations would likely occur:

    (i) The Chinese toys would become costly to the Indian customers and the imports from China would reduce. [1]

    (ii) The domestic toy making companies will have more opportunities to capture the larger share of domestic market. [1]

    (iii) The Chinese government would also bring up the trade barriers. [1]

9. A company that owns or controls production in more than one country is known as Multi-National Company (MNC).

    Multi-National companies manage to keep cost of production of their goods low by:

    (i) Setting up offices and factories for production in countries or places where cheap labor is easily available. USA companies outsourcing production to china. [1]

    (ii) Setting up trade and distribution centers in region close to their markets or stores. [1]

(iii) Setting up production in area where raw material or other resources are available at low cost with an objective to earn higher profits. [1]

10. Foreign trade is all about expanding the business beyond the domestic market. Many foreign traders expand their business in other countries too, e.g. Initially toys were quite expensive in India which was not affordable for every household. China took this as an advantage and brought toys in cheap prices and with different varieties people liked their products and China got a good response from Indian market where as Indian toy sellers get opposite response. So with the opening trade goods travel from one market to another. Choice of goods in the market rises and producers of two different countries get competent. Foreign trade thus results in connecting the markets. [1 + 1 + 1]

11. *(i)* MNCs buy local small companies to sell their products in large areas of the country. For example- Cargill foods bought Parakh, a smaller Indian company having a large marketing network in various part of India and became the largest producer of edible oil. [1]

(ii) Small industries produce raw material for these Multi-National Corporations which helps them to grow as well. [1]

(iii) Sometimes, money for advance investments for setting up new machines are provided by MNCs to increase the production. [1]

12. Our markets have been transformed in recent years in the following ways:

(i) The economy of our country has grown rapidly with the onset of LPG (Liberalisation, Privatisation and Globalisation) reforms in 1991. [1]

(ii) Earlier the production was specified to a particular place. In recent years, production is widely dispersed at several locations with interlinked communication. [1]

(iii) Foreign trade has increased rapidly, connecting and integrating the markets in different countries. [1]

(iv) In the recent years, technology in the areas of telecommunication, computers and internet has developed exponentially. Due to this, many companies have evolved providing services in the field of IT. [1]

(v) Globalization has enabled some large Indian companies like Tata Motors (auto-mobiles), Infosys (IT), Ranbaxy (medicine) to emerge as multi-national companies. [1]

13. Globalization has been advantageous to producers as-

(i) With investment in newer technology and production methods, producers have raised their production standards which have enabled them to produce good quality products and make them available in the international markets. This paves the way to boost exports. [1]

(ii) As the markets expand, the producers now have a large number of well-off buyers. [1]

(iii) Globalization has helped some large domestic companies to emerge as multinationals themselves. Ex. Tata Motors and Ranbaxy. [1]

Globalization has been advantageous to consumers as-

(i) The consumers can choose from a large and different variety of products with improved quality and lower prices. [1]

(ii) Since Globalization paves a way for international markets, people today enjoy much higher standard of living than was possible earlier. [1]

(iii) Globalization has led to the creation of new jobs.

14. Advantages of globalization to customers can be described in the following ways:

(i) The increased competition has led producers to provide products at comparatively cheaper rates. [1]

(ii) Consumers now have the option to select from a variety of products. [1]

(iii) It has increased capital flows, and comparatively greater amount of trade which helps the consumer to fulfill their development goals. [1]

(iv) It has played a vital role in generation of employment and an increase in movement of labour from one country to another by which opportunity and scope of employment increased. [1]

(v) Globalization promotes spread of innovative ideas and technology. [1]

(*vi*) It increases dependency of one country on another as a means of trade which contributes to world peace.

15. Globalization of the Indian economy has come a long way. MNCs have increased in India over the past 20 years, which means investing in India has been beneficial for them. [1]

They are expanding in different industries such as cell phones, automobiles, electronics, soft drinks, fast food or services such as banking in urban areas. [1]

Globalization has mostly had a good impact on Indian economy. Some Indian companies emerged as multidimensional themselves! E.g. Tata Motors, Infosys, Ranbaxy, Asian Paints etc. Because of the expansion of these companies chances of employment have increased on an exponential rate. [1 + 1]

Globalization has increased the opportunity of employment ,which paced the service sector in India . It helped in the upliftment of living standard of our citizens by providing wide range of goods and services at affordable prices. [1]

16. Following are the positive effects of globalization on the Indian economy:

(*i*) Foreign investment has increased over the past years. [1]

(*ii*) New opportunities are created by globalization for Indian companies especially those providing services like IT. [1]

(*iii*) Globalization has increased competition and it is beneficial for some of the top companies like Tata Motors and Infosys because it made them able to get benefit from this increased competition. [1]

(*iv*) The rate of unemployment has been reduced to an extent because because new job opportunities are created due to of globalization. [1]

(*v*) Services which were costly such as data entry, accounting, administrative tasks, and engineering now became cheap in India.[1]

17. Liberalization means the opening of the country for foreign investments and capitals. Countries use trade barriers to protect the domestic industries from foreign products. To protect local markets, countries resort to impose licenses, import quotas or voluntary export restraints. [1]

Following are the impacts of liberalization on the Indian economy:

(*i*) Foreign trade has increased. [1]

(*ii*) Foreign investment has increased. [1]

(*iii*) Countries are exchanging technologies that help in modernization of India. [1]

(*iv*) Better job opportunities are created, which solve the problem of unemployment. [1]

18. Impact of Globalization-

(*i*) Globalization and greater competition among producers has been beneficial to consumers. [1]

(*ii*) Greater choice before consumers like lexcury automobiles. [1]

(*iii*) Availability of standard quality products at lower price. [1]

(*iv*) Foreign investments have increased in many areas like cell phones, auto mobiles, electronics, soft drinks etc. [1]

(*v*) New job, have been created. [1]

(*vi*) Several Indian manufacturing units have shut down rendering many workers jobless.

MULTIPLE CHOICE QUESTIONS

1. Which authority in India has laid emphasis on the development of foreign trade in the five year plans?

(*a*) Election Commission

(*b*) Human Rights Commission

(*c*) Planning Commission

(*d*) All of the above

2. Which of these has been one major factor that has stimulated the globalisation process?

(*a*) Rapid improvement in information and communication technology

(*b*) People's fondness of moving abroad

(*c*) People's curiosity about foreign products

(*d*) Government policies

3. Where do MNCs setup their production units?

(*a*) At a place where they can produce their goods at a minimum cost

(*b*) Close to nature

(*c*) At a place where food is available in abundance

(*d*) At a place where water is available in abundance

4. What is the process of buying and selling goods and services between two or more than two countries is known as?

 (*a*) Foreign investment (*b*) Banking

 (*c*) Foreign Trade   (*d*) None of these

5. Which of these indicate that markets have been transformed in recent years?

 (*a*) Everyone goes to a shopping mall

 (*b*) We have a wide choice of goods and services before us

 (*c*) People do only online shopping

 (*d*) Prices of all goods have reduced significantly

Answer Keys

 1. (*c*)   2. (*a*)   3. (*a*)   4. (*c*)   5. (*b*)

FILL IN THE BLANKS

1. Globalisation and greater competition among producers has been advantageous to____________.

2. ____________________ of an economy means to free it from direct or physical controls imposed by the government.

3. A tax or duty to be paid on a particular class of imports or exports is called as __________.

4. MNCs are setting up their customer care centers in India due to availability of _________ labour.

5. Government has allowed ___________ in the labour laws to attract foreign investment.

Solutions

1. Consumers

2. Liberalisation

3. Tariff

4. Cheap

5. Flexibility

TRUE OR FALSE

1. The impact of globalisation has not been uniform.

2. Tata Motors is an foreign MNC.

3. WTO rules have forced the developing contries to remove trade barriers.

4. The Indian Government had lifted barriers on foreign trade and foreign investment after Independence

5. The idea behind the development of Special Economic Zones (SEZs) in India is to attract foreign investment

Solutions

1. True

2. False

3. True

4. False

5. True

CHAPTER 5

Consumer Rights

Summary

Why consumers movement

* Consumer movement in India took place due to various reasons as-
* Due to dissatisfaction
* Lack of legal system
* Exploitation in marketplace
* Unethical and unfair trade practices
* Rampant food shortage, hoarding, black marketing of goods and necessary food material.

Malpractice in ration shops

* In 1986 COPRA act was implemented by the Indian government to stop unethical trade practices

Consumer rights

* Right to safety.
* Right to be informed.
* Right to choose.
* Right to be heard.
* Right to seek redressal.
* Right to consumer education.
* Right to represent.

Strengthen consumer movements to protect consumer rights

* Consumer protection act on 24th of September enacted by Indian parliament.

* The consumer movement made some progress in terms of number of organized groups.
* The existing laws are not very clear on various issues to protect consumers.
* Consumer movements can be effective only with the consumers' active involvement.
* Consumer movements require the participation of one and all.

Points to know

ISI

ISI mark is a certification mark for industrial products in India. The mark certifies that a product confirms to the Indian Standard(IS), mentioned as CM/L-xxxxxxx on top of the mark, developed by the Bureau of Indian Standards (BIS)

AGMARK

AGMARK is a certification mark employed on agricultural products in India, assuring that they conform to a set of standards approved by the Directorate of Marketing and Inspection, an agency of the Government of India.

COPRA ACT

The act to promote and protect the interest of consumers. Three tier quasi-judiciary machinery at the district, state and national level is set up for the redressal of consumer disputes.

PREVIOUS YEARS'
EXAMINATION QUESTIONS

▶ 1 Mark Questions

1. When did the United Nations adopt the guidelines for consumer protection?
   - *(a)* 1983
   - *(b)* 1984
   - *(c)* 1985
   - *(d)* 1986

   [TERM 2, 2011]

2. Which one of the following logos is used for standardization of agricultural products?
   - *(a)* I.S.I.
   - *(b)* Hallmark
   - *(c)* Agmark
   - *(d)* I.S.0.

   [TERM 2, 2012]

3. In which one of the following courts a consumer should file a case if he/she is exploited in the market?
   - *(a)* Local court
   - *(b)* State court
   - *(c)* Supreme court
   - *(d)* Consumer court

   [TERM 2, 2012]

4. I.S.I mark can be seen on which of the following items?
   - *(a)* Jewellery
   - *(b)* Edible Oil
   - *(c)* Electrical appliances
   - *(d)* Cereals

   [TERM 2, 2013]

5. Suppose your parents want to purchase Gold jewellery along with you; then which logo will you look for on the jewellery?

   [TERM 2, 2015]

6. If any damage is done to a consumer by a trader, under which consumer right one can move to consumer court to get compensation.

   [TERM 2, 2016]

▶ 3 Marks Questions

7. Explain any three factors which gave birth to the Consumer Movement in India.

   [TERM 2, 2011]

8. "A consumer has the right to get compensation depending on the degree of the damage." Support this statement with an example.

   [TERM 2, 2011]

9. How do we participate in the market as producers and consumers? Explain with the help of three examples.

   [TERM 2, 2013]

10. Explain with an example how you can use the right to seek redressal.

    [TERM 2, 2015]

11. "Rules and regulations are required for the protection of the consumers in the market place". Justify the statement with arguments.

    [TERM 2, 2016]

12. How are consumers exploited in the market place? Explain.

    [TERM 2, 2016]

13. "The consumer movement arose out of dissatisfaction of the consumers". Justify the statement with arguments.

    [TERM 2, 2016]

14. How can consumer awareness be spread among consumers to avoid exploitation in the market place? Explain any three ways.

    [DELHI 2018]

▶ 4 Marks Questions

15. Explain any four ways in which consumers are exploited in the market..

    [TERM 2, 2012]

▶ 5 Marks Questions

16. Why are rules and regulations required for the protection of the consumers, in the market place? Explain with examples.

    [TERM 2, 2013]

17. Why are rules and regulations required in the market place? Explain.

    [TERM 2, 2014]

🔑 Solutions

1. *(c)* 1985   [1]
2. *(c)* Agmark   [1]
3. *(d)* Consumer court   [1]
4. *(c)* Electrical appliances   [1]
5. To buy Gold jewellery, one should check for a logo with of Hallmark. [1]
6. Consumers have the 'Right to seek redressal' under which consumers can move to consumer court to get compensation. [1]
7. The three factors which gave birth to the Consumer Movement in India are:

(*i*) In India, the Consumer movement arose out of "Consumer Dissatisfaction". It is like a "social force" that originated with the necessity of protecting and promoting the interests of consumers against unethical and unfair trade practices. [1]

(*ii*) Frequent Food shortage, hoarding, black marketing, adulteration of food products, high prices, etc. which led to inflation. [1]

(*iii*) Lack of Legal system for consumers that led to their exploitation at market places. [1]

8. Consumers have a right to seek redressal against unfair trade practices and exploitation. If any damage is done to a consumer, he/she has the right to get compensation depending on the degree of damage. There is need to provide an easy and effective public system by which this can be done. Under COPRA (Consumer Protection Act 1986), three-tier quasi-judicial machinery at the district state and national levels was set up for redressal of consumer disputes. Thus the Act has enabled us as consumers to have the right to represent in the consumer courts. [1 + 1 + 1]

9. The consumers participate in market by purchasing various good and services. However a Producer work in different sectors of economy such as, Industry, Agriculture and service sector. [1.5]

For examples:

(*i*) Honey produced by Honey bee is a product which is consumed by humans (consumers). [0.5]

(*ii*) Both producers and consumers are mainstay of the market. [0.5]

(*iii*) Clothes supplied in the market by different clothing manufacturers, are purchased by people. [0.5]

(*iv*) Seller sells vegetables and fruits in the market which is further bought by the consumers.

10. Consumer have been provided by the right to seek redressal against unfair trade practices and exploitation. If any damage is done to a consumer, then the consumer has the right to get compensation to recover the damage by filing case in consumer court. For example if I buy gold jewellery and it turns out to be fake, I can approach the consumer court and seek compensation. [1 + 1]

11. Rules and regulations are required to protect consumers in a marketplace, because marketplaces have so many stakeholders and traders or service providers can be unscrupulous at times. When they don't provide a product or service that the consumer has paid for, the consumers need a way to get compensated. For that these rules are needed, which currently are enforced through consumer courts. [1 + 1 + 1]

12. Given below are a few situations which come in the list of consumer exploitation:

(*i*) When shopkeepers weigh less than what they should or when traders add charges that were not mentioned before, or when adulterated/defective goods are sold. [1]

(*ii*) Many times a company tries to sell its items under different schemes and passes wrong information just to convince the consumer. [1]

(*iii*) Sometimes shopkeepers try to sell a product for more than the MRP (Maximum Retail Price) to the consumer who seems less educated to them especially in the rural areas. [1]

13. Consumer exploitation is very easy to see in private sectors e.g. Hospitals, Jobs, lend dealing and many more.

Earlier there was no rule in the favor of consumer so they could not get proper justices in the reversal of what they suffered. [1]

People are getting more into trouble as well as in huge loss due to the different negligence of the medical treatment and many more. Due to all of these issues consumers were dissatisfied and to help them these rules were made after a consumer movement started asking for such rules. Consumers can use these rules and get the compensation in the reversal of their loss. [1 + 1]

14. Consumer awareness among consumers to avoid exploitation-

(*i*) The formation of various organizations such as Consumers Forum or Consumers Protection Council. [1]

(*ii*) To guide consumers on how to file cases in the Consumer Court. [1]

(*iii*) Consumers' education to be promoted through advertisement/mass campaign/ publicity against malpractices of traders. [1]

(*iv*) By writing articles/ holding exhibition/ rallies on relevent topics.

(*v*) Strict laws to be enforced in market places.

15. Consumers are exploited in the market in the following ways:

    (*i*) Shopkeepers and traders use unfair trade practices such as weighing less than they should. [1]

    (*ii*) Traders add hidden charges to goods and indulge in adulteration and hoarding of goods. [1]

    (*iii*) Large companies manipulate the markets with ample resources like providing the consumer with distorted or incomplete information through the media. [1]

    (*iv*) Taking advantage of the fact that consumers are scattered and numerous while on the other hand large corporations are few and powerful, by skewing the market against the consumers. [1]

16. In the market place, individual consumers often find themselves in a weak position. Rules and regulations are required for the protection of such consumers. Rules and regulations are also required, as: [1]

    (*i*) The sellers often try to sell products or services of low quality, sell adulterated/ defective goods, cheat in weighing out goods, and add excess charges over the retail price. [1]

    (*ii*) Companies use media and false advertising to pass on false information about their product. This is done to attract consumers. [1]

    (*iii*) Powerful producers often neglect the concerns of small and individual consumers. Also, they create monopoly in the market and pull down small scale sellers. [1]

    (*iv*) Whenever there is a complaint regarding a good or service that had been bought, the seller tries to shift all the responsibility on the buyer. [1]

17. Rules and regulations are required in the marketplace such that exploitation doesn't take place. Often individual consumers find themselves in a weak position. There are various ways in which exploitation can happen. [1]

    (*i*) Unfair trade practices: Goods sold in the market by the traders are sometimes not properly measured or correctly weighed and at times are followed unfair trade practices such as when shopkeepers add charges that were not mentioned before. [1]

    (*ii*) Unfair prices: Some traders charge a price higher than the prescribed retail price. They do not provide consumers cash memos for their purchase. [1]

    (*iii*) Adulterated goods: Fake or duplicate goods are often sold in the name of genuine parts or goods. Selling goods of substandard quality is also done. Medicines are sold even after their date of expiry. Deficient and defective home appliances are sold by duping the customer. This may result in serious injuries or health problems for consumers. [1]

    (*iv*) False Claims: Whenever there is a complaint regarding a good or service that had been bought, the seller tries to shift all the responsibility on to the buyer. [1]

FILL IN THE BLANKS

1. _____________ is the process of mixing pure and impure products in order to attain profits.

2. Consumer awareness is essential to avoid _____________ in the market place

3. The _____________ logo ensures the quality of gold.

4. COPRA stands for _____________________.

5. Consumers have the _____________ against unfair trade practices and exploitation.

Solutions

1. Adulteration

2. Exploitation

3. Hallmark

4. Consumer Protection Act

5. Right to seek redressal

CBSE
Solved Paper 2019

Social Science
Class X

Time : 3 hrs   MM : 80

General Instructions

(i) The question paper is divided into four sections – Section A, Section B, Section C and Section D.

(ii) The question paper has 26 questions in all.

(iii) All questions are compulsory.

(iv) Marks are indicated against each question.

(v) Questions from serial number 1 to 7 are very short answer type questions. Each question carries one mark.

(vi) Questions from serial number 8 to 18 are 3 marks questions. Answer of these questions should not exceed 80 words each.

(vii) Questions from serial number 19 to 25 are 5 marks questions. Answers of these questions should not exceed 100 words each.

(viii) Question number 26 is a map question. It has 5 marks with two parts 26(A) and 26(B). 26(A) from History (2 marks) and 26(B) from Geography (3 marks). After completion attach the map inside your answer book.

SECTION A

1. How had hand printing technology introduced in Japan? (1)

OR

How had translation process of novels into regional languages helped to spread their popularity?

2. Interpret the contribution of French in the economic development of Mekong delta region. (1)

OR

Interpret the concept of 'liberalisation' in the field of economic sphere during the nineteenth century in Europe.

3. What may be a goal of landless rural labourers regarding their income? (1)

OR

What may be a goal of prosperous farmer of Punjab.

4. How can democratic reforms be carried out by political parties? (1)

5. How is over–irrigation responsible for land degradation in Punjab? (1)

OR

How is cement industry responsible for land degradation?

6. Distinguish between 'primary' and secondary sectors. (1)

7. Explain the importance of formal sector loans in India. (1)

Section B

8. Describe any three main features of 'Rabi crop season'. (3)

OR

Describe any three main features of 'Kharif crop season'.

9. How had Napoleonic code exported to the regions under French control? Explain with examples. (3)

OR

Explain with examples three barriers that are responsible to economic growth in Vietnam.

10. How had the Imperial State in China been the major producer of printed material for a long time? Explain with examples (3)

OR

How had novels been easily available to the masses in Europe during nineteenth century? Explain with examples.

11. Analyse the impact of 'water scarcity'. (3)

12. "Consequences of environmental degradation do not respect national or state boundaries" Justify the statement (3)

13. Why is the 'tertiary sector' becoming important in India? Explain any three reasons. (3)

OR

How do we count various goods and services for calculating gross domestic product (G.D.P) of a country? Explain with example.

14. Explain any three functions of opposition political parties. (3)

15. How can consumers use their 'Right to seek redressal' Explain with example. (3)

16. "The assertion of social diversities in a democratic country is very normal and can be healthy" Justify the statement with arguments. (3)

OR

"Social divisions affect politics" Examine the statement.

17. "Women still lag much behind men in India despite some improvements since independence" Analyse the statement. (3)

18. Describe the importance of formal sources of credit in the economic development. (3)

OR

Describe the bad effects of informal sources of credit on borrowers.

SECTION C

19. "Roadways still have an edge over railways in India." Support the statement with example.
$(5 \times 1 = 5)$

20. Compare the situation of Belgium and Sri Lanka considering their location, size and cultural aspects. $(1 + 1 + 3 = 5)$

OR

How is the idea of power sharing emerged? Explain different forms that have common arrangements of power sharing.

21. Explain five types of 'Industrial pollution'. (5)

22. Who had organized the Dalits into the 'Depressed classes Association' in 1930? Describe his achievements.

OR (5)

Define the term 'Civil Disobedience Movement'. Describe the participation of rich and poor peasant communities in the 'Civil Disobedience Movement'

23. "Indian trade had played a crucial role in the late nineteenth century world economy" Analyze the statement. $(5 \times 1 = 5)$

OR

"Series of changes affected the pattern of industrialization in India by the early twentieth century" Analyze the statement.

OR

"Industrialization had changed the form of urbanization in the modern period." Analyze the statement with special reference of London.

24. Describe any five factors that make democracy is a better form of government than other alternatives. $(5 \times 1 = 5)$

25. Explain any five facilities available in the special economic zones developed by the Central and State Governments to attract foreign investment. $(5 \times 1 = 5)$

SECTION D

26. (A) Two features A and B are marked on the given political outline map of India. Identify these features with the help of the following information and write their correct names on the lines marked near them. $(1 \times 3 = 3)$

    (a) The place where the Indian National Congress Session was held.

    (b) The city where Jallianwalla Bagh incident took place.

  (B) Locate and lanel any three of the following with appropriate symbols on the same given outline political map of India. $(1 \times 3 = 3)$

    (i) Kalpakkam   –   Nuclear Power Plant

    (ii) Vijayanagar   –   Iron and Steel Plant

    (iii) Noida   –   Software Technology Park

    (iv) Paradeep   –   Sea Port

    (v) Sardar Sarovar   –   Dam

Solution

SECTION A

1. Buddhist missionaries from China introduced hand-printing technology into Japan around AD 768-770. The oldest Japanese book, printed in AD 868, is the Buddhist 'Diamond Sutra'. Containg six sheets of text and woodcut illustrations. Pictures were printed on textiles, playing cards and paper money which made publishing very interesting. (1)

OR

English novels translated into regional Indian languages were initially not very popular as the Indian people could not relate the stories and characters to their own lives. But translation process of novels bring different spoken languages of people closer. These novels produce the sense of a shared world between diverse people in a nation. Novels also bring understanding of different cultures and values. (1)

2. The French began by building canals and draining lands in the Mekong delta to increase cultivation to bring about economic development. They used labour for construction of irrigation facilities to improve rice cultivation, built infrastructure and transportation facilities for the export of agricultural produce. (1)

OR

The term 'liberalism' is derived from the Latin word 'liber' means free. In the economic sphere. liberalism stood for the freedom of markets and the abolition of state–imposed restrictions on the movement of goods and capital. (1)

3. Development goals for, landless rural labourers regarding their income would be: (1)

    (i)   To get more days of work and better wages.

    (ii) To get quality education for their children.

    (iii) No social discrimination

OR

Development goals for prosperous farmers of Punjab would be (1)

    (i)   Low price of food grains.

    (ii) Assured high family income through higher support prices for their crops.

    (iii) Hardworking and cheap labourers.

4. Political parties need to have strong internal democracy, avoid dynastic succession, money and muscle power and by offering meaningful choice to the voters which could lead to democratic reforms. (1)

5. Water is very important for the growth of plant but excessive irrigation of field leads to water logging of soil. Therefore, over–irrigation is responsible for land degradation due to water–logging which leads to increase in salinity and alkalinity in the soil. (1)

OR

Excessive mining of limestone, silica and gypsum which are used as raw material for cement industry leads to land degradation. It later on settles down in the surrounding areas, affecting infiltration of water and crop cultivation. (1)

6. **Primary Sectors:** The primary sector is also called agriculture sector. It constitutes the backbone of our economy and the major sources of employment. Primary activity which is involved with the production or extraction of natural resources. (1/2)

   Secondary Sectors: Secondary sector involves use of natural goods and transform them into something more valuable by the manufacturing process. It is also called industrial sector. (1/2)

7. Importance of formal sector loans in India:

   (i)   The rate of interest charged on formal sector is lower than of informal sources of credit. (1/2)

   (ii) Reserve Bank of India supervises their function. (1/2)

Section B

8. There are three main features of 'Rabi crop reason'

   (i)   Rabi crops are grown in winter from October to December and harvested in summer from April to June. (1)

   (ii) Some Rabi crops are wheat, barley, peas, gram and mustard. (1)

   (iii) These crops are grown in large parts of India such as Punjab, Haryana and Himachal Pradesh etc. (1)

OR

There are three main features of 'Kharif crop season'

   (i)   Kharif crops are grown with the onset of monsoon and harvested in September–October. (1)

   (ii) Some important crops are paddy. maize, jowar, bajra, toor, moong, urad, cotton etc. (1)

   (iii) Rice is an important Kharif crop. Some important rice growing regions are Assam, West Bengal, Coastal region of Odisha, Andhra Pradesh, Tamilnadu etc. (1)

9. The civil code of 1804, known as the Napoleonic code.

   These codes were the revolutionary principles of administration and were exported to the regions under French control. (1)

   For example, in the Dutch Republic in Switzerland, Italy and Germany. Napoleon simplified administrative divisive, abolished the feudal system and freed peasants from serfdom and manorial dues. (1)

   Peasants, workers and new businessman enjoyed a new–found freedom. Businessmen and small–scale producers of goods in particular, began to realise that uniform laws, standardised weights and measures and a common national currency would facilitate the movement and exchange of goods and capital from one region to another. (1)

OR

According to an influential writer and policy–maker Paul Bernard, several barriers to economic growth in Vietnam such as:

   (i)   High population level in Vietnam proved to be and obstacle to economic growth. (1)

   (ii) Low agricultural productivity was another barrier that hindered the economic growth. (1)

   (iii) Excessive indebtedness among the peasants that did not promote economic growth in Vietnam. (1)

   (iv) The French colonialists did little to industrialise Vietnam and in the rural areas, landlordism spread and the standard of living declined. (1)

10. The earliest print technique developed in China. The imperial state in China was a large bureaucratic system, that sponsored the printing technique by the way of conducting examinations. China possessed a huge bureaucratic system which recruited its personnel through civil service examinations. Textbooks for this examination were printed in vast numbers under the sponsorship of the imperial state. (2)

From the sixteenth century. the number of examinations candidates went up and that increased the volume of print which node the Imperial state in China a major producer of printed material for a long time. (2)

OR

The Novel was one of the first mass–produced items to be sold in Europe. Novels created a sense of belonging on the basis of ones language. They dealt with the life of common people and they were cheap. Publishing markets helped in more sell and production of novels which was available to the masses in Europe during nineteenth century. (2)

Technological improvements in printing brought down the price of books and innovations in marketing led to expanded sale. In France, publishers found that they could make super profits by hiring out novels by the hour. (1)

11. Water is an essential resource for humans. Water scarcity is indeed the outcome of large and growing population. Humans require water for their various activities and more the number of people more the consumption. Water scarcity may lead to following impacts:

(i) Ground water level will decline. (1)

(ii) It may adversely affect water availability that shall impact agriculture and industry. (1)

(iii) Food grain production will be affected which may affect food security of the country. (1)

12. It is true that environmental degradation do not respect national or state boundaries. It has international and global affects because our future is linked together through common environmental and ecological system. Global warming, acid rain etc are the issues that cannot be tackled by one nation. It is a global concern. (2)

For example, if Indian Thermal power plants are causing massive air pollution, it affects our neighbouring countries like Pakistan, Bangladesh, Sri Lanka and others as well. Similarly, deforestation in Brazil has caused disturbance in rainfall pattern throughout South America. (1)

13. Importance of Tertiary Sector in India:

(i) In any country, several services such as hospitals, educational institutions, post and telegraph services, defence, transport, banks etc, are required. These can be considered as basic services. (1)

(ii) In development of agriculture and industry leads to the development of services such as transport, trade, storage etc. Greater the development of the primary and secondary sectors, more would be the demand for such services. (1)

(iii) With the increase in income levels, certain sections of people start demanding many more services like tourism better educational facilities, communication services etc thereby, giving a boost to the tertiary sector. (1)

OR

The various goods and services are counted on the basis of the value of each goods or services, not on the basis of actual numbers.

(i) The value of final goods and services produced in each sector during a particular year provides the total production of the sector for that year. The sum of all the three sector's production within a country is known as Gross Domestic Product (G.D.P) of a country. (1½)

(ii) For example, a farmer sells wheat to a flour mill for ₹ 18/kg. The mill grinds the wheat and sells the flour to a biscuit company for ₹ 20/kg. The biscuit company uses flour, sugar and oil to make the packets of biscuits. It sells biscuits in the market ₹ 45/packet. Now, biscuits are the final goods. So, only the value of all final goods and services produced within a country during a particular year is counted as GDP. (1½)

14. Those parties that lose in the elections play the role of opposition to the parties in power. There are three functions of opposition political parties:

(i) By voicing different views and criticizing government for its failures of programmes and wrong policies and their implementation. (1)

(ii) It keeps people aware of wrong policies and programmes of the government. (1)

(iii) It provides alternatives to choose from as it voices those views which are different from the party in power and helpful for the peoples of that country. (1)

15. **Right to Seek Redressal** : Consumers have the right to seek redressal against unfair trade practices and exploitation. If any damage is done to a consumer, he or she has the right to get a compensation depending on the degree of damage. There is a need to provide an easy and effective public system by which this can be done. (2)

For example, Deepak had sent a money order to his village for his daughter's marriage. The money did not reach to his daughter at the time when she needed it nor did it reach month's later. Therefore, Deepak can filed a case in the district level consumer court and exercised right to seek redressal. (1)

16. Social diversities in a democratic country is very normal and healthy. It divides similar people from one another but also unite very different people belonging to different social groups. (1)

The assertion of social diversities in a country does not require to be seen as a source of danger.

(i) In a democracy, political expression of social divisions is very normal and can be healthy. This allows different disadvantaged and marginal social groups to express their grievances and get the government to attend these. (1)

(ii) This leads to strengthening of a democracy. People who feel marginalized, deprived and discriminated, have to fight against the injustices. Such a fight often takes the democratic path, voicing their demands in a peaceful and constitutional manner and seeking a fair position through elections. (1)

OR

All social differences and diversities do not lead to social divisions. A combination of social divisions and politics can be really dangerous. A democracy involves competition among various political parties. The cases of Sri Lanka and Yugoslavia are clear examples.

While political competition along religious and ethnic lines led to the disintegration of Yugoslavia into six independent countries, the situation in Sri Lanka is also very explosive. Social divisions between the Sinhalese and Tamils are affecting politics of the country and have brought it in a civil war situation. (2)

In a democracy, political parties would talk to these divisions, ask for votes on this basis, make different promises to the people and talk of politics to redress the grievances of the disadvantaged communities. (1)

17. Women still lag much behind men in India despite some improvements since independence. There are some factors to analyse the given statement:

(i) Literacy Rate : The literacy rate among women is only 64.6% compared with 80.9% among men. A smaller proportion of girls go for higher studies.

(ii) Low Sex – Ratio : Parents in India prefer to have sons. They also find ways to abort the girl child before she is born. Such sex–selective abortion has resulted in a decline in female child sex–ratio.

(iii) Political Representation : In India, women representation in legislature has been very low, while in America, England etc, women are given seats in Parliament even though there are male members.

18. Formal sources of credit are beneficial in the sense that they provide credit at reasonable rates without any undue exploitative practices as faced under informal sources of credit. Importance of formal source of credit:

   (i)   The formal source of credit includes loan from banks and co–operatives.   (½)

   (ii)   RBI supervises the functioning of formal sources of loans.   (½)

   (iii) RBI ensures that loans are given not only to the profit – making business man and traderss but also to small– cultivators, small–scale industries, small borrowers etc.   (½)

   (iv) Banks and co–operative societies need to lend more. This would lead to higher incomes and many people could then borrow cheaply for a variety of needs. They could grow crops, do business, set up small– industries etc.   (½)

   (v)   Cheap and affordable credit by the formal sector is crucial for the country's development.   (½)

OR

Informal sources of credit are the moneylenders, traders, employers, relatives and friends. There are some bad effects of informal sources of credit:

   (i)   The borrowers tend to find themselves in a debt–trap   (½)

   (ii)   The rate of interest can be really high as it depends on the wishes of the lender.   (½)

   (iii) There is no organization to supervise its lending activities.   (½)

   (iv) The cost to the borrower becomes much higher that leads to less incomes.   (½)

Section C

19. In India, roadways have preceded railways. They still have an edge over railways in view of the ease with which they can be built and maintained. The growing importance of road transport vis–a–vis rail transport is rooted in the following reasons:

   (i)   Construction cost of roads is much lower than that of railways lines.   (1)

   (ii)   Roads can traverse comparatively more dissected and undulating topography.   (1)

   (iii) Roads can negotiate higher gradients of slopes and as such can traverse mountains such as the Himalayas.   (1)

   (iv) Road ways tend to provide door to door service, therefore the cost of loading and unloading is much lower.   (1)

   (v)   Road transport is economical in transportation of few persons and small amount of goods over short distances.   (1)

20. Belgium is a small country in Europe while Sri Lanka is an island nation is Asia. In Sri Lanka and Belgium, there were ethnic conflicts for power on the basis of the language.   (1)

Belgium has a population of a little over one crore, about half the population of Haryana. whereas Sri Lanka has about two crore people, about the same as in Haryana.   (1)

People of Belgium practice Christianity while people of Sri Lanka follow Buddhism. Out of Belgium's total population. 59% lives in Flemish region and speaks Dutch language and another 40% lives in Wallonia region and speak French while Sri Lankan social groups are Sinhala – speakers and Tamil speakers.

In Belgium, the Dutch community has advantage of its numeric majority and could forced its will on the French and German speaking population. In Sri Lanka, the Sinhala community enjoyed an even bigger majority and could imposed its will on the entire country.   (3)

OR

It is true that the idea of power sharing emerged in opposition to the notions of undivided political power. In modern democracies, power sharing arrangements can take many forms.

Power is shared among different organs of government such as legislature, executive and Judiciary Power can be shared among governments at different levels. A general government for the entire country and governments at the provincial or regional level. (2)

Power may also be shared among different social groups such as the religious and linguistic groups. 'Community government' in Belgium is a good example of this arrangement.

Power sharing arrangements can also be seen in the way political parties, pressure groups and movements control or influence those in power. In a democracy, the citizens must have freedom to choose among various contenders for power. (3)

21. Although industries contributes significantly to India's economic growth and development, the increase in pollution of land, water, air, noise and resulting degradation of environment that they have caused cannot be overlooked.

(i) **Air Pollution :** It is caused by the presence of high proportion of undesirable gases, such as sulphur dioxide and carbon monoxide. Air–borne particulate materials contain both solid and liquid particles like dust, sprays mist and smoke. (1)

(ii) **Water Pollution :** It is caused by organic and inorganic industrial wastes and affluents discharged into rivers. The main culprits in this regard are paper, pulp, chemical textile and dyeing, petroleum refineries, tanneries and electroplating industries that let out dyes, detergents, acids, salts and heavy metals like lead and mercury pesticides (1)

(iii) **Thermal Pollution :** Thermal pollution of water occurs when hot water from factories and thermal plants is drained into rivers and ponds before cooling. (1)

(iv) **Noise Pollution :** Noise pollution not only results in hearing impairment, increased heart rate and blood pressure among other physiological effects. (1)

(v) **Pollution from Nuclear Power Plants :** It causes cancers, birth defects etc, which is life – threatening. (1)

22. Dr. B.R. Ambedkar sought reservation for dalits in educational institutions. For him, political empowerment was the only way of achieving upliftment for dalits. Dr. B.R. Ambedkar and other dalit leaders demanded separate electorates for the depressed classes in order to protect their interest and extending political power to them. Dr. B.R. Ambedkar formed the depressed classes Association in 1930 and demanded the following:

(i) To bring about political empowerment of the depressed classes. (½)

(ii) To have reserved seats in the educational institutions. (½)

(iii) He also mooted the idea of reservation for dalits which brought him in clash with Gandhi. (1)

(iv) Demanded separate electorates and bring about social justice. (1)

(v) It was with Ambedkar's constant persuasion which was eventually resolved with the Poona Pact of 1932, which provided for reserved seats in Provincial and central Legislatures for them. (1)

(vi) He also launched Kaiaram temple movement that sought entry of dalit in the Brahmin dominated temples. (1)

OR

The civil Disobedience Movement led by M.K. Gandhi, in the year 1930 was an important milestone in the history of Indian Nationalism, it began with Gandhi's famous salt march of about 240 miles from Sabarmati Ashram in Ahmedabad to the costal town of dandi in Gujarat.

(i) Civil Disobedience Movement was one of the most significant movement launched by Mahatma Gandhi where people were asked not only to refuse co–operation but also to break colonial laws. (1)

(ii) The rich peasants became enthusiastic supporters of the civil disobedience movement participating in the boycott programmes. (1)

(iii) For the rich peasants, the fight was a struggle against high revenue. (1)

(iv) The poorer peasants were not just interested in the lowering of the revenue demand but also wanted the unpaid rent to the landlords to be remitted. (1)

(v) Apprehensive of raising issues that might upset rich peasants, the congress was unwilling to support 'no rent' campaigns in most places. (1)

23. Indian trade has played a crucial role in the late nineteenth century world economy which can be explained as:

(i) Export of raw cotton from India increased from 5 % to 35 %. (½)

(ii) Indigo used for dyeing clothes was another important export for many decades. (½)

(iii) Opium shipment to china grew rapidly to become India's single largest export. (1)

(iv) Money earned through the sale of opium was used to finance its tea and other imports from china.

(1)

(v) Britain had a 'Trade Surplus' with India Britain used this surplus to balance trade deficit with other countries resulting in multilateral settlement. (1)

(vi) Food grains and raw material export from India to Britain and rest of the world increased. (1)

OR

A series of changes affected the pattern of industrialization in India by the early twentieth century due to various reasons. They are

(i) **Swadeshi Movement :** Swadeshi and Boycott movement provided impetus to Indian industries leading to higher demand of Indian goods. (1)

(ii) **Formation of Business Association :** Formation of FICCI also helped them to protect their collective interest against increasing tariff. (1)

(iii) **Decline of Indian Goods to China :** It was due to production of cotton goods rather than yarn.

(1)

(iv) **Impact of World War I:** World war I created a different situation where import to India declined as the British factories were producing to meet the war needs. (1)

(v) At the same time, Indian factories were called upon to supply war needs such as jute bags, clothes and shoes etc. (1)

Hence these changes resulted in creation of resilient and sustainable industrial growth to meet the domestic demand.

OR

Industrialization changed the form of urbanization in the modern period.

(v) Road transport is economical in t

(i) The early industrial cities of Britains such as Leeds and Manchester attracted large number of migrants to the textile mills set up in the late 18th century. **(1)**

(ii) London was a colossal city and its population expanded four–fold from 1 million to 4 million, as the Industrial revolution attracted more and more people. **(1)**

(iii) The city of London was a powerful magnet for migrant populations, even though it did not have large factories. **(1)**

(iv) Apart from the London Dock yards, five major types of industries employed large numbers: Clothing and footwear, wood and furniture, metals and engineering, printing and stationery and precision products such as surgical instruments, watches and objects of precious metals. **(1)**

(v) During the first world war (1914–18), London began manufacturing motor cars and electrical goods and the number of large factories increased until they accounted for nearly one–third of all jobs in the city. **(1)**

24. Democracy is a better form of government than other alternatives because:

(i) **Promotes Equality Among Citizens:** It promotes equality among people by providing equal rights for everyone. It brings social, economic and political equality among all. **(1)**

(ii) **Enhances the Dignity of the Individual :** Democracy provides rights for the protection of disadvantageous group where by dignity of every individual irrespective of any differences is upheld. **(1)**

(iii) **Improves the quality of decision making :** Decision making takes place through debate, discussion and deliberation leading to quality decision making. **(1)**

(iv) **Provides a method to resolve conflict :** Conflict and disagreement is obvious in multi–cultural society but these conflicts can be resolved through constitutional and democratic means. **(1)**

(v) **Allows room to correct mistakes :** Democracy enshrines a system of check and balance which allows timely rectification of mistakes if any. **(1)**

(vi) Democracy provides an accountable and responsible government. **(1)**

25. There are five facilities available in the Special Economic Zones developed by the central and state governments to attract foreign investment:

(i) Single window clearance for setting up of a Special Economic Zone. **(1)**

(ii) Exemption from Import duty. **(1)**

(iii) Five years tax holiday (Income Tax). **(1)**

(iv) Liberalizsation in labour laws and availability of skilled and semi–skilled labour forces. **(1)**

(v) Will connected with the network of transport and communication. **(1)**

Section D

26. (a)   (2×1=2)

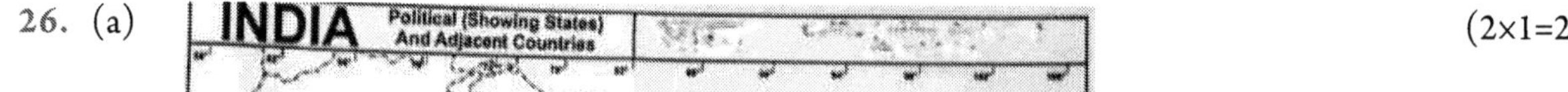

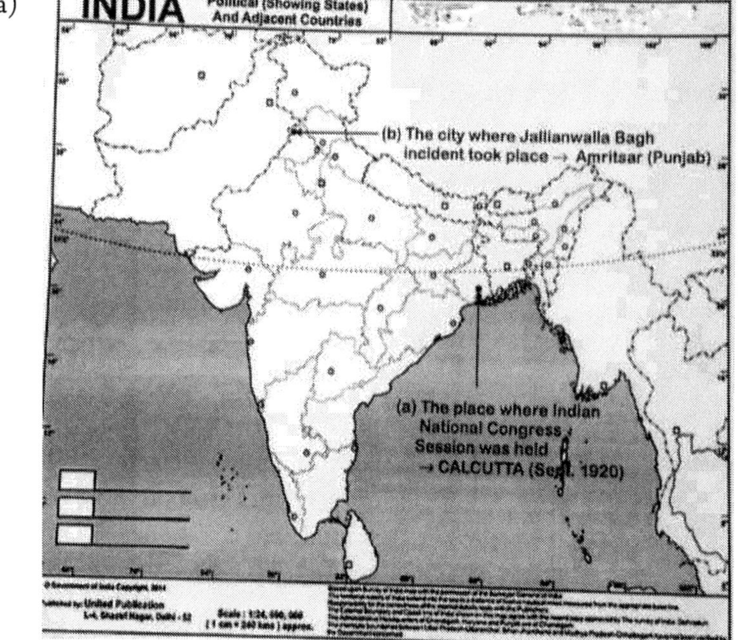

(b)   (3×1=3)

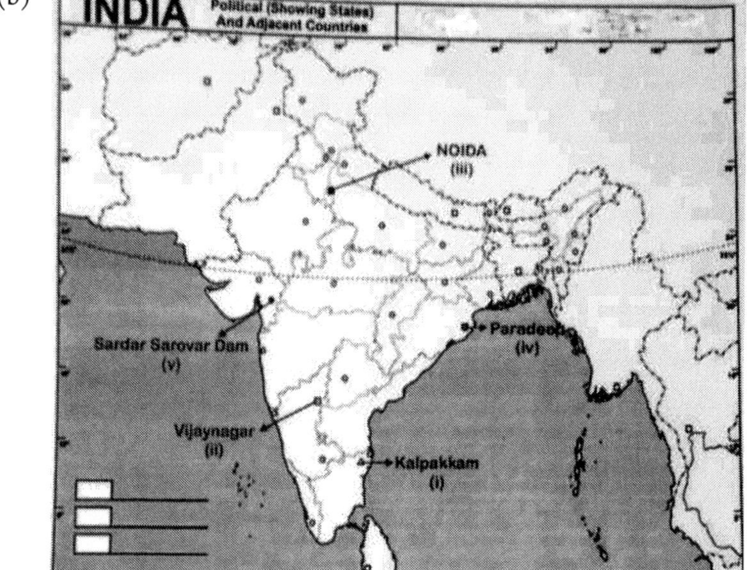

CBSE
Solved Paper 2020

Social Science
Class X

<table><tr><td>Time : 3 hrs</td><td>Maximum Marks : 80</td></tr></table>

General Instructions

Read the following instructions very carefully and strictly follow them :

(i) The question paper comprises **four** Sections **A, B, C** and **D**. There are 35 questions in the question paper. **All** questions are compulsory.

(ii) **Section A** – all questions no. **1** to **20** are very short answer type questions, carrying **1 mark** each.

(iii) **Section B** – question no. **21** to **28** are short answer type questions, carrying **3 marks** each. Answer of each question should not exeed **80 words**.

(iv) **Section C** – question no. **29** to **34** are long answer type questions, carrying **5 marks** each. Answer of each question should not exceed **120 words**.

(v) **Section D** – question no. **35** is map based carrying **6 marks** with two parts **35a** from History (2 marks) and **35b** from Geography (**4 marks**).

(vi) Answer should be brief and to the point, also the above word limit be adhered to as far as possible.

(vii) There is no overall choice in the question paper. However, an internal choice has been provided in few questions. Only one of the choices in such questions have to be attempted.

(viii) Attach **MAP** along with your answer book.

(ix) In addition to this, separate instructions are given with each section and question, wherever necessary.

SECTION A

1. Name the Civil Code of 1804 which established equality before law and secured the right to property in France. (1)

2. Who among the following wrote the Vande Mataram ?
   (a) Rabindranath Tagore
   (b) Bankim Chandra Chattopadhyay
   (c) Abindranath Tagore
   (d) Dwarkanath Tagore (1)

3. Which one of the following was NOT the reason for the popularity of scientific ideas among the common people in eighteenth century Europe ?

   (a) Printing of ideas of Isaac Newton

   (b) Development of printing press

   (c) Interest of people in science and reason

   (d) Traditional aristocratic groups supported it   (1)

4. Name the two hostile groups of Second World War.   (1)

OR

Name the two industrialists of Bombay who built huge industrial empires during nineteenth century.   (1)

5. Which among the following best signifies the idea of liberal nationalism of nineteenth century Europe ?

   (a) Emphasis on social justice

   (b) State planned socio-economic system

   (c) Freedom for individual and equality before law

   (d) Supremacy of State oriented nationalism.   (1)

6. "When France sneezes, the rest of Europe catches cold". Who among the following said this popular line ?

   (a) Guiseppe Mazzini   (b) Matternich

   (c) Otto Von Bismarck   (d) Guiseppe Garibaldi   (1)

7. Certain events are given below. Choose the appropriate chronological order :

   1. Coming of Simon Commission to India

   2. Demand of Purna Swaraj in Lahore Session of INC.

   3. Government of India Act, 1919

   4. Champaran Satyagraha

   Choose the correct option :

   (a) $3-2-4-1$ (b) $1-2-4-3$

   (c) $2-3-1-4$ (d) $4-3-1-2$ (1)

8. Complete the following table with appropriate terms in places of A and B.

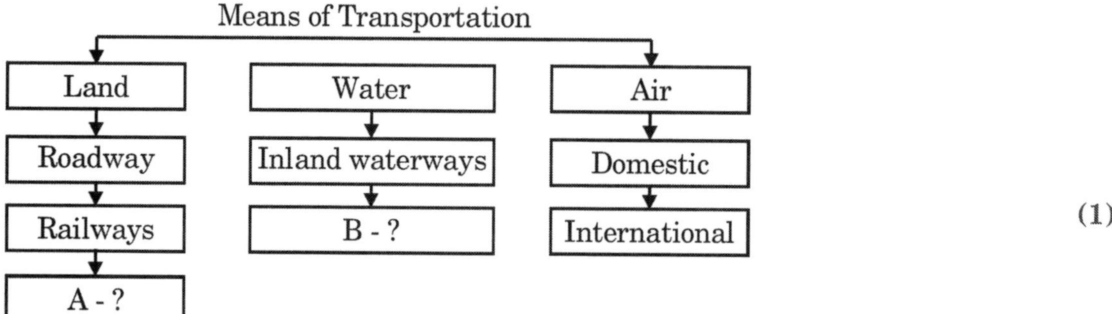

      (1)

9. India has emerged as a software giant at the International level. Suggest any one way to enhance the export of information technology. (1)

10. Business Processes Outsourcing (BPO) is an example of _____ industry in India (1)

OR

Lime stone, silica, alumina and gypsum are the raw materials of _____ industry. (1)

11. Read the following features of a soil and name the related soil :

(a) Develops in high rainfall area.

(b) Intense leaching process takes place.

(c) Humus content is low. (1)

12. Write the temperature requirement of Maize crop. (1)

OR

Write the amount of annual rainfall required for the cultivation of Wheat. (1)

13. Read the following information and write a single term for it.

The Constitution of India provides freedom to profess and practice any religion to all its citizens. The Constitution of India prohibits discrimination on religious grounds. (1)

14. Consider the following statements regarding language policy of Indian Federation.

(1) Hindi was identified as the official language.

(2) Besiders Hindi, there are 21 other languages recognized as scheduled languages.

(3) English can be used alone with Hindi for official purpose.

Choose the right option from the following :

(a) 1 and 3   (b) 1 and 2

(c) only 1   (d) 1, 2 and 3 (1)

15. In the question given below, there are two statements marked as Assertion (A) and Reason (R). Read the statements and choose the correct option :

Assertion (A) : Democracy is a legitimate government.

Reason (R) : Regular, free and fair elections are the spirit of democracy.

Options :

(a) Both (A) and (R) are true and (R) is the correct explanation of (A).

(b) Both (A) and (R) are incorrect.

(c) (A) is correct, but (R) is incorrect.

(d) (A) is incorrect, but (R) is correct. (1)

16. Suggest any one way to make political parties more responsive to the people's need and demand. (1)

OR

Suggest any one way to promote the public participation in the Political Parties for enhencing the quality of democracy. (1)

17. Correct the following statement and rewrite it.

Removing barriers or restrictions by the government is known as Globalisation. (1)

OR

International Monetary Fund (IMF) is an organization whose aim is to liberalise international trade. (1)

18. Which among the following issues currency notes on behalf of the Central Government ?

(a) State Bank of India　　　　　(b) Reserve Bank of India

(c) Commercial Bank of India　　(d) Union Bank of India (1)

19. Choose the incorrect option from the following :

List I	List II
(a) Courier	(1) Tertiary Sector
(b) Fisherman	(2) Primary Sector
(c) Carpenter	(3) Primary Sector
(d) Banker	(4) Tertiary Sector

(1)

20. Define the term Per Capita income. (1)

OR

Define the term Literacy rate. (1)

SECTION B

21. Describe the implications of First World War on the economic and political situation of India. (3)

OR

Describe the role of poor peasantry in the 'Civil Disobedience Movement.' (3)

22. How had Indian trade been beneficial for the British during seventeenth century ? Explain. (3)

OR

Why did the elite of Britain prefer handmade goods in the mid nineteenth century ? Explain. (3)

23. "A concerted effort has to be made in order to use mineral resurces in a planned and sustainable manner." Suggest and explain any three measures. **(3)**

24. "The pace of change in the communication sector has been rapid in modern times." Support the statement with examples. **(3)**

OR

"Roadways have an edge over Railways." Support the statement with examples. **(3)**

25. Describe the rationale behind the implementation of Decentralisation in India. **(3)**

26. Read the sources given below and answer the questions that follow :

Over a hundred countries of the world today claim and practice some kind of democratic politics: they have formal constitutions, they hold elections, they have parties and they guarantee rights of citizens. While these features are common to most of them, these democracies are very much different from each other in terms of their social situations, their economic achievements and their cultures. Clearly, what may be achieved or not achieved under each of these democracies will be very different.

(1) Explain the fascination for democracy amongst various countries. **(1)**

(2) Explain democracy on the basis of expected and actual outcome. **(2)**

27. Why is the tertiary sector becoming more important in India ? Explain. **(3)**

OR

Why is organized sector preferred by the employees ? Explain. **(3)**

28. Describe the significance of the Reserve Bank of India. **(3)**

SECTION C

29. Read the sources given below and answer the questions that follows :

Source – 1 : Religious Reform and Public Debates

There were intense controversies between social and religious reformers and the Hindu orthodoxy over matters like widow immolation, monotheism, brahmanical priesthood and idolatry. In Bengal, as the debate developed, tracts and newspapers proliferated, circulating a variety of argument.

Source – 2 : New Forms of Publication

New literary forms also entered the world of reading lyrics, short stories, essays about social and political matters. In different ways, they reinforced the new emphasis on human lives and intimate feelings, about the political and social rules that shaped such things.

Source – 3 : Women and Print

Since social reforms and novels had already created a great interest in women's lives and emotions, there was also an interest in what women would have to say about their own lives.

Source – 1 : Religious Reform and Public Debates

(1) Evaluate how did the print shape the nature of the debate in the early nineteenth century in India. (1)

Source – 2 : New Forms of Publication

(2) To what extent to do agree that print opened up new worlds of experience and gave a vivid sense of diversity of human lives ? (2)

Source – 3 : Women and Print

(3) To what extent did the print culture reflect a great interest in women's lives and emotions ? Explain. (2)

30. Explain the factors which are responsible for location of industries. (5)

OR

Explain the ways through which the industrial pollution of fresh water can be reduced.

(5)

31. 'Communalism can take various forms in politics.' Explain. (5)

32. Describe the necessity of political parties in democratic countries. (5)

OR

Describe the efforts to reform political parties in India. (5)

33. "The impact of globalization has not been uniform." Explain with examples. (5)

34. Why is sustainability important for development ? Explain. (5)

SECTION D

(MAP BASED QUESTION)

35. (a) Two places A and B are marked on the given political outline map of India. Identify them and write their correct names on the lines drawn near them.

(A) The place where Indian National Congress Session was held.

(B) The place where Indigo Planters organized Satyagraha. (2)

(b) On the same outline map of India, locate and label any four of the following with appropriate symbols :

(i)	Haldia	– Major Sea Port
(ii)	Mohali	– Software Technology Park
(iii)	Vijayanagar	– Iron and Steel Industrial Centre
(iv)	Naraura	– Nuclear Power Plant
(v)	Tehri	– Dam
(vi)	Thiruvananthapuram	– International Airport

(4)

Solution

SECTION A

1. The Napoleonic code (1)

2. (b) Bankim chandra chattopadhyay (1)

3. (d) Traditional Aristocratic groups supported it. (1)

4. The two hostile groups of second world war were –

   The Central Powers and

   The Allies (1)

OR

   Purshottandas Thakurdas and G.D Birla

   (1)

5. Freedom for individual and equality before law. (1)

6. Matternich (1)

7. 4 – 3 – 1– 2 (1)

8. A- pipelines (½)

   B- Overseas waterways (½)

9. International trade (1)

10. Information Technology and Electronics Industry (1)

OR

   Cement Industry (1)

11. (a) Forest soils

    (b) Laterite soil

    (c) Forest soils (1)

12. Between 21°C to 27°C (1)

OR

   50 to 75 cm (1)

13. Secularism (1)

14. (d) 1, 2 and 3 (1)

15. (a) Both (A) and (R) are true and (R) is the correct explanation of (A). (1)

16. A law should be made to regulate the internal affairs of political parties. It should be made compulsory for political parties to maintain a record of its members. (1)

OR

One way to promote public participation in political parties is that those people who want this join political parties. (1)

17. Incorrect: Removing barriers on restriction by the government is known as <u>Globalisation</u>.

Correct: Removing barriers or restrictions by the government is known as <u>liberalisation</u>. (1)

OR

Incorrect : International Monetary Fund (IME) is an organisation whose aim is to liberalise International Trade

Correct: World Trade Organisation (WTO) is an organisation whose aim is to liberalise International Trade. (1)

18. (b) Reserve Bank of India (1)

19. (c) Carpenter   (3) Primary sector (1)

20. When the total income of the country is divided by the total population is called as per capita income. (1)

OR

It measures the proportion of literate population in the 7 and above age group.

(1)

Section B

21. The war created a new economic and political situation.

- It led to a huge increase in defence expenditure which was financed by war loans and increasing taxes: customs duties were raised and income tax introduced. (1)

- Through the war years prices increased- doubling between 1913 and 1918, leading to extreme hardship for the common people. (1)

- Villages were called upon to supply soldiers.

- Then in 1920-21 and 1918-19, crops failed in many parts of India, resulting in famine.

- This was accompanied by an influenga epidemic. (1)

OR

The poor peasantry were not just interested in the covering of the revenue demand.

- Many of them were small tenants cultivating land they had rented from landlords. (1)

- As the Depression continued and cash incomes durindeed, the small tenants found it difficult be pay their rent.

- They wanted the unpaid rent to the landlord to be remmitted. They joined a variety of radical movements. (1)

- Apprehensive of raising issues that might upset the rich peasants and landeords, the congress was unwilling to support 'no rent'campaigns in most places. (1)

22. Trade with India was greatly beneficial to the Britishers in 17th century.

(i)   India exported products like Cotton, Silk, Indigo which was in high demand in Britain. **(1)**

(ii) India was the source of high value products like spices for Britain.   **(1)**

(iii) All these items were in demand in Britain and their availability at cheaper rate from India enhanced the quality of life for the Britishers.

(1)

OR

This is because :

(i)   The upper classes preferred the expensive hand made products for their exclusiveness, which were not shared by all.   **(1)**

(ii) Hand made products were better finished, individually produced and designed carefully.   **(1)**

(iii) Handmade products came to symbolise refinement and class.   **(1)**

23. A concerted effort has to be made in order to use our mineral resources in a planned and sustainable manner.

- Improved technologies need to the constantly evolved to allow the extraction of minerals at low cost and to allow use of low grade ores at low costs.   **(1)**

- Another way can be recycling the metals and using scrap metals to avoid wastage.   **(1)**

- Substitutes can be used instead of metals. This would lead to conservation of our mineral resources for the future.   **(1)**

24. The pace of change in the communication sector has been rapid in

- Long distance communication is now easier without pysical movement of the communicator or receiver.   **(1)**

- Personal communication and mass communication including television press etc.are the major means of communication.   **(1)**

- The Indian postal network is the largest in the world. It handles parcels as well as personal written communications.   **(1)**

OR

Roadways have an edge over railways.

- Construction cost of roadways is much lower than railways.

- Roads can transeverse comparitively more dissected and undulating topography.   **(1)**

- Roads can negotiate higher gradients of slopes.

- Road transport is economical in transportation of few persons and relatively smaller amount of goods over short distances.   **(1)**

- It also provides door- to- door service.

- Road transport acts as a link between other modes of transportation.   **(1)**

25. The basic idea behind decentralisation is that there are a large number of problems and issues which are best settled at the local level. **(1)**

- People also have better ideas on where to spend money and how to manage things more efficiently. **(1)**

- At the local level, it is possible for the people to directly participate in decision making. This helps to inculcate a habit of democratic participation. **(1)**

26.1 Over a hundred countries of the world today claim and practice some kind of democratic politics. They have formal constitutions, they hold elections, they have parties and the guarantee rights to citizens. **(1)**

2. Democracy can be measured on the following basis :

(i) Accountable, responsive and legitimate government.

(ii) Economic growth and development. **(1)**

(iii) Reduction of inequality and poverty.

(iv) Dignity and freedom of citizens. **(1)**

27. In any country several services like hospitals, educational institutions, police stations etc., are considered as basic services. In a developing country the government has to take responsibility for the provision of these services. **(1)**

- The development of agriculture and industry leads to the development of services such as transport, trade, storage etc. Greater the development of primary and secondary sectors, more would be the demand for such services. **(1)**

- As income levels rise, certain sections of people start demanding many more services like eating outs, tourism, shopping, private hospitals etc. **(1)**

OR

Organised sector is preferred by the employees because it gives the following advantages over unorganised sector.

- It is registered with the Government.

- There are fixed working hours. **(1)**

- Employees get fixed salary on a fixed date every month. **(1)**

- Salary is not deducted for holidays.

- There are other facilities like provident fund, maternity leave and paid leave etc. **(1)**

28. The Reserve Bank of India supervises the functioning of formal sources of credit.

- The RBI monitors the banks in actually maintaining cash balance. **(1)**

- The RBI ensures that banks gives loans not just to profit-making businessmen and traders, but also to small cultivater, small industrialists, the small borrowers etc. **(1)**

- Periodically, banks have to submit information to the RBI on how much they are lending, to whom, at what interest rate, etc. **(1)**

Section C

29.1 From the early nineteenth century there were intense debates aroud religious issues. Some criticised existing practices and campaigned for reform, while others countered the arguments of reformers. (1)

2 Print culture was not just a development, a new way of producing books; it transformed the lives of people, changing their relationship to information and knowledge and with institutions and authorities. It influenced popular perceptions and opened up new ways of looking at things. (2)

3. Lives and feeling of woman began to be written in particularly vivid and intense ways.

- Liberal husbands and fathers began educating their womanfolk at home, and sent them to schools. (1)

- Many journals began carrying writing by women, and explained why women should be educated. (1)

30. Industrial locations are complex in nature.

- They are influenced by availability of -

1. Raw material
2. Labour
3. Capital
4. Power
5. Market (2½)

- Manufacturing activity tends to locate at the most appropriate place where all the factors of industrial location are either available or can be arranged at low cost. (1)

- Sometimes, industries are located in or near the cities. Because cities provide markets and also provide services such as insurance, transport, labour etc. to the industry.(1½)

OR

Some suggestions are :-

- Minimising use water for processing by reusing and recycling it in two or more successive stages. (1)

- Harvesting of rainwater to meet water requirements. (1)

- Treating hot water and effluants before releasing them in rivers and ponds. Treatment of industrial effluents can be done in three phases:

  1. Primary treatment by mechanical means. (1)

  2. Secondary treatment by biological process. (1)

  3. Tertiary treatment by biological, chemical and physical means. This involves recycling of wastewater. (1)

31. The most common expression of communalism is in everyday beliefs. These routinely involve religious prejudices, stereotypes of religious communities and belief in the superiority of one's religion over other religions. (2)

- A communal mind often leads to a quest for political dominance of one's own religious community. For those belonging to majority community, this takes the form of majoritarian dominance. **(1)**

- Political mobilisation on religious lines is another frequent form of communalism. **(1)**

- Sometimes communalism takes its most ugly form of communal violence, riots and massacre. **(1)**

32. Political parties are necessary because they perform the following functions-

- Parties contest elections. **(1)**

- Parties put forward different policies and programmes and the voters choose from them. **(1)**

- Parties play a decisive role in making laws for a country. **(1)**

- Parties form and run governments. **(1)**

- Parties shape public opinion. **(1)**

OR

The constitution was amended to prevent elected MLAs and MPs from changing parties.

- This was done because many elected representatives were indulging in defection in order to become ministers or for cash rewards. **(2)**

- The supreme court passed an order to reduce the influence of money and criminals. **(1½)**

- The election commission passed an order making it necessary for political parties to hold their organisational elections and file their income tax returns. **(1½)**

33. **The impact of globalization has not been uniform because :**

(a) It has largely enhanced life style of well off in society as MNC's mostly focused on cell phones, automobiles, electronics, soft drinks fast food or services such as banking in urban areas. **(½)**

(b) New jobs have been created in these sectors. **(½)**

(c) Local companies supplying raw materials for these industries also prospered. **(½)**

(d) Globalisation has also created new opportunities for companies providing services, particularly those involving it, call centers. **(1)**

Globalisation also brought its negative impact in terms of :

(a) Smaller businesses were impacted badly as they lost their market share due to rising competition and cheaper products. **(1)**

(b) Consumers started opting for cheaper products against quality products as technology upgrades become frequent and shelf life of products decreased. **(1)**

(c) Unskilled labours turned jobless as small scaled industries closed down. **(½)**

34. • It takes care of the needs of the future generation. (1)

• It promotes efficient use of natural resources. (1)

• It lays emphasis on equality of life. (1)

• It suggests measures for growth and development effectively (1)

• It ensures equal distribution of resources to everyone. (1)

Section D

35. (a) (A) Calcutta

(B) Champaran (2)

(b) (4)

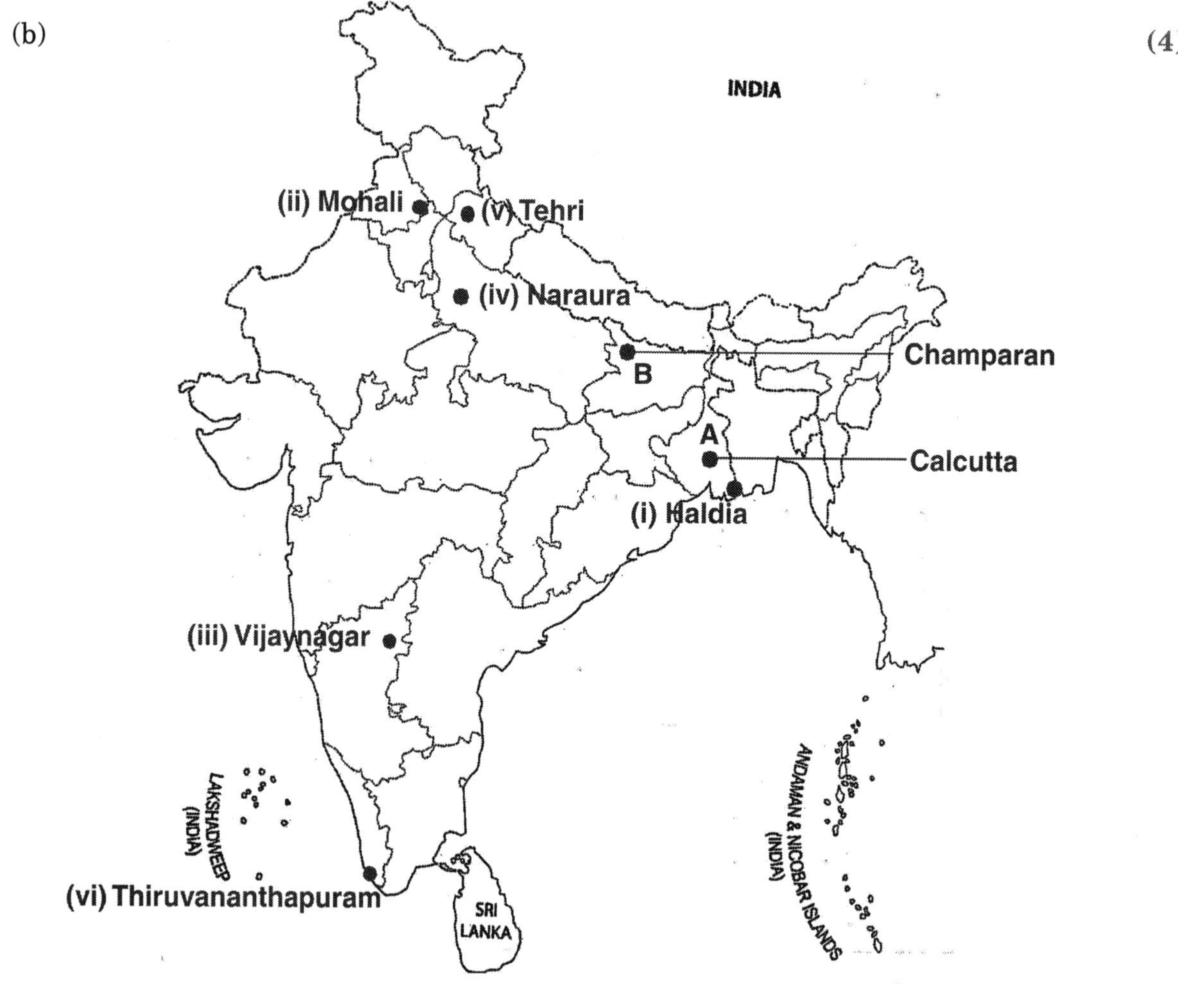

Printed by Libri Plureos GmbH in Hamburg,
Germany